HOW TO BE A DUDE IN THE 21ˢᵀ CENTURY

BY ALEX CORDERO

Library of Congress Control Number: 2024925227

ISBN: 979-8-89228-160-7   (Paperback)
ISBN: 979-8-89228-161-4   (Hardback)
ISBN: 979-8-89228-162-1   (eBook)

Printed in the United States of America

CONTENTS

ACKNOWLEDGEMENT

Wow, I don't even know where to start. Many people have been instrumental in helping me write this book! First, I thank my parents. They are, without a doubt, the most amazing, loving, caring, and wise parents anyone could ever ask for. All the morals, values, and traits I possess are largely due to the extensive life lessons I learned from Mom and Dad. I am far from perfect and have many character flaws, but these are despite my parents, not because of them.

I hope you two are doing well. Dad, I imagine you golfing with your brother, Uncle Julian, while Mom is preparing a delicious lunch of sinigang na bangus, adobong pusit, and kanin in heaven. Dad and I always had something in common: we are both self-proclaimed coffee snobs. I hope, one day, to once again brew a cup of coffee for Dad with my treasured steel French press and prepare tinolang manok for Mom.

To my ex-wife, Maria, and my sons, Alex and Seve: I know the process of writing this book was not easy with me not being there very much for the last four years! For this, I truly apologize and say I'm so sorry! Without you guys, this book would not have been possible! Rest assured that our sacrifice will benefit many young men and young people around the world. Thank you so much for all your support! Love Dad.

To my siblings, especially Rob and Odette! Salamat sa lahat ng tulong niyo! And to all my extended family, in-laws, nieces, nephews and cousins, a big thumbs up.

To my parents' caregivers: Thank you for taking such good care of both Mom and Dad.

To my driving students: A massive shout-out to all of you! A large part of my inspiration and understanding of modern society comes from our time together. Ty!

Also, I apologize for two things: 1. That I am a massive pain in the ass at times as a teacher! It's because I give a fuck! 2. That I absorbed three days of your youth like a vampire having a mid-life crisis. Thanks for helping my life force get younger by ten years!

To the Victoria tennis and music community: I have been enriched and blessed to have befriended many hundreds of people on my four-year odyssey to complete this book! There are far too many individuals and businesses to name, but rest assured, the next time I see you, I will thank you in person!

Robin—my publisher's rep in Victoria; Nathan—my tennis buddy who helped me with edits; Sever and Tim—both of you gave me invaluable advice and direction.

Donnie, Lee, and the Wednesday Volleyball crew—I'm buying a round at the Beags the next time I'm in town!

To the Filipino crew at Banfield, especially Abner—thank you for helping me get my mojo back in tennis!

To my amigos and amigas at the Hill—I miss you guys mucho!

And Brett Smith Daniels—you were the first musician I met on this magical carpet ride. Ty mate!

And finally, to my soulmate and eternal love, Marie: Reuniting with you after thirty-six years was the fuel I needed to complete this book. Remembering our past love—frozen in time—and continuing where we left off awakened my soul completely. You gave me the inspiration and motivation to finish my life's work. Thank you, my love.

Lastly, everything is possible because of You, O Lord! Please use me and my book to bring Your message and light to those in need.

Thanks be to God. Amen.

Use By Alex Cordero

How to be a dude in the 21st century

INTRODUCTION: The Modern Male's Journey

- My name is Alex Cordero. I was born in the Philippines in 1971 and moved to Vancouver Canada seven years later. I traveled back and forth for the next twenty years, met Maria in Manila, got married at 24 and finally moved back to Canada at 28. This book Chronicles my 51 years of life experiences from an early age to the present day 2023.

- I have observed and noticed massive changes, especially when it comes to the average guy. Society has made significant strides, but with this progress comes a downside: the growing impact on young males and their place in modern society. Their role in today's world is shifting, and it's important to address the challenges they face as we move forward. There are still normal dudes, but that number is much less than thirty years ago. This book will share a variety of stories about my life, from things I have observed and learned working as a CPGA Class A golf professional to the thousands of driving school students that I have taught in Victoria, British Columbia, Canada.

I'm not a writer or an author and have not taken any formal writing classes in college. The book is meant to be written as raw and authentic as possible to convey my true thoughts. Many students comment on how I have no filter when I teach or speak. They call me "dope" and that I "spit facts and drop truth bombs" about things we talk about that are considered too taboo to discuss in our modern society. Because these sensitive topics are often left unsaid, many young people are unsure and confused about what to believe. This confusion can cause them to follow societal norms without critical thought often at the expense of developing their own authentic and genuine points of view.

The style of this book is organic, and it will feel like I'm talking to you directly.

With the combination of social media, COVID restrictions, school curriculums, and the redefinition of masculinity, I am noticing that modern dudes are more anxious, trepidatious, lack self-belief, have poor decision-making skills, are less assertive, unathletic, lack initiative, are more easily offended, overly sensitive, not looking for a girlfriend/mate/wife and less sexual than dudes in the past. At the end of the book, I have a designed developmental model to help be a dude in the 21st century. It is patterned after the LTAD that develops high-performance athletes in Canada used by coaches for every sport.

I describe a dude as a competitive, fun-loving guy, who has a solid group of friends. This dude may play sports or have other hobbies. He is respectful, disciplined and enjoys the company of a woman, and is generally obsessed with sex and intimacy. He still displays male characteristics from over 200,000 years of human evolution; who still exhibit strong instinctual behavior.

In biology class, it is taught that mammals have 2 primary goals, to live (survival) and reproduce (mating.) When there is an imbalance between these two goals, negative consequences are bound to happen.

This book will try to develop dudes in the 21st century to be gentlemen. Relearning all that comes with being a strong, confident man with all the chivalry and ideal traits that the best 21st-century man can possess.

Another important aspect of this book is to understand the difference between masculinity and toxic masculinity. Most people in society group both without really knowing or critically thinking about the difference between them. Dudes should/can be masculine and assertive in a relationship but can also be respectful and in control of their behavior. Essentially, it is important to learn chivalry to become a gentleman. Sadly, many of the traits of how to act like a gentleman have been squeezed out of most men in modern society.

Though I write this book mainly for the benefit of young males and most of the content refers to a male/female relationship, these stories are for everyone. I have met and taught people from various religions, orientations, beliefs or non-believers. By sharing my life experiences and perspectives, I hope this book can benefit everybody.

I fully support and agree with equality and embrace strong women in a relationship, but this does not stop a normal dude from also being a protector, provider, and rock. Both things can be true.

All the thoughts and opinions are my own. People may agree, disagree, or dismiss me completely. I fully respect and expect that not everyone will like or agree with the topics and messaging of my book. I am not trying to force people to change their minds but, instead, I hope that by reading my book, it will give them the choice to critically think about modern society with a more open and balanced viewpoint.

Lastly, I do not profess that I know everything or that I'm always right. I will be the first to admit when I'm wrong, that's what a dude does!

CHAPTER 1
FOUNDATIONS OF FAMILY AND EARLY LESSONS

Early Age

I'm the youngest in a family of eight. There were six boys and two girls. Back in the 60s and 70s, it was common to have large families. There was no social media or technology and with fewer distractions in life, everyday living was much simpler and less complex. My theory is that couples were much more in tune and had more time for each other which led to stronger family connections, greater intimacy, and lovemaking, resulting in bigger families. It is more common today to have between zero and two kids. I have two sons. When my youngest was five, Maria asked if I wanted more kids. I didn't think it was ideal and we both decided to be happy with 2 kids.

Growing up in a typical Filipino family, we had lots of drama, fights, love, and great food from my mom who would cook for a family of 10! Her name was Natividad (Naty) and she was an amazing lady. Mom would tell us stories about how she met my dad, Vicente (Vic.) They both worked extremely hard to become successful. Right after WWII, the Philippines was rebuilding with the invaluable help of the Americans. If a person worked hard, they would have an opportunity to be successful and live the "American Dream". My mom graduated with a Pharmacy Degree from the University of the Philippines, and my dad was an engineering student in college but dropped out in 3rd year to start working and support his family. With street smarts, determination, and luck, my parents became successful.

Mom would tell stories about her childhood growing up in a big family. She was also the youngest of six children. It was an amazing thing to hear about honor, envy, love, hate, jealousy, greed, and all the strong human emotions that we show less of today. In my parent's generation, courtship and dating were much different than they are now. Ladies were more feminine, conservative, and reserved. They would wait for their knight in shining armor. It was common practice for men that had serious affection for women, to endure a long courtship. If the man did not strive to attract a mate through education, hard work, and an undying show of love, he would be discouraged or not allowed by the woman's family to date her. Men would even serenade in front of her house to profess their eternal love through songs (Harana). How times have changed? Today, guys wait for girls to text/DM them, giving little or no effort to courtship and not enduring any of the traditional mating rituals seen in the past. It's great for equality, but it is influencing relationships and resulting in a lack of connection. Men are not trying as hard which leads to apathy and a lack of initiative. This is creating a dating environment for most young people that they describe as horrible.

If a lady agreed to a date, she would not be allowed to be alone with the guy and would need a chaperone. There was a fear of something happening sexually. The Philippines was and still is fairly conservative, like a lot of countries around the world in the early to mid-20th century. If a couple were seen alone in the park or at a movie theater, it would be gossiped about, and the girl would be branded in a very negative light.

I also experienced this as a teen in the Philippines. A girl would invite me over to her house to meet her family. We would be sitting in the living room watching tv and having some snacks. Me, this horny dude from Canada, just wanting to get laid with the girl I am seeing, in total bliss for me to just meet her family. What an eye-opener, but also an important life lesson. It taught me the beauty of courtship and patience. It gave me the foundations to act like a gentleman. I gained much more appreciation not just for physical acts but also, more importantly, for emotional connections that led to the deeper intimacy that I see less and less of today. In 2023, hookup culture is the norm. Couples are still intimate, but I have heard from many people that the sex is more expected and not nearly as spontaneous and organic. Modern dating apps are the most common way to meet a mate. Once a couple swipes, there is a certain understanding about sex even before meeting that person in real life. For sure, some couples experience amazing chemistry through these apps, but we are losing or have lost thousands of years of traditional ways to attract a mate.

Chivalry is dead today. Courtship and flirting are nowhere to be found. As I joke with people, in a life-or-death situation a lot of dudes would expect their girlfriend or wife to save them instead of the other way around!

Early Childhood Memories: Learning Life's First Lessons

I don't remember too much from my early childhood, other than some very distinct memories. When I was four, we brought my siblings to school in a big Volkswagen van. I got out of the van and ran across the parking lot for God knows why. My mom spanked my ass and pinched me for the next 5 minutes. I learned never to run across a parking lot without looking both ways and how much a spanking hurt!

My mom also taught me to have good body posture with my shoulders back, head up, and back straight so that you could rest a heavy textbook on your head while walking. As a kid, I thought this was absolutely, ridiculously stupid but, little did I know that this would lay the foundation for my inner confidence later in life. Even average-looking at best, women of all ages will give me a friendly smile or a second look. Thanks, Mom!

At a kindergarten afternoon ceremony, we were all dressed in native attire. I had traditional face paint and native Filipino clothing that exposed my chest and stomach. I was petrified as a 5-year-old, to be so exposed and felt insecure about my body and how people would judge me. I was born a shy, insecure introvert, afraid of what people's opinions were of me. Not dissimilar to how a lot of my younger male students feel now in 2023. The only difference is that I was five, and my students are 16+. Another important life lesson is not to be too self-conscious and not to give a shit about being judged.

CHAPTER 2
EMBRACING CHANGE: A NEW COUNTRY AND THE SPIRIT OF COMPETITION

Moving to Canada

In the 60s and late 70s, Ferdinand Marcos was president of the Philippines until he was deposed and exiled to Hawaii in 1986. The former president was young, charismatic, good-looking, and idealistic. He captivated the Philippines with his vision, charm, and intellect- President Marcos was brilliant! The country was an up-and-coming tiger economy in Asia and ranked very highly in terms of rice production and other agricultural goods. It had a major advantage against its ASEAN neighbors with English being one of its official languages. Companies from the US and around the world would have fewer problems setting up manufacturing and other industries with minimal language barriers. But as the old saying goes, power corrupts and absolute power corrupts absolutely. President Marcos took this to a whole new level. His wife Imelda famously had a closet of more than ten thousand designer shoes! By the mid to late seventies, the Philippines began to have civil unrest with corruption embedded in all levels of government. As a young boy, I remember passing through numerous police and army checkpoints while driving home from school. Martial law was declared and the rule of law was dictated by President Marcos. My mom and dad were relatively successful. They started a business driving jeepneys, which were converted military Jeeps that looked like small buses. My dad eventually set up a barge and tugboat business. They would achieve enough success to have the means to leave the Philippines if my parents chose to do so. While on vacation to the US in the late seventies, they drove over the Cascade Mountains in Washington State from Seattle through Bellingham before crossing the border into Vancouver. When my mom saw the beauty and tranquility of Vancouver, she immediately told my dad to move the whole family. In August 1979, eight kids moved to an unknown foreign land. My older siblings were not thrilled with the move, I was six and had no fucking clue what was happening. I just remember eating my first Big Mac. It was an orgasmic experience- I didn't know what an orgasm was , but that's what it felt like!

The 1980s was a great time to move to Canada, with multiculturalism being very en vogue. I went to school with kids from all over the world and we were exposed to different cultures. On my first day, I was walking to school with a white Canadian boy named Steve. My first English sentence to him was, *how is your age?* To this day, when I tell the story, it brings a smile to my face.

In 1979, Vancouver was a medium size town. A hockey and sports-crazed city that had a small-town chip on its shoulder. It was not a world-class city as it is now known. The local and provincial governments did a great job growing the city. I remember going to school, playing road hockey, soccer, football, pick up basketball after school, little league baseball, tag, hide and go seek, dodgeball, square dancing, and Mrs. Smith's shortbread cookies in a brown paper bag during Christmas. We would still pray before class and sing God save the Queen. Holidays like Christmas, Easter, and Remembrance Day were celebrated with the utmost importance. Stores were open Monday to Saturday and most were closed on Sundays. Sunday was a day of rest and worship. Then, in grade three or four, to promote the inclusion of all peoples and cultures, changes began to happen to the status quo. Watching TV, I remember the pundits talking about political correctness. It was a very lively debate going back and forth that left an indelible memory. One of the debaters spoke about the benefits but also, if left unchecked, the serious consequences of political correctness in the future. Consequences that are manifesting themselves like a virus in modern society today.

Lake Placid 1980 Winter Olympics

The Winter Olympics were held at Lake Placid, New York in 1980. Having only three or four channels on TV, I had the choice of watching Sesame Street, painters sketching the skyline of NYC, Local and world news, or wall-to-wall Olympic coverage. I chose sports.

I remember Eric Heiden winning five gold medals in speed skating for the US, the dominance of the Eastern Bloc countries, and the US shocking the Soviet Union in the semi-final hockey game dubbed "the miracle on ice." That Soviet team was stacked and played such a beautiful brand of hockey which I instantly fell in love with. To this day, the Olympics are the catalyst for why I'm such a big sports fan and athlete, watching both the thrill of victory and the agony of defeat. Competition and sports offer great learning tools that, sadly, we are missing out on today. I have observed this firsthand with many of my students, especially my younger male students. They don't seem as competitive or have the will to win and are okay with any result. Athletes in the past would do almost anything to win. They would relish the opportunity to compete, enduring blood, sweat, and tears. If they lost, it would be so painful that they either gave up or they worked even harder to find a way to improve themselves for their next opportunity for redemption. If they won, it was the most euphoric feeling. Athletes would have such an intense feeling of accomplishment and satisfaction for all the hard work and perseverance that they endured. Mediocrity was not tolerated!

This is a topic I will get into deeper, later in the book and I call it meritocracy. To earn everything and not expect winning to be easy or to be given to you. To develop a growth mindset and high-performance competition skills.

CHAPTER 3
RECOGNIZING MODERN MASCULINITY'S CHALLENGES

Men in crisis

I've been writing this book for the last two years and have been struggling to finish the final few chapters. For the last six months, I had writer's block and I couldn't understand why. Subconsciously, I felt like I was missing something. This is probably why I fully invested myself in many different sports and activities. Talking to people, playing tennis, volleyball, and basketball, and going out to different clubs and bars to fully immerse myself in people's daily lives. It was what I needed to give me a much deeper insight into modern society. To be honest, since my sons were born, I felt like I had been frozen in amber and my life was in stasis. This was perfect to write this book as I am pretty much the same person as I was 35 years ago. Society, social norms, and values of people have definitely changed within that time, however. I often feel like a time traveler transported from the 1980s to present-day 2023 or that I'm in a time capsule or a spaceship that traveled 35 years in the future.

I first started noticing a crisis in men several years ago. This was the time that I had taught a rower and saw the first signs of trouble for young men. The crisis was in its infancy but as I unfortunately predicted, would accelerate to where it is right now- a tsunami of broken down, weak men.

It's now February 2023, I started this book in March 2021. During this time, the landscape for young men has changed even more drastically. I'm currently teaching several high school students from different institutions around town. The first student is a lacrosse player from a local high school that has a good lacrosse program. The academy program aims to send kids to play college lacrosse in the US. My student is in grade 11 and committed to playing Division One lacrosse. I had taught his brother a couple of years back and have known "G" for 3 years. When I would see G and his family, we would say hello. Through a lot of hard work in the gym and lacrosse field, G looked extremely fit. He was a chubby kid growing up. We start our lesson and I ask him how he's doing in school and lacrosse. He says that their high school team was heading to California to play a tournament in the spring. I asked why they weren't going to the east coast instead. East Coast lacrosse tournaments are where most of the college recruiters are and, logically, Canadian teams would benefit most from the exposure and competition playing the best instead of going up against inferior teams in California. His response was that they were just going to California to play for fun. He seemed a little irritated with my question. We talked about the importance of playing the best and the benefits that it would provide to their team. Competing against the best provides numerous learning moments and growth opportunities. Win or lose, the team and players would know what things to work on and to improve. If you play weaker competition, it just reinforces a false sense of competency and may lead to a mindset that you're good enough and don't need to improve anything.

During my son, Seve's lacrosse journey, Canadians were always considered tough inside players who were coveted by American colleges for their ability to take extreme physical punishment and verbal abuse. I ask G about the difference between American and Canadian players and teams. His answer absolutely shocked and floored me. In the past, Canadians were known for having really good stick skills which translated to inside players able to score big goals under pressure. Canadians could play through contact, get slashed as they shot the ball, or dodge towards the net. In other words, we were known as dumb, tough, plumbers who could put the ball in the back of the net. Americans on the other hand were known to be very fit and athletic. Most Americans were amazing student-athletes who played multiple sports like football, baseball, soccer, golf, and other sports. The quarterbacks, wide receivers, pitchers, and the most athletic athletes made really good lacrosse players. But because they weren't 100% full-time playing lacrosse, their stick skills and shooting weren't as good as Canadians. I then asked G the main difference today between us and them, he answered that the Canadian players were softer than the Americans. I almost spit out my coffee! In no way and in no time would I have ever thought that those words would come out of a Canadian lacrosse player's mouth. When we used to go down to the US to play club or high school lacrosse, Canadian teams would always joke that the American players were soft and whiny. American teams would always try to avoid getting in physical games with the big, bad Canadians. The parents, players, and coaches would regularly complain to the refs about the rough, physical style of play and for the refs to call more penalties against the rough-and-tumble Canadian teams. So, when G said that Canadians were soft, I asked him why. He said that what they were learning in school and the way the game was being played, officiated, and coached was making all the players soft.

At the same time, I started lessons with another student named B. He was enrolled in a hockey academy. B and G had a lot of similarities. Both were hesitant, pensive, reserved, and unsure about their decisions on the road. Traditionally, hockey and lacrosse players were considered the toughest, regularly getting in fights, and being a little bit crass, rude, and rough around the edges. The boys would typically always have scratches, bruises, or black eyes. Hockey and Lacrosse were really ferocious, violent, and brutal sports that the more refined and Bougee people would often shy away from for their kids.

That toughness is a stark contrast to B during his first driving lesson. B was nervous and afraid to make his own decisions and in busier traffic or unknown scenarios, he would always tense up.

My lacrosse and hockey students from even two or three years ago did not have these same issues. It's so shocking for me to see how big the difference is. As I start to get to know B, I tell him about my book and thoughts about modern society. He starts to feel a lot more comfortable and opens up about how things have been for guys in school and on social media. B says that a lot of the anxiousness and insecurities are being learned in school. Both G and B mentioned to me that the very athletic students, who exhibited traditional masculinity and strength were now the outcasts in their respective schools. Both would always be around their team or small group of friends but would rarely interact with the majority of the other students. The athletes and jocks were now viewed as the weird ones and for most of the school, they did not exist. How times have changed! This has resulted in these young men being frustrated, disillusioned, and angry about being excluded or ignored by fellow students and teachers. Then B shares a story from grade 10 social studies class. He tells me that in front of the whole class, the male teacher suggests to all the boys that it is better to be gay than straight and that the teacher is encouraging the males to be gay. This shocked me but also gave me new insight into what was happening with these young men. Furthermore, both G and B tell me that it is now considered cool to come out as trans or gay. And that the social studies teacher would be sexist towards the straight male students in his class showing favoritism to everyone else and giving the straight male students a harder time. Though I've heard of similar things happening in the US and Canada by watching podcasts on YouTube and seeing tweets on Twitter, this is the first time that I have experienced this with students telling me outright about the school curriculum and teachers directly having a hand in weakening or emasculating these young men.

I have another grade 11 student from an exclusive private school in town. Student "N" was a rugby player and his parents immigrated from South Africa. At his school, it wasn't as severe, but he also noticed a lot of the similar things that my other students were mentioning. In their lesson plans, teachers would regularly introduce and use LGTBQ themes in their quizzes and tests. The school would bring in different speakers to lecture in different classes and subjects. On a daily basis, LGTBQ topics were discussed and taught. A common thing I am hearing from these students is that they are respectful and accommodating to different types of people whether they're LGTBQ or of different races. But I also sense a growing, yet silent, frustration, anger, and fear because they are being inundated by these topics and it is being given more importance than traditional subjects in school such as STEM subjects, Science, Math, or PE. These are being replaced with a lot of classes that deal with empathy, kindness, and general themes of diversity, equity, and inclusion. My students also feel silenced about being able to simply ask or question anything that goes contrary to these topics. Any views that are not in alignment will land them in trouble with the teacher or principal. This is causing a lot of hidden mental strain and depression. In my driving school, my students identify by the gender they freely choose. I am very comfortable teaching a variety of people and see them only as people. Being a minority myself, I see everyone the same regardless of their orientation or race. With that said, if I have a student who is straight asking for dating advice, I will give them the best dating advice that I can. If I have students who identify as gay or trans, I will equally give them the best dating advice that I can. I do not try to convince them to become straight if they're gay or trans and to become gay or trans if they are straight. I respect who they are and how they identify. It is not my job to influence or try to convince them of anything else. This is originally what the LGBTQ's purpose was, to be accepted for who they were. They weren't trying to overtly convert anyone to their lifestyle but just to be respected for who they were and what their preferences were. From what I've been hearing from my high school students these last two weeks, I'm both shocked and concerned because straight students are being influenced by school and society to identify as gay or trans just to fit into society's ideal modern mold. All three of my students are so happy to just be able to talk to me. They generally feel so isolated and scared to speak up for fear of being ridiculed or canceled. The fear of being canceled, being silenced, and not being able to speak or even suggest or ask a question must be such a heavy burden. It's total obedience and any sort of query is immediately considered transphobic or homophobic. These sentiments are all freely shared from my students without me putting them up to it or planting any ideas in their heads. My car is a safe space to think and speak about any ideas or topics. There are no topics that cannot be discussed, as controversial or as sensitive as they are. I believe that everything can be discussed and if there's an idea that seems outside the boundaries of normalcy, people should still be able to debate and discuss it calmly and logically without triggering an immediate negative emotion and visceral reaction.

I have two more high school students whom I started teaching last summer. Both of these students were very good athletes. One was a rower and went to a private school and the other was a three-sport athlete that went to a public school. Both students were athletic, big, and strong but were extremely shy when we started the lessons. Both did about 10 lessons each last summer. We worked on their self-confidence and learning to be comfortable talking and communicating. We would talk about their lives, their sports, and plans for the future. Last summer, I didn't really consider why both students were shy and introverted, but now I'm getting a better understanding. My high school students after COVID are generally more introverted, shy, and quiet as compared to my students in the past. Fast forward to this week, I see both of my students again. The runner has become a track star. While playing tennis at Beacon Hill last week, I bumped into him in the parking lot. He confidently approaches me to say hello. His mannerisms and aura were that of a young gentleman with his chest out, looking me straight in the eye while we talked. This was such a monumental difference from the young man I saw just 8 months ago. We didn't have that much time to chat but I asked him what he had learned the most in our lessons. I was so happy to hear that he could talk to random people and be able to freely communicate confidently without any fear. Some of his friends did not like taking the bus for fear of interacting with random strangers. Student "T" was able to come out of his shell.

He's a three-sport athlete in track, basketball and soccer but has now focused on cross country after dropping the other sports. In track, he has worked hard to be a top cross-country runner for his age group in the province and was nominated for cross-country runner of the year in BC! He is now focused on attending a top D1 school for track in the US! On our last lesson, T thanks me for everything he learned in the car. He is what this book is hoping to do- to inspire and develop young men to be gentlemen. To be strong, masculine, motivated, and disciplined. To have the best traditional traits of men in the past, thrive in the present, and to adapt for the future. Student T is the model to which this book is all about.

Student A goes to a private school, and he has made tremendous growth in terms of his confidence, demeanor, and, overall, he's becoming an awesome young man. In our lesson yesterday, we were talking about the pressures of society particularly when it came to girls. He has never had a girlfriend and didn't really feel like he was ready to have one. Student A asked me what my thoughts were. I said that if he wasn't ready for a girlfriend, he shouldn't feel pressured by society to have one. Too many times, young people are under tremendous pressure to conform and will do things that they really don't want to do but feel compelled to do so. There are expectations that by a certain age or certain grade, that you should have a girlfriend, you should have done this in sports, etc. but in reality, we need to give young people a chance to mature at their own pace without being pressured when they're not ready. Student A was so happy with my advice because he said that I was one of the few people that he could actually talk to about this or anything else on his mind. He was focused on his rowing and his school, with the goal of trying to be admitted into a really good college or university in the US.

A common theme for all my recent young male students is how happy they were to just be able to talk. They have no one except for maybe one or two really close friends with whom, they feel that they can discuss these topics freely. This is causing so much frustration, fear, anger and depression. What's disturbing is that these are traditionally the strongest and most masculine young men. Now, they were all fearful, reticent, hesitant, shy, introverted, and generally afraid. Our lessons have helped awaken these young men. They can open their eyes, minds, emotions, and feelings so much more than before. I'm so happy about this, but also extremely concerned about the crisis amongst men. I see this when I'm out and around town playing sports, going out at night in bars, or having a bite to eat at a restaurant, or coffee shop. I had a business meeting on Friday at a family restaurant similar to Applebee's. I sat down around 6:00 pm and the restaurant quickly filled up with a diverse group of people from seniors to young families with young kids. We looked around and observed the energy of the people and their mannerisms. Most were very polite and cordial, but the one noticeable thing was that a lot of the men seemed gentle, docile, polite, and passive. They all looked less masculine. The person I was meeting was in his late 40s. He said the same thing, that none of the men that we saw around the restaurant looked like men.

I dropped by a neighborhood pub before a lesson the day before and sat down for a quick meal. The server approached me and gave me a really warm smile. She was in her mid-forties and because of everything that my students have been sharing with me this week, I asked her for her take on the situation concerning men. I asked her how long she's been at the pub and she said, "25 years." I asked her if she had noticed if men were different now from before and if that change was in the last couple of years. She actually said that "the change started at the same time as the 'Me Too Movement' from several years ago." She further explained that after the movement, men were either becoming "very weak or becoming "very toxic." A very small percentage were absolute assholes and dicks, the rest were weak and acted like boys. She then complained and said, "there are no men, where are the men?!" I told her that I was writing a book to try to reignite more masculinity and to develop more gentleman. She was so happy to hear that, but unfortunately for her, this book will probably come out too late for her to find a real man. It's a similar theme that I've been hearing from my female students the past year and a half, regardless of what school they attend. They all complain that there are very few datable guys in their schools, if any. More and more, these young women would date guys a couple of years up to twenty years older. I ran into an ex-student this past weekend. She was 22 and has been dating and hooking up with guys as old as 42!

Two years ago, I started seeing the signs of the problem with the lack of men and I theorized back then that with the scarcity of men, females will start to become very aggressive in the search for men and will probably have to resort to dating much older men. Instead of being empowered, they have become desperate. With feminism, equality, female empowerment and the opposite emasculation of men, the quest to empower women has succeeded extremely well. It has made them so powerful that it has become almost impossible for them to find a real man because real men are almost extinct. This is humanity's irony and twisted sense of humor!

Starbucks

During the last stages of writing my book, I was trying to find a place to write. I went to the Starbucks close to Beacon Hill. It's nice because not only can I sit down and grab a coffee, I can also charge my phone, with free WiFi and super clean bathrooms. Still having writer's block, I sat in Starbucks for a good 2 hours trying to find inspiration, but I was just blankly staring at the people inside. While I was observing, I noticed something pretty interesting. That day, there were four guys working behind the counter and 2 female managers all in their mid-late twenties. I noticed that all the guys seemed a lot softer, and very obedient. The women on the other hand were very strong with alpha personalities. The first thing that I thought of was the inverted role structure. In the past, it would have been the other way around with a lot more male bosses and female counter persons. Now in 2023, guys were more like the females back in 1980, and the women were more like the men. The other thing I noticed, was that most of the male patrons were also very passive and soft. Both the male workers and the patrons up-talked to present themselves in a more kind, gentle, and polite way. There is nothing wrong with this, it's just an observation on the direction and trajectory of the modern male.

Burn-out

In the 1980s, there were a number of teen tennis prodigies blowing up on the men's and women's professional circuit. Unfortunately, most flamed out within a couple of years which was described as "burn-out". To reduce burn-out, money and effort was invested to understand and make changes to how athletes were being coached and developed.

They found that there was a big drop in participation in young athletes once they hit their later teen years. We theorized burn-out was happening because of the obsession with competition and winning at all costs attitudes. With the best of intentions, people set out to redefine how to maintain participation in all sports and activities. They found that too much pressure and competition at a young age had a negative effect in their desire to continue once they reached their late teens and early 20's.

There are pros and cons with competition, too much too early may lead to burnout but not enough will lead to athletes lacking the competition skills in sports or more importantly in everyday life. Finding a balance is crucial to develop an elite athlete who will enjoy their sport for a lifetime. Ironically, competition skills or lack thereof affects confidence, decision making abilities and belief or lack of self-belief in daily living.

To combat burn-out, coaches developed a framework model with a series of stages from the start of the activity or sport all the way to the highest levels of competition. In Canada, we call this long-term athlete development (LTAD). Within these stages, there are suggestions and guidelines on how to develop athletes from when they start playing (Active Start) progressing all the way to lifetime participation (active for life.) LTAD also has more specific timelines, when to practice, have fun, learn fundamentals and at which stage to introduce competition and the value of winning and losing.

Interestingly, burn-out is still present, and hearing from many student athletes today, it is equal to, if not worse, than in the past. This has led me to think deeper and ask my students how and why they burned out, even with more modern coaching and awareness. It may not be the competition but the pressure from external sources such as school, teams, parents, societal expectations that, in the end, is more the cause of burnout than the actual intense competition that we originally thought caused this decades ago.

Competition Skills

Competition skills is the ability to perform consistently in any situation whether in practice or under the most intense pressure of a test or high-level event without any significant changes in performance. The more constant your performance is under all conditions, the higher your competition skills are. Therefore, it is important not only to perfect your technique, but to use your technique in different situations, conditions, and scenarios. This will teach you the ability to adapt, reassess, and improve whether in practice on a Tuesday evening or the championship game on Sunday. Your performance should be the same and as Michael Jordan famously says, the score is always 0-0. He never changed the way he played and would even play harder during those Tuesday evening practices.

In golf, we are trained to teach the fundamentals through Blocked Practice (technical) and develop sports IQ and game strategy with Random Practice (competition skills).

Examples of blocked practice would be to repetitively shoot hoops by yourself trying to improve your form, to use step ladder drills to improve your footwork, to hit golf balls in a driving range working on technique to groove your swing, and to practice any sport with the intention of technical improvement.

Examples of competition skills are trying outrun the other kids on the playground, diving for a loose ball in basketball to help the team win, doing anything possible to get the ball back in tennis without worrying about shot mechanics and playing golf for money or in a tournament with the goal of winning, putting more emphasis on how to win and less on perfect technique.

"Drive for show and putt for dough" is an old saying in golf. Golfers more concerned with form would routinely spend hours in the driving range trying to hit a perfect, straight ball and they would endlessly worry about their form and how their swing looked. Golfers that wanted to win were not as concerned about technique, but they put more effort adapting and employing strategies that will help them win.

Golfers then would not only want to improve their drives, they would also spend more time working on their short game and putting. Usually, for every 1 hour of practice in the range, seasoned competitors would spend 2-5 hours on the chipping/putting green. They understood that no matter how pretty their swing looked, the ultimate goal in golf is to play a round of golf with the least number of strokes. Therefore, they could accept less than perfect shots knowing that they could still get the ball in the hole with an expert short game. Legends like Tiger Woods and Phil Mickelson had amazing short games and could win big tournaments hitting some less than perfect drives off the tee with their chipping and putting saving the day. In the end, a competitors ultimate goal is to lift the trophy, whether it looked pretty or not. Win ugly!

Other examples of competition skills are playing basketball after school in a pick-up game trying to win, or individual games like 21 or horse. Competing against friends or strangers in other sports or activities with the only goal of winning. Technique is a very important component to becoming elite in a sport or activity, but it must be combined with competition skills. If not, you end up looking good but often, it's just for show and not for dough!

In the past, most people hated losing. Flying elbows, bruises, black eyes, and the occasional bloody nose were normal playing pickup basketball or in other sports. Meritocracy was the norm, people had to pay their dues and earn everything, nothing was ever easy. An example was on the playground when captains would pick teams to play a game or sport. As a young child, the worst thing in the world was to be picked last. It would mean that you were the worst athlete, clumsiest kid, most uncoordinated and least desirable. It was embarrassing, humiliating, and felt like the end of the world. You had two options, stop playing with the kids, or try to get better through practice and hard work. These life lessons are harsh, but that was the reality in the past. Though we try to lessen the importance of competition today, people with the strongest will, work ethic, and intensity generally succeed in life today.

Most games and activities would have winners and losers. At home, we would play games like Monopoly, Battleship, or cards. At the carnival, games of skill were extremely popular with dudes spending a fortune for the chance to win a teddy bear for their girlfriends. Most guys would play golf, tennis, team sports, bowling or even join a darts league. We would try to guess how many gumballs were in a glass jar or play charades at home trying to win a prize. Video games, pinball machines and arcades were extremely popular. Getting the highest score and putting your initials on the pinball machine top 3 ranking was like the greatest thing ever and a monster flex!

All these memories seem like they existed in a parallel universe. More popular activities today are more participatory like cycling, working out at the gym, hiking, rock climbing and walking with no defined winning or losing outcome. People still play sports but since we have lessened the importance of winning and have placed greater emphasis on participation, the games are not as intense or fierce with competitors not able to perform under pressure when something is on the line.

When I see competition today, it is so different. There may be increased participation, but it has also caused people to shy away from more competitive sports or activities. This has resulted in many people being uncomfortable with tests or intense competition, making them more brittle in the face of adversity.

I developed competition skills at 10 years old. I started playing tennis with my older brothers, who were 4 years older. It forced me to try much harder to be able to compete with them. By the end of the summer, my skills were on par or better than my brothers. Because of this, I had a competitive advantage with kids my own age. I played U12 tennis tournaments against kids with better technique but because my competition skills were more advanced, I was able to come up with strategies to beat them. Examples of this would be if I was losing, and momentum was on my opponent's side, I would delay a point by tying my shoelaces, turn my back briefly to gather myself and recollect or interrupt my opponent mid serve to try to throw off his rhythm. I learned that taking deep breaths when I was nervous helped calm me down to play better tennis on the very next point. Bouncing the tennis ball the same way each serve helped me not overthink and this allowed me to serve with no fear. If I was winning, I learned not to let up and keep my foot on my opponent's neck until I won. Momentum was key and helped me get into the zone, known today as the "flow state." The longer I can stay in the zone, the better chance I have to win. Though I exhibit better sportsmanship now, the obsession to win pushed me to develop and invent various ways to come out on top.

All these simple techniques were ways to adapt in competition for the purpose of winning. These are the same techniques that high performance sports psychologists teach to world class athletes. I learned them organically at age 10 because I wanted to give myself the best chance to win. These strategies were developed with no guidance or coaching, just with the utmost will to win.

I hated losing with all my passion! As a young tennis player, I would throw my racket in frustration and anger. One day, my favorite Prince tennis racket broke after a toss into the back fence. Because I broke it in anger, my parents did not replace the racket. I had to learn to control my emotions in the face of defeat and it strengthened my competition skills even more. There's a saying in sports that before you learn how to win, you must learn how to lose! Because in modern society, we place less emphasis on competition, and more on participation, the lessons I learned when I was 10 are not being passed down to the next generation, especially young males.

Lastly, it is crucial in competition skills to be a fair and gracious loser. While I hated losing, I had great coaches that instilled in me to always look your opponent in the eye and say good game/great job while shaking their hands after a tough loss. This ability to accept and understand that losing is not only a possibility but reality strengthened my will and confidence. I was not afraid to lose and instead, I focused on giving 100% effort no matter the situation. This is the key to competition skills and is not nearly as emphasized, that losing is always possible. This is extremely important in daily life. . The ability to accept and admit when you're wrong and that the chance of losing or making a mistake is always present. It overcomes the anxiety of trying to be perfect. Having a Growth Mindset!

CHAPTER 4
REFLECTIONS ON GROWTH, RESILIENCE, AND THE POWER OF SELF-BELIEF

Dating in my teen years

As an awkward 13-year-old, I started liking girls. Some of the scariest memories I had as a kid were asking a girl out on a date. I would have to summon up all my courage just to say hello! If she responded and talked to me, I would ask for her telephone number. That's step 1. The next obstacle would be to phone her and hope that she would answer the kitchen phone. If her parents answered, it was a problem. You would have to ask nicely and say, "could I speak with your daughter please?" There was only a 50% chance that her parents would give her the phone. If you were lucky enough to get her on the phone, it was a toss-up if she would keep talking to you. And if you came up with even more courage, there was only another 25% chance that she would agree to go out on a date. Trying to ask a girl out 35 years ago was a real challenge, but also ingrained courage and conviction. Guys would routinely get turned down and you needed to develop thick skin and resolve to try again in the face of failure. Being rejected either face to face or on the phone was one of the most difficult and scariest things I've ever faced in my life. But again, these experiences have increased my belief in myself and the ability to adapt and improve. Though it's easier for guys these days because, most of the time, girls will take the initiative and ask guys out by dm or text, I wouldn't trade all those failures and rejections for anything in the world. I appreciated those relationships, they felt more satisfying, more real, because I had to work so much harder to find a partner and mate. Love making, spending time together, even the fights were much more satisfying. This is why the music 30 years ago was based more on relationships, intimacy, getting back together, and the most intense heartbreak. When I was dating, I would play music from artists like Atlantic Starr, Klymaxx, SOS Band, Jeffrey Osborne, Bobby Brown, Keith Washington, Brian McKnight, New Edition, Gerard Le'Vert, and many others. When I play these songs today, my students find them really mushy. Though most of them would comment that they feel more emotions in the older music than they do in most modern songs today.

I asked a lot of my male students if they have partners. A lot of them do not and seem to not be that interested in finding a girlfriend at the moment. Some of the reasons are: that they are too busy, they don't have money to go on a date, or they are concentrating on school. A common theme is that they like girls but are afraid to ask girls out for fear of rejection. They will often wait for girls to make the first move. The guys are afraid of rejection, their friends finding out about the rejection and how they would be judged by their peers. I always recommend to them to try and ask a girl to hang out. If she says no, to try again. If she still says no, assess what went wrong, refine your approach, and try again with another girl. Most of my students are mortified of this advice and would not think of putting themselves in the position to fail. Low competition skills are likely the reason for my young male students lacking the confidence to ask girls out. They do not have the processes to deal with failure if a girl says no.

Marie, my 1st love

Your first love is always the most memorable and mine was with a girl named Marie. She worked at Duffin's Donuts, known for their delicious donuts and hot coffee. I can't remember why I passed by but when I looked through the glass doors, I saw an angel dressed in a donut shop uniform. I couldn't stop looking at her and had to go inside to try to talk to her. I'm not sure how I introduced myself, it's still really foggy after all these years. All I know is that I talked to her and got her phone number. Later that evening I gave her a call and we started talking. Finding a mate in the '80s was not easy and was survival of the fittest. The one thing going for me is that I was a Scorpio man and Marie was a Cancer woman. Though I'm not heavily into astrology, our zodiac signs are a perfect match. We shared the most intense emotional, physical, and psychic connection. I instantly realized that we were a match made in heaven. We started dating and after a year, I would sleep over and spend the night in her room. Remember that this is 1987, and people were still pretty conservative. I would be at Marie's around 10:00 p.m. My problem was I had to wait until her dad fell asleep before she would let me climb through her bedroom window. There were nights I would wait up to three hours! This was an important learning moment for me about delayed gratification. I teach my students to be patient in learning and not just take shortcuts to pass their tests. After waiting for hours, I would sneak into Marie's bedroom into her loving arms. Marie was the first girl that I made love to. It was magical, euphoric, and intense. Not only did we have an amazing emotional synergy, our sexual connection was incredible. Scorpio men are very passionate and inventive when it comes to making love, while Cancer women are very sensual-this combination was extremely explosive! We experimented with strawberries, whipped cream, and ice cubes. We both learned from each other, but sometimes good things must come to an end. I was immature and I made many mistakes. Because we were so madly in love, my mom with the best of intentions, sent me by force, back to the Philippines for 2 years to finish high school and to break up the relationship with my soulmate, Marie! It essentially ended our love story or so I thought? It was the most painful event I've ever experienced in my life! These powerful emotions gave me appreciation for all that humans experience. Both the highest highs and the lowest lows. When I see my students today, it seems as though they experience the same emotions, but not to the same extremes. It's like people are conditioned to feel less emotion or show less to shield them from experiencing extreme pain and suffering. I'm not sure if it's just what people show on the outside, I just don't see the same passion and intensity that was present in the past.

I try to ignite intensity in my male students, yet most are hesitant and afraid to make decisions. They don't want to take a chance for fear of failure. They also second guess themselves and decisions they make or have made.

When asking a girl out, guys shouldn't hesitate. If they like someone, don't overthink and just act on your instincts without worrying about what may go wrong.

In driving, it is essential to not be too anxious. Since driving is all about the decisions that you make, indecisiveness and a lack of self belief is not ideal and needs to be improved. Therefore, it is critical for my students to learn confidence by doing and achieving! Real belief is developed not only through affirmations but also through action. Try, fail, and try again until you succeed!!

First signs of trouble

About 4 years ago, I started teaching an 18-year-old student named Ben. He was a rower with goals to compete in college. Like most of my students, I get to know Ben pretty well. Ninety minutes is a long time in the car, and it gives us a chance to talk about more than just shoulder checking and parallel parking. I asked Ben about college, his senior prom and if he was excited to graduate with his friends. I also asked if he went to parties. He attended some but since he was a rower, he didn't go to all of them. When he would go, there would be guys and girls having a great time. I asked him if he had a girlfriend, he said no. Then I asked him if he met any girls at the parties, or made out with them. He was really into girls, and they were into him but, to my surprise, he hesitated to hook up with any of them. I asked why, his answer shocked me. He said that "girls would always come on to him at parties, and he was really turned on, but he had to resist all their advances." He was afraid that if the girl woke up the next day and had remorse, she could go to the authorities, and he would be charged with assault or rape. Even if everything was consensual that night, the girl could change her mind at any moment. This was what he was truly afraid of. I was surprised, but it also opened my mind to the fact that if Ben had full consent from the girl and was hesitant to act on his urges, how this would have an impact on his psyche later in life. This is the reason I'm writing this book. This happened 6 years ago, and young males are even more afraid to follow their instincts not only in a sexual way, but in everyday life, school, and work. I have more examples of this with other students. Today most guys are afraid to be dudes.

Getting my driver's license

I got my driver's license in Vancouver when I turned 16. At the time, you could go to the DMV, get your learners license and take your road test the following week. Most kids were so excited to turn 16! It meant that they could go for their license to gain independence, be able to go places with friends, use the car for work, and take girls out on dates. Being this very confident dude, I got my learner's permit, then I asked my older brother Rob to come practice driving with me. I had never ever driven a car before and only practiced on two separate occasions for about thirty minutes each time. In the 80's, people just tended to wing things and figure shit out without actually having all the skills to do so. I was fucking crazy that way and I thought that I could do anything! I even felt like if I had to, I could jump from a two-storey building or run through a glass window. There was nothing that I thought was impossible to accomplish. The following week, with one hour of driving experience, I went for my road test. It was at the Macdonald office in Vancouver which, at the time, had the rep for being the hardest DMV to get your license. I planned to be extra polite to the examiner and follow all his instructions intently. After thirty minutes of driving around the city and parallel parking, I passed my road test. This was really bad because I really didn't have the driving skills or maturity to safely drive on the road. I'm not sure how I survived my teen years because I drove like a maniac. But the learning moment here is to have supreme confidence in yourself that you can do anything that you want to accomplish. In 2023, many of my students will never try to take their road test without some form of driver training. It's a great thing for them to learn defensive driving skills from a professional, but I sometimes wish that there were more people that had the courage to just wing it with no fear of failure. If they fail the test, keep improving and take the test again with no frustration or remorse. Fail going 100%!

Driving stick

After getting my license, the only car I was allowed to drive was a 1981 Toyota Celica with a manual transmission. Unfortunately, I had never driven a stick shift before, but with the winging it attitude, got the keys and headed to the garage. I put the key in the ignition and tried to start the car. It suddenly lurched forward. Ahh, I need to have the gear in neutral, press the clutch and then turn the key. This isn't so hard! Car is started, what the fuck do I do? I put the car in first, let go of the clutch, car shakes violently, engine stops, car stalls. Restart car again, repeat, put gear in first again, this time let go of clutch slower, wow, car moving, press gas but car now too fast, freak out, slam on brakes, stall, almost smash a car. Repeat, start car, let go of clutch, press gas, here we go, woohoo, turn right on Oak St. super busy road. Shit, almost crash, switch to 2nd gear, why is engine so loud, wrong gear, switch to 3rd gear, repeat process, now I'm going. Head back home, 4th gear, 3rd , 2nd , neutral, brakes, stop in driveway. Get out, grab coke in the fridge, phone Marie. And that's how people DID shit in 1987.

My students think I'm crazy, learning to drive stick solo, and that it took only 15 minutes!

Coup d'etat in Manila

In 1988, I was finishing high school in Manila. Driving around the metropolis was so crazy. There were no rules. Roads had; cracks and potholes 3 feet deep, severe flooding during monsoon season and manhole covers stolen and sold for scrap metal. Armed carjackers were everywhere trying to steal your ride. If you were unfortunate enough to be inside the car, you become a hostage held for ransom! There were so many cars, buses, pedestrians, bicycles, motorcycles, and street vendors in a city of 15 million. Coming from Vancouver where driving was calm and orderly, I had to instantly adapt to this new driving environment. To be able to change my mindset, observe, learn and as Bruce Lee would say, "be like water my friends!" There were too many insane stories that I could share, maybe the craziest was in 1989. I was staying with friends in Makati, which was the financial hub of the Philippines. Rebels within the Philippine army staged a week-long coup d'etat to try to overthrow the duly elected government of Corazon Aquino. Stuck in my friend Brian's condo for 3 days, I was going crazy so I decided to go out and buy some food. Driving to a nearby restaurant, I didn't notice the soldiers smoking on the sidewalk. They had an army checkpoint set up on the corner. Finally, I heard men yelling and I saw the soldiers running towards my car. I slammed on the brakes and abruptly stopped with my car screeching to a halt. Eight Philippine Army soldiers surrounded me and had me lay face down on the ground with their M16s pointed at my head. The soldiers searched my trunk suspecting that I was helping the rebels move guns and ammo. Luckily all I had inside was my awful-smelling basketball uniform that I had not washed for 2 weeks. The soldiers let me go, and warned me in the future to stop for an army checkpoint. If I had driven another 10 feet, they would have sprayed my car with bullets. As I was about to leave, the soldiers shouted in Tagalog *"putang ina mo, pag pinapara ka namin, huminto ka, tang ina mo"*, which loosely translates to "when we tell you to stop, you fucking stop, you fucking son of a bitch!" I was shook for the next 10 minutes, with the car shaking and lurching forwards and back uncontrollably. Maybe 'coz I almost died driving in a middle of a Coup d'etat in search of *chicken and pork adobo* with *garlic rice*!

Learning moment #1: Don't be a fucking idiot and drive during a coup d'etat!

Learning moment #2: Don't be distracted, always look up and see the big picture. Nowadays, we are so used to looking down on our phones, that we miss real life events happening all around us!

Anthony Bourdain

My love of food developed from an early age because of my mom. She was an amazing cook and would often prepare traditional Filipino dishes. Weekends were a big deal, all the boys would go with mom to the outdoor wet market(palenke) and follow her around while she shopped for the freshest ingredients that we would later cook in the kitchen. Our job was to be her shopping assistants, and carry the numerous bags of meat and veggies she purchased from her favorite vendors(suki.) In the kitchen, my brothers and I would be my mom's prep cooks, chopping, dicing, and cutting. She would make the most delicious Filipino dishes imaginable such as lengua estofada, pancit palabok, adobo, adobong pusit, kare kare, sinigang na sampalok, nilagang baka, and the most delicious pancit malabon ever which our town is famous for! Being exposed in my mom's kitchen, I developed a deep passion for food! I am willing to try anything at least once and will seek out delicacies in the most far flung, sketchiest places.

I've been to east LA for goat tacos, a ghetto in DC for Uncle Maddio's Pizza, Golden Krust Jamaican food in Queens, and the best breakfast birria soup at a random street corner in Ensenada.

When I was 17, I explored different areas of Malabon and found a local Filipino congee house, Akong Lugawan. They served congee-*lugaw* topped with your choice of ingredients. Utilizing every part of the cow and pig, I have tasted exotic items like; pig intestines, cow's tongue, cow's brain - *which is absolutely fucking gross,* pig's blood and cow's eyes - *crunchy and tasty.*

Manokan Country in Bacolod City, is in my top 5 all-time favorite places to eat! They serve inasal na manok - *Bacolod style BBQ Chicken.* Local, free run chicken marinated and grilled over charcoal, to create the most succulent and delicious BBQ chicken I have ever tasted! Must haves are their chicken leg and breast combo with garlic rice smothered in *chicken oil* paired with sinamak na suka - *spiced vinegar* and soy sauce.

I've enjoyed sea urchin, deep fried crickets, frog legs, deer jerky, corned bear. This year, I was at Fridah Kahlo's hometown of Coyaocan Mexico. At the local mercado(market), I ate chapulines(grasshoppers) and el escorpion(scorpion) with Mezcal. It is said to have supreme aphrodisiac properties. I'm normally not a believer in these Viagra-like foods but the following day, the scorpion worked it's magic to a T! 😊

In the early 2000's, there was a show called "A Cook's Tour" featuring Anthony Bourdain. He was a brilliant chef at Les Halle in NYC. The show was so captivating because of Bourdain's authenticity and sincerity while presenting. He would travel to different countries and cities to try the foods that the locals ate. He would also meet and be toured around by the people whose lives he documented. It was a great show that lasted for a couple of seasons. He moved on to a new show on the Travel Channel called "No Reservations". It had a similar feel but dug deeper into different cultures, their history, and the relationship with their food. Bourdain was a master storyteller and would be so enthralling to watch. He was the epitome of a modern dude- confident and humble. Bourdain was friendly and authentic, respectful of the different cultures and their customs. His show filmed content that was sincere and realistic instead of looking for shock value material to get better ratings. He was committed to showcasing the authenticity of the food and people he met. He didn't give a shit about money or fame, and he inspired millions of viewers like me. Though I have yet to visit most of the countries that he went to, I felt like I had after watching his shows. I learned about the places, cuisines, and cultures of the people that he touched. Bourdain has tried almost every possible food that exists in the world: Cobra blood wine, eel livers grilled on the stick, blood sausage, beef intestine, whole pig's head, pig knuckles, beef tongue, pig's trotter, elk liver, sea barnacles, bull penis, duck embryo, maggot fried rice, raw seal eyeball, Cobra heart, fermented shark in Iceland (tastes like ammonia), and many more exotic foods to name. He was a savage and really didn't give a fuck. Bourdain, who was and will always be one of my inspirations, passed away a few years ago. It's awesome watching his shows and seeing his character shine on camera. He was very confident but also extremely humble never forgetting his past and being very open about dark times in his past. Bourdain loved women and really enjoyed having sex, as he proclaims on many episodes. Bourdain was a real dude!

My sons Alex and Seve

I have two kids: Alexander (Alex) 23 and Seve 18. They are very different, but both are amazing sons.

Alex was a shy kid growing up. Born in the Philippines, we moved to Canada when he was two. As a toddler, Alex would always play with balls and toys in his crib. We started bringing him to the driving range at three and he would start hitting balls with a cut down golf club. Our whole family is into golf. Maria was a member of the Philippine National Golf Team and I was a Canadian PGA Class A teaching professional. My dad, brothers, sisters, and friends all enjoy playing. Alex loved spending time at the course, going on the putting green, cut down putter in hand, trying to sink putts or just sitting on the grass. He was 5 when we moved to Victoria. Unfortunately, he stopped playing golf. When he was fourteen, Alex suddenly developed the itch to start playing again. We never forced him to play and made sure that it was his decision. Once Alex decided to play again, he was hooked and kept asking me to teach him at the driving range or take him golfing on the course. After three months, Alex's game took off and he was hitting 280-yard bombs with his driver. He also inherited Maria's short game which is great because it is 1000x better than mine. She is also the best putter I have ever seen!

My advice to Alex when he was starting out was to swing as hard as possible and not worry about where it goes. We sometimes have a tendency to over-coach new players but, as in the past examples, it's good for people to just figure things out on their own. The only other thing I taught him was the fundamentals; how to grip the golf club and to swing in balance with good posture. Everything else, I wanted Alex to develop naturally. He swung like there was no tomorrow and would outhit almost all the adults in the range. He joined a local club as a junior member and started playing every day, as a single, with friends, or joining random people. When he came home, he would either be so happy or be royally pissed by the way he played. There was no middle ground, and his moods were dependent on his performance on the given day. He started playing tournaments and did ok but he would have wildly inconsistent results. Undeterred, he was determined to improve and keep getting better. Alex worked very hard on his game. With many failures and disappointments, he learned to be resilient and patient until finally seeing results and becoming a +1 handicap. In his last two years as a member of the Camosun Chargers golf team, he helped lead the team to nationals. He has won locally and has played in the BC amateur, Pacific Northwest amateur and other regional events. We're so proud of him!

Seve's path to lacrosse was like a movie script. He was born in Victoria and, as a kid, spent all day building stuff with Lego blocks. Seve loved watching Lego videos on YouTube subscribing to different channels. He also watched a ton of Disney Channel on TV. Seve was diagnosed with asthma at six months and was hospitalized twice. He was extremely unathletic growing up and out of 100 kids, Seve would have been at the bottom 10% for physical literacy. While Alex and I were outside throwing a ball or playing road hockey, Seve preferred staying indoors doing his own thing. His only physical attribute was his strong, powerful hands and arms. When he was eight, a friend asked him to play lacrosse. We had no clue what lacrosse was, I never played as a kid. Lacrosse has a small, loyal following in Victoria and the city has produced some all-time greats like Paul, Gary Gait, and Tom Maracek. All three starred for the Syracuse University Lacrosse team which won the National title in 1990. On his first day, he wore used hockey pads and helmet not made for lacrosse, and looked like a total newbie. Seve was the very worst player out of around 200 kids when he started playing. Uncoordinated and unfit, he couldn't pass or catch the ball. Due to his asthma, Seve could barely run 10 yards without needing to take a break. Luckily, he joined a team that was coached by an ex-Junior A Victoria Shamrock, Rob and his buddy, Jesse. Rob's daughter Amelia was on the team. These guys were hardcore and real dudes! They would treat these eight-year-olds like they were eighteen and would have them do sit-ups, push-ups, fitness, and lots of running. They also taught them to be physical, and how to give and take a hit, which are fundamental skills in lacrosse. In one practice, Coach Rob had the kids do a shooting drill, if the shot missed, they had to do ten push-ups. Seve ended up doing 200, Coach apologized to us after practice, but we were good with it and Seve was too, even at 8! He developed a deep love for the game. In the early years, his role on the team was more of the enforcer (goon) than scorer due to his solid, stocky frame. Seve would routinely lay out kids with massive body or cross checks that may or may not have been completely within the rules. After 3 years of playing, he was still on the C team which is the lowest tier. His goal was to be on the A team. Seve tried out on multiple occasions, but his skills and fitness were not good, and he never made it on the top team. Because of his love of lacrosse, he had a deep desire to improve and he was willing to finds ways to do so. We enrolled him in non-lacrosse activities to work on his coordination and fitness. First, he did Kendo. It is a traditional Japanese martial art that utilizes wooden swords. This helped with his footwork and hand-eye coordination. We then signed him up for boxing. He did this for a couple of months and really enjoyed it until one day, the trainer Nate, accidentally landed a punch on his head. He stopped boxing and started cross fit. This started his love of working out and he eventually became fitter. Seve was still slower than everyone else, but his fitness and stamina were trending upwards. Finally, we enrolled him in track and field training to improve his running style, speed, and footwork. All along, he would go to the outdoor lacrosse box for hours and do wall ball (pass the ball against the wall to himself) and shoot 100+ balls a day in the net. My wife and I would pass him the ball as he shot. His development did not come easily, and he devoted himself tirelessly to improve. With all this work, Seve finally cracked the Peewee A team in year 4, though he was a marginal player on the team. The other players and coaches still viewed him as a fringe C player and from time to time, he would be made fun of because of how bad and unathletic he was in the past. To this day, I'm not sure what drove Seve to stick it out with lacrosse. He endured subtle bullying but was unbothered and he kept pushing on. During year 4, I found TedTalks about Mental Strength on Youtube. It covered growth mindset, its importance and how to develop it. Seve and I would watch together and discuss the different principles in the videos. I think this was the key for him. He learned that through patience, hard work, determination, and working on the process, he could develop into the player he wanted to be. His big picture goal was to play D1 lacrosse. Secretly, I thought he was delusional and fucking nuts, but we just kept supporting his dream. The turning point for his lacrosse came when he joined a team coached by Brian Spaven. Coach Spaven was as old school as they came. He had knowledge and wisdom from 60+ years of playing and coaching. Coach Spave had a thunderous loud voice and would scream at players incessantly if they were not meeting his standards. He instantly took a liking to Seve, maybe he saw how hard he worked and how much Seve loved the game. Seve learned so much that season that by the end, he was the leading scorer on the team. At this time, Seve also played with a local travel team, called Victoria Seaspray and went to try out for Team BC which represents the province at Nationals. A couple of years back, Seve tried out for Team BC but was cut immediately and questioned why he was there. Undeterred, he tried again. There was a small ID camp conducted on Vancouver Island, if you were selected, you were invited to the main camp in Vancouver. On the day of the announcement, Seve was on pins and needles, he was so happy when he was invited to the main camp. Seve was defying all the odds as a first year U15 player. At that time, only second-year players were selected to the Team BC roster (Seve was 13 at the time.) This later became known as "Seve's rule," to consider and pick deserving first year players to the Team BC roster. Main camp started and there were really good players, all big, strong, fast, and athletic. Seve was still chubby and on the slower side but he had good hands and scored a lot of goals that season with Coach Spaven. He had a really good camp, but he only made the team as an alternate. Seve would only be moved to the main roster if there was an injury. Miraculously, an attackman injured himself while on holidays and they invited Seve to be part of the team! This was huge and he took full advantage of his opportunity. During practices, Seve worked tirelessly until he earned the trust from Coach Brian. Seve tried his best in every drill, and he gained respect from the whole team. Team BC had 3 events that year and on the first one, the team clicked. Seve kept scoring goals as he was flanked by absolute studs Ryan Sheridan (Hofstra), Pat Dodds (Shamrocks) on the starting attack line. The team was made up of the best players in BC; Arthur Miller (Timbermen), Mitch Sandberg (Ohio St.), Kevin Sobey (Cleveland St.), Noah Armitage (Stony Brook), Isaac Swan (Shamrocks). At Nationals, Team BC's nemesis was Team Ontario. They were almost unbeatable and would always have multiple D1 players on their roster. The first game was against Ontario, BC came out firing with Seve scoring a hat trick and we won the game by a goal. Ontario was pissed. In the finals, the teams met again. We were up 8-7 in the 4th quarter but couldn't hold on, eventually losing to Team Ontario. Seve made the all-tournament team (all-star) which was unexpected. He was a first year, unknown player and he beat out more established studs, for the all star nod. Losing to Ontario was so painful that on the flight home, Seve and I talked about Nationals the following year and how to avenge the loss to Ontario. We spoke with the team manager a couple of weeks later to inform him that Seve was fully committed to tryout again for Team BC the following year to finish the job and win. The next year at Nationals, it was again BC and Ontario in the finals. The game went to overtime and serendipitously, Seve scored the game winning goal. BC slayed the dragon and finally beat Team Ontario! He waited a full year but achieved his goal and got revenge for the heartbreak he experienced a year prior. That was a savage move and very dude-like behavior. By this time, Seve was starting to receive attention from both boarding schools and colleges in the US. Though he was only 14, we saw that his dream was getting closer. In grade 10, Seve attended Claremont Secondary which had a world-renowned lacrosse program headed by Darren Reisig and Chris McKay. Both were former Victoria Shamrocks and ex NLL pros. They had lots of contacts with their ex-teammates in the US and were well known in getting kids into US Colleges to play lacrosse. Teams were inquiring about Seve and let it be known that they would have a roster spot for him in the 2020 recruiting class. Seve though, always wanting to improve, saw that his best chance was to go to a US boarding school and play against the top us high school players. He risked a guaranteed full ride scholarship which is extremely rare in lacrosse and instead flew off to Washington D.C. to attend Georgetown prep. Prep had an amazing reputation for both its athletics and academics. In Canada, Seve was top dog but at Prep, he was unknown and had to prove himself again. He played on the Varsity team, which was stacked, and Seve found out how competitive it was at Prep. Every minute of playing time had to be earned and if you had an off shift in a game or practice, you immediately lost playing time. Seve had a good season scoring big goals against rivals Landon, Gonzaga and 2 goals in the IAC semi final loss against St. Stephens and St. Agnes. Though he didn't play as much as he hoped, Seve learned a valuable lesson that you're only as good as your last shift and never to take anything for granted. It was pure meritocracy that is less common today. I see more emphasis placed on equal playing time, inclusion and fairness which on the surface sound good, but it does not breed into players the competitive streak needed to compete and win at all costs. He transferred to Westminster School in Connecticut, but his junior season was cut short due to COVID. Now in his senior season, Seve is currently leading the team in goals and points. These are valuable life lessons that he will keep forever. Seve is committed to play D1 lacrosse at Marist College in the class of 2021. He keeps working hard every day to hopefully achieve his dream of winning an NCAA National Championship. The resiliency and never give up attitude is something that I teach my students. To be a dude and always have full belief in yourself even when everyone says that you can't do it, and to never give up. We're so proud of both our kids!

The car ride home

Having two sons play competitive sports, we have spent countless hours in the car driving to different events. These were some of our greatest memories as parents, watching our kids play in competition. Maria and I have driven all around Canada and the USA. From Creswell Oregon for the Pacific Northwest Golf Amateur to Baltimore MD for the Under Armour All-American Lacrosse. I miss and wish I could relive those moments in the car with my family. The other important thing was the car ride immediately after a game or tournament. Especially after a disappointing loss, what was said and not said. For many young athletes, the development doesn't start and stop on the field but starts from the hotel, while eating breakfast before the competition and most importantly on the car ride home. These are very crucial moments that determine how an athlete performs in competition and how they will deal with and handle disappointments after a poor showing or tough loss. With Alex, I wouldn't really say much and just give him space to unwind. If he talked to me, I would give input, but this more passive style worked well for him. For me to say less, it gave him the time and space to process the frustration. With Seve, I would immediately ask how he felt and what he could improve. Each athlete is different and it's up to the parents to understand what the best environment is for the car ride home. One thing I have observed is that many parents will be very frustrated after the disappointment and will immediately share their emotions in the car. We all must remember that the sport is for the kids, not the other way around and what is said in the car ride home shapes your kid's mindset for competition in the future and how they deal with and handle adversity later in life.

CHAPTER 5
BUILDING CONFIDENCE, AUTHENTIC CONNECTIONS, AND ACCOUNTABILITY

The Power of the high five

A few years back, I was watching a documentary about basketball teams and how their success was greatly influenced by the number of high fives, fist, and body bumps that the team did either in a game or practice. Teams that had more physical touches would play more unselfish and generally, support each other on and off the court. The study also found that teams lacking that connection criticized each other more, and that they would not have the same cohesion and teamwork. Players would place more emphasis on individual stats over team success. This resonated with me and has been magnified by Covid and the lockdowns that we experienced. In the summer of 2021, when we were able to resume teaching, it was discouraged to shake someone's hand, fist bump or have any sort of human connection. I noticed that all road users, whether they were drivers, cyclists, pedestrians were detached and seemed to not understand what the other road users' intentions were. Before starting a new lesson, I asked students to take off their masks so that we could form a human connection . It helped us create a symbiotic relationship and helped us communicate better inside the car. After passing their road tests, I would shake hands or do a fist bump with my students. Modern life is becoming more isolated and detached everyday. To combat this, I suggest registering your kids for a team sport. It will do them a world of good and help them to relearn the skill of communication!

Lessons with a big-time drug dealer

I teach students from diverse backgrounds and life experiences. A few years back, I had a memorable series of lessons with an ex-big time drug dealer. Student X spent years in jail for not snitching on one of his closest associates… or so I was told. He was from the prairies and attended a school with lots of Filipino kids. His ex-girlfriend was Filipina and he would tell me stories about how her and the Filipino food that her mom cooked like lumpia (pork spring rolls) and pancit (Filipino noodles.)

On our first lesson, Student X's driving style was crazy, fast and erratic. He had a really heavy foot and would floor the gas pedal zooming in and out of traffic. When he reverse stall parked, it was like he was being chased by a rival gang trying to kill him. I was trying to figure out the best lesson plan for him and how to change his mindset and behavior. This would be a daunting task for Student X as he seemed like the kind of guy that was not used to taking orders, especially from a middle aged, Filipino driving instructor. I figured out that the best way to get through to him was to get to know him and see how he ticked. I started to ask about his past, where he was from, attempting to form a human connection. I then asked what his goals were in the present and future. He wanted to get his license so that he could get a good paying job in construction. He would make a lot less than his previous profession, but it was a good, honest day's pay. I talked about my time in the Philippines and different foods that I ate growing up. By the middle of the lesson, I suggested a more relaxed cruise around town and for him to chill out and drive like an 80-year-old grandma. I was hoping that it would work, he was the 1st ex-big time drug dealer that I ever taught. Student X was open and willing to try to change his driving style, but this proved to be more difficult than we both expected. He was hardwired to be really aggressive and paranoid which translated to his Uber over-the-top driving style. I would have him get up to the posted speed limit, 50 kph but he would have trouble keeping his foot from the gas once he was up to speed. He kept wanting to floor the gas when there were cars around us. I suggested that he detach from the flow of traffic and instead of riding the gas with his foot, to ease off the gas pedal once he got up to 50 kph. After 2 lessons, he slowly began to improve his speed control. Next, we worked on staying calm and not rushing to beat a red light. Most aggressive drivers will try to speed up when the light turns yellow, this may be one of the hardest habits to break because aggressive drivers get into tunnel vision with their only goal to not get stuck at a red light. While driving around, I discovered that Student X was just a normal guy with the same dreams and aspirations as anyone else, except that he was an ex-big time fucking drug dealer! During our next lesson, I met his dog, which was a medium sized pitbull. It had a gentle temperament and was good with people and kids. As I saw them walking, I realized that Student X was just like me and we could make a true connection in the present without any judgment of his past. This was the turning point of the lessons. Student X started to trust me and my teaching style. He failed the road test twice because it really was hard to change his aggression but after a few months and more hard work, he finally started to improve his driving to the point where he developed the patience needed to be successful for his road test. He again took his test and on his third try, passed with flying colors (he gave me a $100 tip!) I was so proud of student X for his effort and willingness to change his habits. It shows that anyone wanting to make meaningful change in life is able to do so, it just takes patience and a can-do attitude. Neurologists call this neural plasticity, which is developing and activating new pathways or connections in your brain, allowing the ability to do something that you previously were not able to do. The key to this is to "want" to change instead of "need" to change.

Montreal

I visited Montreal a couple of times in 2012 on a business trip. What an amazing city with an awesome and unique vibe. Montreal's energy is cool and sexy which sets it apart from other big cities in Canada. The birthplace of poutine, it's fries with cheese curds smothered in gravy, loved by Canadians from coast to coast. The food in Montreal is so good that it is a must go to, for the truly serious foodie. And I remembered that anywhere I went, the women were fun, passionate, gorgeous and sexy. The men were equally friendly, personable, playful and handsome. Everyone exuded confidence and openly flirted with each other. The human connections were so clearly obvious and the sex in that city must have been so orgasmically over the top. Whenever I have high school or university students considering going to university in Montreal, I strongly recommend doing everything possible to live in that city. To this day, I have never had an ex-student disagree.

Hong Kong 1993

Back in 1993, I was this young, handsome (debatable) 21-year-old dude going out with a 27-year-old flight attendant stationed in Hong Kong. When I visited her, I would stay in her flat which was really small compared to how spacious apartments were in Vancouver. Hong Kong was still a British colony but their 200-year agreement with China was set to expire in 1997 with control of Hong Kong set to be handed back to China. It was a dynamic city geared towards capitalism and making lots of money. The people were pushy, aggressive, and straight to the point. If you went into a store, window shopping, the shopkeeper would give you the dirtiest look. She might even rudely ask you to leave their store if she thought that you were not seriously shopping and just browsing. You could find all kinds of electronics, cell phones, Walkmans, karaoke machines and designer brands that were hard to find in Vancouver at the time. The food was spectacular, and it was the first time that I had Roast Goose on steam rice. Roast Goose is a leaner, gamier version of duck (it was another orgasmic foodie experience just like my 1st big mac!) Back to the people, I miss the days when people just said and acted on what was on their minds with true authenticity. Though it could come across as rude and unkind, at least you knew exactly what people were thinking and where you stood.

Societal Conditioning

I was doing a lesson with Andrew, a second-year computer science student from UVic. The first time I met him, he was very shy and nervous. He had a hard time talking to me and making eye contact.

The previous summer, he had done a series of lessons in Vancouver, tried and failed his road test. He hadn't driven in a long time and during the first lesson, he was very apprehensive and lacked confidence. I told him that my lesson objectives for lesson 1 was just to get from point A to B without hitting something or getting hit. We didn't need to worry too much about the road rules, road test requirements or anything even remotely close to getting ready for the road test. All we needed to do was to relax and not crash. When we were exiting his driveway to turn left, he was frozen in fear and the car was not moving. I realized that Andrew was overthinking and obsessing about the rules and not about driving the car. As with other examples in the book, he was stuck in conscious thought, but his instincts or lack thereof was his biggest obstacle. Because of social media, the curriculum in schools, and new modern norms, people are trained and conditioned to think and overthink about what to say, their actions, and how their actions would be perceived by others. It eliminates creativity and human instinctual behavior. So, when it comes to kinesthetic activities like sports, driving or dating, many modern young people are having a much harder time. I've since coined the term societal conditioning. He's aware of this and knows that he's trapped in the "Matrix". Whenever he struggles with a simple task, I ask him why. Logically, he understands the mistakes, but he has a hard time breaking free when a similar situation arises again. He's both frustrated but also intrigued and he is motivated to make the changes needed to break free from this societal conditioning.

Yesterday afternoon, I showed Andrew a story of me and a tennis buddy. I was getting a video when all of a sudden, my buddy says, "we're tanned and beautiful!" I didn't expect him to flex like this, but it was a funny moment, so I posted this on my stories. But I added to subsequent clips with the next being, "my friend is a little delusional!" 😜 😜 😜 and the last clip, "but still love ya brother!" When I showed Andrew the stories, he had an interesting reaction. He really liked my stories, but he also said that most of the people today would never post anything like this. It would be very difficult because of the constant worry of being judged. Andrew further states that they are continually thinking and overthinking on their posts every spoken word and action. This puts them in a position to doubt and second guess every scenario leading to what I call "paralysis by analysis." It's a term in golf instruction when we're teaching students. Because of so many theories about the golf swing, many golfers will overcomplicate and have between 10-20 conscious swing thoughts as they try to hit a golf shot. The actual swing from backswing to follow through takes less than a second to execute. This is why many golfers never improve even after years of playing!

This happens in everything from tests in school, social media posts, tennis tournaments, everyday interactions and especially, DATING!

With my bout with pneumonia and almost dying, the one benefit for me was losing 13 lbs. after cutting salt and beer from my diet. After 3 weeks, I felt much lighter on the court. This helped me run faster, track down balls, play longer points and have more energy in matches. I decided to join the Victoria fall classic 4.5 tournament in both singles and doubles. I've always been able to play doubles even at a heavier weight, but the excess pounds made singles much harder. It was much more demanding because of the need to cover the whole court, requiring more athleticism, stamina, and agility.

I partnered up with one of my young tennis buddies Sam, in doubles. He's in his early twenties, and a product of the modern societal conditioning. On the outside, he seemingly has everything: good looks, well educated, has a great job, and is a very athletic tennis player. The first time I met Sam at the Hill, he was much more introverted and less confident. His groundstrokes and technique were very solid but he struggled with consistency and putting it all together. He would hit tremendous shots followed by a series of errors. There are 2 mantras that I believe in sports; 1. God does not bless you with everything except in rare cases (i.e. Tiger Woods & Roger Federer) 2. Rome wasn't built in a day! It takes time and lots of patience to become better at anything. To become elite, it is critical to develop a strong mindset, to practice hard, get reps, achieve-fail-achieve, until you start to develop complete belief in yourself!

One day, he joined us for a beer at the beagle with Vegas Dean. Dean was an OG in his late '60s. His jokes and demeanor were from the early days of Vegas reminiscent of the rat pack; Sinatra, Sammy Davis Jr and Dean Martin. While we were having drinks, Sam was shocked but also extremely amused at the lively conversation happening. He wasn't used to the openness of Vegas Dean, Pizza Matt & Mark (who are in their 40's) and I were engaging in. It's unusual now to have such openness. To be able to make crass jokes without worrying too much. Sam was surprised that there are people like Vegas Dean who still exist. The world has conditioned many people to live in walls and barriers where free thought and free speech are distorted and feel more like a maze or labyrinth instead of a wide-open field to freely roam with ones ideas. After an evening of jokes with lots of laughs, everyone went home in a much better mood.

In the fall, Sam went back to school, but he always remembered his summer at the hill and his experiences with all the people. He started to become less sensitive. While in school, we would video chat from time to time just to catch up. He decided to move back to Victoria in large part, because he missed playing tennis with us. We played for the first time since last summer. I notice a vast improvement in both his skills and his mindset. He wasn't nearly as sensitive which helped him play better tennis. He was on a good trajectory to climb out of the social conditioning until the BC Team Tennis provincials last month. In provincials, he played on the 4.0 team which was a level below our team at 4.5. Sam had a really good tournament only losing 1 match. Their team finished second overall. Our team on the other hand, the Beacon Hill boyz struggled. We didn't have our full roster due to different commitments, but we represented, fought hard, and tried our best. But in the end, got killed by the Vancouver teams. I only won 1 out of 4 matches, which was so fucking frustrating. I gave it my all but, in the end, we were just outplayed and outgunned. The next week, I partnered up with Sam and we played doubles at the Hill. Sam was on a high from provincials and was playing very well. We took on some of the strongest players and managed to unexpectedly win a few sets. I was encouraged by this, so I asked him to play in the Fall Classic tournament the following week. I was very excited but that's when everything changed. The moment that we were officially entered into the tournament, his mindset switched, and he became much more serious about the following week's tournament and about how he thought we should be preparing and playing. The next day, we played again. Everything was okay until I was up at the net and went to poach. My volley hit the top of the net and we lost the point. It was a solid play but for whatever reason instead of a clean winner, the ball clipped the net. I hit a good shot but sometimes even when you have done everything right, shit happens and you miss! I was ready to play the next point but Sam on the other hand was pissed. He said, "you shouldn't take those balls that aren't yours," meaning that I should have left the ball for him.

We restart the match and lose the next 3 points. I thought that was the end our disagreement. Sam on the other hand couldn't let it go and a little later in our set, decided to argue about that same volley. In the middle of the match, I called a timeout (timeouts are not a thing in tennis) and I went over to talk to Sam. He was still obsessed about that one error I made. We ended up losing and after the set, I tried to talk to him about that volley. He started to reason to me about statistics and probability and what a right and wrong shot was. I had mentioned to him that it was a good doubles strategy, but I simply missed the shot. I also reminded him of my doubles prowess and record throughout the season. I'm known around Victoria as a doubles specialist and have earned a reputation as one of the top doubles players in town. But because of his newfound success the week prior at provincials, he felt superior and that his way and his strategy was the only strategy. I've had a very successful season in doubles. To qualify for provincials, our team finished first on the Island. I went 26-4 in sets for the season! I try not to flex because I don't need to, my results speak for themselves. So, when I missed that shot and Sam got very upset, it was the beginning of the end for our team. After a couple of days, we were still arguing about that volley, so I suggested to him that we try to avoid blaming each other and instead, give support when needed. Everybody misses shots, it's how quickly you forget about the miss, and get back to a neutral, balanced state of mind, that is the key for us to have a chance to win. I'm pretty successful in doubles not only because of my technique, and creative style but also due to my ability to adapt to different situations and have a short-term memory of my errors. I play an aggressive game up at the net and possess good hands, but I think my most important attribute is the kind of teammate I am. I can play with almost anybody. If my partner misses a shot, I never look at him, blame him or her, and conversely if I miss a shot, I always take accountability and say my fault, my bad. And even if my partner misses a shot, I will even take the blame for it because of a prior shot or two that I hit or did not hit. A lot of people find this very strange because I'm always taking the blame but in a very subtle way, it takes a lot of pressure off my partners. I'm always taking accountability for points we lose. What Sam did was the inverse and he just didn't get it.

The singles event was up first followed by doubles later in the week. With my newfound svelte physique, I was excited. My first singles match was against the #3 seed. Tony was one of the top juniors in Victoria a few years ago. In his early twenties, he was the heavy favorite to win with very few people giving me a chance. Obviously, I wouldn't be playing in the tournament if I didn't think I could win. My only strategy in the match was that if I got the lead, I wouldn't let up and I would keep applying pressure on Tony. Before my singles match, I had a warm up set of doubles with Geoff vs Matt and Josh. We demolished them 6-2 playing superb tennis! The key to tennis when you're winning and in the zone; is to keep riding that wave.

For my singles match with Tony, I did the same. I started off and won the first game, then after a couple more hard-fought games, I was up 3-0. I think Tony was a little bit stunned and he tried to hit the ball harder, but I kept applying pressure and playing consistent. He kept making more and more mistakes. I won the first at 6-0 which was a little bit of a shock for both of us. After the set, he took a bathroom break to talk to himself and regroup. As I waited, I kept reminding myself to just keep pushing and applying pressure. That's always been my mentality in tennis is to keep my foot on my opponent's neck and keep applying steady pressure until they submit. We were tied 1-1 but I stuck with my strategy. Tony kept making error after error. When the score was 3-1, I saw the life exit his body. With his will to compete completely gone, I finished him off 6-0 6-1. People watching were in complete shock, Tony was in shock, I was in shock! But I knew that I could do it. This is a very important lesson for young people today. Belief, grit, strategy, and competition skills are much more important than just having good technique. Because there's less competition (winning and losing) opportunities, what I did to Tony would not have been possible because of the mercy rule. Teachers, coaches, and parents are not allowing such one-sided games to happen and the total destruction of an opponent. The game would be stopped, and the powers of authority would insist on fairness. To give an opportunity for the player getting badly beaten to either catch up or quit the game. But it's not allowing young people the space to develop a killer instinct, to keep pushing when they're ahead. Instead, they're told to take their foot off the gas and let the other player catch up.

Therefore, a very important life lesson is missed, which is to ride that wave when winning. To keep pushing higher and higher. Great things can be achieved by learning this skill!

Conversely, when athletes are down, they are not being encouraged to just get the fuck back up. To feel uncomfortable, to feel defeated, to feel down. We are not allowing young athletes to experience adversity and we are quick to hold their hand and help them up. As painful as it is for Tony to get demolished, 6-0 6-1, it will benefit him in the long run.

 I think that's why so many people these days are having problems in tests, in competition, and in overall pressure situations. They're not experiencing this high pressure, winning and losing moments and learning how to handle them and just get the fuck back up. Instead, games are paused, or the importance ignored when these situations arise. But because past generations learned and enjoyed competing, this was just like breathing for me, like muscle memory. Tony, on the other hand, was perplexed and had no answer. Even though at the end of the match I personally felt bad for him, I would not have changed one thing and let up. I knew that if he had won the second set, I would have probably lost the match due to his youthful energy, better stamina, and conditioning.

Back to Sam. Our doubles tournament started Saturday at 9:30 a.m. We were playing Jeremy and Nick. I played Jeremy in the singles quarterfinals on Friday losing 6-1 6-3. He's one of the top players in Victoria. Eleven years younger and overall, just a better tennis player. In our match, I played well, but Jeremy was just better. I tried to make adjustments, change strategies, but for every adjustment I made, he had a counter. I never gave up, giving 100% effort but in the end, he was just too damn good. Though I hate losing, I wasn't upset because I gave it my all. Plus, that loss motivated me. I'm already planning on how to get better in singles by improving my fitness and conditioning, plus doing weekly drills to improve my groundstrokes. You learn so much from losing. That's why it's so important. It teaches you to accept and learn from the loss, to delete the emotion from your memory, but to also retain what improvements are needed in the future. The opposite is happening for young people today. They get emotionally invested in a loss and are not able to see rationally what to do in the future. Back to our doubles match, Jeremy and Nick are experienced players 30+ years old. They have played and won multiple tournaments in Victoria. In the first set, it was close. We were 4-5 down with Sam serving. That's when his problems started. Sam tensed up and had a hard time getting a serve in. After serving a couple of double faults, he started to overthink. On the very next serve, he froze for a couple of seconds, and struggled to toss the ball in the air. He served consecutive double faults, and we lost the first set 6-4. After the set, he stood by himself in the corner looking up at the sky, rattled. He walked over to me on the bench, and said "oh I'm just chilling." This is a very common attitude that I see in young people when they fail at something. They've been taught to feel like it's ok to lose, "to just chill" and "it's okay." I wasn't chilling, I was so pissed off but I didn't want to show Sam. But deep down inside, I was seething and this anger helped motivate me to try harder in the second set. Conversely, Sam looked shell shocked and was already defeated. When the second set started, he made even more errors and could hardly run or hit the ball. We went down early 3-1 but I kept battling because as everyone knows, I hate losing. And I rarely give up. When we were down 5-2, I started playing my best tennis. Getting angry helped me get even more focused. I willed us back to win the next game and was still fighting on every point, encouraging Sam to do the same. Unfortunately, Sam was already checked out and he asked me, "Alex what do I do?" But at that moment, it was too late for him. He should have asked me what to do last week, not at 3-5 down in the second set. At that moment, he was a lost puppy trying to find his way home. He had no chance, he had no clue, he was panicking, and he felt helpless. This is what I'm seeing with a lot of young people, especially young males, is that feeling of helplessness when they're down. They try to show competence and confidence in real life, acting like they know everything and have the situation under control. But the reality is disparately opposite of this. If the plan goes the way it's supposed to go, they're fine, but once they experience the first moment of adversity, they don't have the grit or tenacity to get back up. Again, as I've written in the earlier chapters, we're not letting young people lose. If we let more young people get destroyed earlier in life, it will give them the chance to try to find a way to get back up, as painful as this is. But because they haven't had that opportunity to really feel that pain of losing, of being slaughtered, of being obliterated, they really don't have the capabilities to deal with failure and take full accountability. To hate losing, and just get the fuck back up! So, at that moment, at 3-5 down, Sam was dead. Unbelievably, we almost came back but Jeremy and Nick were just too strong. I had no regrets, I played as well as I could possibly play. If Sam just played reasonably normal, we probably would have had a chance to win. After the match, I took a picture and posted it on Instagram. I'm not afraid to show my losses. My page is transparent, and I will post the raw events happening, win or lose, good or bad. I'm not ashamed or afraid of people seeing my weaknesses or vulnerabilities. And I think that is the key. To have less ego so that you're not so worried about being judged. That's where Sam had problems, he was too worried about every error and mistake he made, and that people would see it. Every time he made an error during our match, he would blame something like dust in his eye, the sun, or the ball taking a funny bounce. He couldn't accept that it was him who screwed up and just say my bad, and then move on the next point. It reminds me a lot of my female students when they say that modern guys will keep mansplaining even though they're 100% wrong. Sam was doing the exact same thing, he was mansplaining to himself and to me, but he couldn't accept that it was his mistakes. There are no easy fixes or easy solutions to this problem. It's going to take a lot of hard work, patience, self-reflection and understanding to eventually start the process of healing this lost generation. But the very first thing that we need to do as a society, is to realize and accept, that as parents, educators, coaches, community leaders that we all fucked up. To start reversing this social conditioning which has led to all the behavioral and emotional problems plaguing our youth.

Adam Sandler

I started lessons with Mateo a couple of months ago. I've taught both his siblings and have known his family for years through lacrosse. His brother played with Seve 9 years ago. Mateo's mother and grandfather were originally from Chile and moved to Canada during Augosto Pinochet's dictatorship years in the 70's. It's been interesting to teach all 3 siblings and observe the changes in each of them. I taught Michelle 6 years ago and Arturo 2 years after. In my lessons with them, we talked about school, work and just some random shit! The vibe was laid back with chill music playing as they learned how to drive. Arturo and I would talk about lacrosse and trash the guys on other teams. Fast forward to 2023, my conversations with Mateo had a more serious tone. We talked about societal issues, politics, wokeness and current events. Because his family fled Chile to move away from an autocratic and repressive regime, Mateo's grandfather sees the similarities from the past to those that are manifesting with political correctness today.

On lesson 4, I asked Mateo how everything was going? In the 3 weeks between lessons, Mateo's grad class was organizing events for Spirit Week. It's an annual tradition for graduating students and a major theme is to pick or dress up like a celebrity. In the past, students would choose themes like Freddy Kreuger, Jason from Friday the 13th, Paris Hilton, Cross dress, sports stars like MJ and other original and creative genres. This year, Mateo's class agreed to dress like Adam Sandler. Everyone was stoked to wear baggy pants and a baseball cap. But as crazy as this sounds, the school admin refused to allow it because they did not deem Adam Sandler to be "INCLUSIVE" enough! Like WTF!! How is this possible?

The students got together and agreed to change the theme to Barbie and Ken. Again, the school admin found them to not be "INCLUSIVE" enough! Hahahahaha, this is now becoming very funny in the most dystopian way! The students were not allowed to dress like normal people because of "INCLUSION!" I don't even know what that word, "INCLUSIVE" means anymore when almost everybody is "EXCLUDED!"

Eventually, they were allowed to dress in "MONOCHROME!" Everyone will dress in the same solid black outfits:)

My Buddy Nathan

It's a Sunday morning in September 2023. I got up bright and early with extra motivation and purpose to finish this book. I headed over to Parsonage Cafe, to write a few chapters. I texted my tennis buddy Nathan to join me for coffee. We met at the Hill earlier this spring. He was an elite junior and is currently running a tennis club. Nathan hadn't played in a while and was extremely rusty though you could tell that he was a really good tennis player in the past. We played and ended up losing to Geoff and John 6-2. He looked very frustrated but was cordial when we left the court. We played a lot over the next few months. As his game started coming back, we had some epic battles on the court. One day, he wasn't playing his best and he was off, so I asked him if everything was okay? He confided that he was having major issues with his wife. Nathan asked me to go out for a drink that night, he needed someone to chat with. We met at Irish Times, I ordered a beer, he had a non-alcoholic one. He shared that he and his wife were recently married but had separated because of a night of drunken IG texting Nathan had done with another woman. His wife was so upset about his momentary indiscretion and the damage it caused was too severe that it ended their marriage. Nathan was confused, upset and wanted to find a way to get back together with her. A few weeks later, we met up at Craft Brewhouse and as we were walking inside, I saw Nathan's face turn white, like he had seen a ghost! He saw a dude sitting with his arms around his ex-wife. Nathan asked to go elsewhere, and we grabbed food at bar next door. He was devastated to see his wife already dating only 2 months after they had separated. He was still clinging on with the hope to get back together but she on the other hand had clearly moved on. It was a difficult moment for him but a much needed one. It was a clear sign and a catalyst for him to end this chapter of his life and, as painful as it was, to get back up and start a new chapter. After a week, we sat down for coffee again. We talked about my book and my take on dating. Nathan was intrigued and reads the rough draft. He says that he likes the authentic and genuine feel of my book, finding the stories to be simple, without trying to sound smart or academic.

Nathan asked if I had an editor and if I didn't, that he would be interested in editing my book. Fast forward 6 weeks, he has started to use some aspects of the book for his own dating. One of the main things he's learned is to be more proactive. Nathan has been using dating apps but instead of just chatting online, he's been more assertive in asking the women on face-to-face dates. And it's worked, he's been on several dates, playing tennis, mini-golf, and waterfront walks. He's also been very transparent and honest about his status and what he's looking for in these dates; to meet different women, get to know them and see where it goes. He said, it's something he's learning by reading my book, to be genuine and honest without the optics or way that modern society is conditioning people to think they have to be. He had been so down for the past few months. I was so happy to see Nathan benefit from my book and its message having such a profound and positive impact on him. It's so dope!

Guys Need To Care More

I ran into Nathan at the tennis store while looking for shoes. He was planning on watching my doubles match last night but missed it and asked how we did? I went over Sam's struggles in the match against Jeremy and Nick. He agreed that younger guys are having a hard time with accountability; to admit their mistake and to own it. When Sam made an error, he would say, "I'm just chilling," "I'm just having fun" and would generally just check out for the rest of the match and not care. It's not that they don't care, maybe, they're afraid that they are not good enough and their ego can't handle the truth. So instead they say, "I don't give a fuck." It's actually fear and insecurity leading to apathy. And instead of fighting, they just give up. Today's society has promoted and encouraged this, that it's ok to lose and not to care about the loss. Men today are becoming more brittle in tough situations and lack the resiliency and grit to fight. This is causing mental and emotional stress in situations that makes them uncomfortable. Well, to be honest, we need young men today to be more uncomfortable and "to give a fuck and care!"

Overconfidence

So far, I have talked about how dudes can develop more confidence. However, there is a fine line between confidence and overconfidence. In 1988, after a few months of driving, I was feeling invincible behind the wheel and on top of the world. There was a girl that I liked named April who went to a school across town. She was very pretty and kind with a bubbly personality. I asked her to hang out with a couple of friends on a Friday night. It was a fall evening; the roads were slick and wet from the afternoon rains. After a great night eating and partying, it was time to take everyone home. We were driving from Surrey to New Westminster over the Alex Fraser Bridge. Around midnight, the bridge was empty with no cars in sight. It took about a minute to go to the top of the bridge and the descent was like a roller coaster. Feeling invincible as the 16-year-old dude that shouldn't have passed his road test, I felt an adrenaline rush buzz through my body. I floored the gas in my 1984 Honda Civic. As we climbed the bridge, all I wanted to do was keep going faster. By the time we reached the apex, our speed was around 150kph. As we descended, our speed increased to around 200kph. At the bottom of the bridge was a long curve to the right with solid cement barriers which separated the traffic. As we approached the bend, I finally tried slowing down and turning but we were like an out-of-control train that jumped its tracks. I'm not sure what happened next but, about 10 metres before the cement barrier, I was able to slow down enough to regain partial control of the car and avoid the barrier by about a foot! If we had hit the cement divider, I would not be here writing this book. Maybe by divine intervention, God had me experience this ridiculously stupid maneuver so that 30+ years later, I am able to share this story with my students on the dangers of being too overconfident.

I often talk about what real power is. Power is having the ability and capability to do something but discipline, restraint, and capacity, if the situation is not ideal, to refrain from exercising said power. Again, as with numerous real world examples, power corrupts, and absolute power corrupts absolutely. Once dudes regain their inner confidence, it is imperative that they also develop the control and self-discipline to only use power in the most ideal situations. Do not be toxic with your masculinity!

P.S. April never went out on a date with me again :(

CHAPTER 6 LESSONS IN STRENGTH, PERSEVERANCE, AND STAYING TRUE TO YOURSELF

Basketball back in the day

When we were younger, basketball was extremely popular because of Michael Jordan; everyone wanted to "be like Mike!" A Lot of dudes played on their school team, on the playground or in various competitive men's leagues in town. My brother Rob and I formed a team to play in the Filipino league. Back in 1991, a lot of the players had alpha-male mindsets and they hated losing. We competed against a number of good teams as well as a perennial juggernaut team of really amazing players; Baldo, Tin Tin, Estee(ex pro player,) and Mariboy. We would also play with these dudes from time to time at Kits Beach where the highest-level players in Vancouver played pick-up.

They would sometimes ask Rob and I to play with them even though we were a few years younger. We took on the best players in the area who were mostly black. I relished the chance to play against the top players in Vancouver and appreciated the older Filipino crew for giving us a chance to join them! I got elbowed, scratched, roughed up, and threatened by the older players. I didn't back down, and elbowed them back. If you gave an inch, they would have taken a mile, and you were already defeated. You had to man up and look your opponent straight in the eye without flinching. If you looked away, you already lost, and these lions would smell fear and destroy you. We won a lot of games but, of course, we also lost a couple, but the lessons that I learned at Kits beach, I try to instill with my students today. Never back down from a challenge, and relish the opportunity to play the very best. Win, lose, or draw, never ever look away!

Back to the Filipino league. Our team consisted of younger guys my age around 19 with Rob being the oldest at 23. Our team played well all year only losing to the juggernaut team of Baldo and his boys, in the regular season. We made the playoffs but in the first game, due to injuries, only 4 of us were available to play. Because of league rules, our team was disqualified for not having the minimum 5 players. Since everyone was already at the gym, with stands packed, we played the game 4 against 5. They had a full bench of subs. Even shorthanded, we knew that we were better than the other team. Our team played a box zone defense and a fast break offense. Miraculously, we won the game 4 on 5 but couldn't advance in the playoffs, and unfortunately, we were disqualified. It was probably the best game we ever played and the feeling of accomplishment in beating the odds is something that I carry with me to this day. For dudes in 2021, life isn't fair. You will face similar no win situations, so relish the opportunity to beat the odds and try to come out on top. Even if you don't succeed, give it your maximum effort without bitching or complaining about equality and fairness.

"I would rather die on my sword trying, than give up and be butchered in the slaughterhouse!"

Marlboro Reds

In 1990, it seemed like more than half of the men in the Philippines smoked cigarettes. It was part of society and the only place that people were not allowed to smoke was in a gas station or inside the church. Once mass ended, there would be a stampede to go outside and have a dart. I started smoking while on vacation with friends in grade 12. We were in the mountain resort town of Baguio and spent the week eating, drinking, and hanging out with my guy friends from school; Dot, Migs, Josh, Brian, Lex and Cary. One night while drinking, we all started smoking at the same time. It was a rite of passage for young men. Looking back, what the heck was I thinking? But those days were amazing. In a smoke filled living room with a case of San Miguel Pale Pilsner, chilling with your best buds talking about things eighteen-year-olds talked about.

- I almost died driving down the mountain. We left during a typhoon and the van we were riding in was swept by a massive mudslide towards a 5000-foot drop. Miraculously, our driver was able to regain control of the van maybe 10 feet before the edge of the cliff. We jumped out of the van and started walking down the mountain wading through knee height water which was just as dangerous as the 5000 ft cliff.

-2 weeks later a massive earthquake hit Baguio City and flattened parts of the city including the Hyatt Terraces Hotel. I have faced death many times and it's probably why I'm not fazed by inconsequential or trivial things and why I try to live life everyday to the max. Carpe Diem!

Fast forward 10 years, my son Alex was a very curious 4-year-old. Maria asked me to quit smoking because he would see my cigarettes in our room and, on occasion, put one in his mouth. I decided to quit, cold turkey but this was not easy since I had been a pack a day chain smoker for 10 years. The first night of quitting was the hardest. I woke up numerous times trembling and shaking from the massive nicotine withdrawal. The following morning, I had withdrawal symptoms again and started trembling. I thought about what to do and decided to go outside for a run every time I was feeling an urge to smoke. It worked! After a few days, the symptoms weren't as bad and as a bonus, I lost 20 lbs. with the increased exercise. I knew that I had kicked the habit 2 weeks later when I saw a homeless man smoking on the street. I passed by him, through the waft of the smoke and though I enjoyed the smell, I was not tempted to have one. To this day, I enjoy the smell of cigarettes and don't mind people smoking around me. I try to teach willpower to my students, the ability to stick with something even through the most difficult adversities. I want to inspire dudes to not back down from a challenge and to develop the strongest willpower to achieve a goal that they set out on, no matter the difficulty.

Mr. Clark

I attended Eric Hamber secondary, and as a sophomore, tried out for and made the Varsity Basketball team. I was the only player to make it, the rest were all junior and senior boys. Our coach was Mr. Clark, who was an ex-college player hailing from California. Mr. Clark is what the definition of "old school". I was excited to make the team and even happier to be named the starting point guard. My teammates consisted of kids that immigrated from all over the world. We had Amos from somewhere in the Eastern Bloc, Kneven from the former Yugoslavia, Cary from Hong Kong, Gurshan from India, and me from the Philippines. We were an eclectic mix that played for the hardest, hardcore coach in the history of hardcore coaches! Mr. Clark's practices were legendary for their intensity and focus on fitness. We would first do static stretches, then ball handling drills before finally doing lay-up lines to finish the warmup. I first learned basketball playing on the street and developed flashy moves and liked to attack the basket with ferocious drives. I didn't care if the players guarding me were 5 '6 or 6' 6, I always believed that I could score against anyone even if I was double or triple teamed. Mr. Clark had other ideas, he wanted to mold me into a pass first, disciplined traditional point guard. That was like fitting a square peg into a round hole. As the preseason wore on, he taught our team good fundamental basketball with set plays and unselfish ball movement. If double teamed, pass the ball quickly. He did not like streetball-type fancy layups preferring to use the backboard when driving to the hoop. He was so savage that if anybody on the team dropped a pass, did an underhand layup or walked through a drill, he would make us do a suicide (lines) as was a form of punishment. To do 1 line, a player starts on the baseline, runs to ¼ of the court, back to the baseline, ½ of the court, baseline, ¾ court, baseline, full court, baseline. The whole team needed to finish the line within 1 minute or we would have to start over. We had some slower players on the team and on numerous occasions, we would have to redo a line. On an average practice, the team would do around 20-30 lines which was a lot. Our team played pretty well during the season and had fun playing together. We loved away games and road trips, but we had a terrible game near the end of the season. We had a bad feeling about practice the next day. I'm not sure that balls were even on the court and all I remember was Mr. Clark calmly saying, "On the line boys." We kept count 1,2,6,16,25. When we reached 40, I thought that we would start doing scrimmage or drills. That wasn't the plan and we just kept hearing Mr. Clark's whistle and seeing his fucking stopwatch; 56, 62, 71 still going, some of my teammates were exhausted and a couple were close to throwing up. 76, 82, 2 guys start puking, we try to support and encourage them to keep going, 88, 95, ¾ of the boys are doubled over and ready to quit. 99, 100, 101, the only thing that I could remember was that I wasn't going to let this son of a bitch defeat me. My whole body was in shock and lactic acid was building up all over but my mind would not let this guy destroy me! 102, 103, 104 ,105, 106, Mr. Clark leaves the gym without saying a word. What a fucking asshole, but I was still standing. When he left the gym, I collapsed for a few minutes until I was able to crawl to the water fountain. That first sip was glorious and I stayed hunched over the fountain for the next few minutes. I hated Mr. Clark at that moment and thought that he was the devil for making us suffer for close to 3 hours of suicides. Many years later, I realized that he cared deeply for his players and the foundation that he instilled in us transcended the basketball court. That season taught us the importance of teamwork, and to stick together through adversity. It also ingrained the value of hard work, resiliency, grit, will power, and commitment. When I play basketball now, I'm still able to compete against guys half my age even though I can't jump as high or run as fast. I always remember the lessons I learned from this ultra old school coach and use some of his techniques in how I teach my students today. I don't make them run suicides, but the life lessons about resiliency, will power, commitment, overcoming intense anxiety and learning the true meaning of hard work are all compliments to my best ever coach, Mr. Clark.

T Score

Last summer, I dropped by Beacon Hill to hit against the old wooden wall to work on my groundstrokes and volleys. At 7am, I watched 2 guys rallying feverishly on the court 1. I immediately noticed the older player and his incredible footwork, balance and technique. In tennis, a very important skill is the split step. To be able to move quickly towards the next shot, good players will jump slightly as the opponent hits their shot. As your feet land on the court, you are able to explode in any direction towards the ball. The highest-level tennis players will split-step on every shot they take. I was in awe watching this old guy rallying for ten minutes and I asked him who the heck he was. His name was Glen, a retired financial advisor and national level player. He has represented Canada in many international competitions. Glen moved to Victoria from Calgary for the high caliber tennis players here in town. After Glen's lesson, I asked if he could do an evaluation on my game. We hit for 20 minutes, and he said that I have decent skills, fast feet but need to improve my strokes and, more importantly, my game strategy. Glen invites me to join a bi-weekly high performance morning training session for junior, college and ex professional players. The VETS group, as Glen calls it, practices Tuesday and Thursday mornings from 6:30-8am. These sessions are perfect for me to develop into a higher-level player, to keep active through the winter months and more importantly, to meet and play with some of the best players in Victoria. Our training sessions are super intense with guys having played the highest levels of tennis. Right away the one thing people notice about the group is how competitive, abrasive, aggressive, everyone is always. Being naturally aggressive myself, I fit right in. The level of testosterone exhibited by this group of mainly older guys is a stark contrast to what I see daily with my students and modern athletes competing in other sports. I enjoy watching lacrosse, hockey, baseball, soccer and anything else that is highly competitive. I sometimes play pickup basketball at Crystal pool against a lot of young ballers. It is very evident how much more passive and accommodating everyone is these days. Though it is generally positive for guys to be polite and respectful they seem to be lacking intensity, grit and the dog mentality needed during the heat of competition. I was watching a podcast last year about testosterone levels in modern males. It was about 4 guys in their 20's with a YouTube channel called the Try Guys. For fun, they tested their testosterone levels and were surprised that three out of the four guys had levels of an 80-year-old. There was only one guy that had relatively normal levels. Other studies have shown that testosterone levels have dropped dramatically over the last 30 years. The podcast theorized that changes in diet, societal norms, microplastics and an increase of estrogen intake by males through foods and the release in the environment by unused birth control pills have all contributed in lower T levels for modern men. I understand the push to reduce toxicity and misogyny in modern males. They definitely existed in my generation but to categorize every male as toxic and misogynist has led to policies and social norms that have nearly wiped-out average testosterone levels for the vast majority of normal guys. The Chinese believe in balance and harmony, the yin and the yang. I'm not sure what the ideal balance is for testosterone in males but I do know that the levels today are so low that it is leading to many behavioral problems, and a lack of strong, confident young men.

Parents in denial

Last night was my sister Odette's 60th birthday. We celebrated her special day at my brother Rob's house with a bunch of her closest friends and relatives. Her boyfriend Rick ordered a variety of delicious Filipino dishes and my sisters-in-law Ellen and Ruby, prepared delicious pasta and served some wicked cocktails. Everyone had a great time. After dinner, I sat down with Odette and the rest of her friends. Sitting beside me was a couple in their '50s who had kids in their 20's. The husband and I hit it off right away. I mentioned my book and the things I've noticed and learned about modern society over the past few years. He worked in technology and, in his free time, coached top tier minor hockey over the last 25 years. I mentioned changes I've noticed when it comes to competition skills, grit and resilience within the younger generation. He agreed and shared his thoughts. The major change he noticed were the parents. In the past, everything was much more competitive and fun. The parents, kids and coaches all got along, enjoying the games, practices and travel tournaments. Today, people would drop off their kids, leave them, do their Costco shopping, and then come back. He called them Costco parents. Or on the flip side, helicopter parents hovered over every move that their kids and coaches made. What's missing are parents that cared deeply but let the coaches coach and allowed their kids to play. His wife agreed but the tone and vibe of our conversation turned. When her husband and I shared ideas about the younger generation, his wife seemingly interjected every time and started to say that her husband always generalized. We then talked about the lack of interpersonal and face-to-face communication skills young people have today. His wife countered that because of technology, they learned a different way of communicating. I immediately picked up on her energy and though I wanted to explore and exchange more ideas with her husband, I started changing the subject. She made excuses and defended everything about their kids. Then we talked about cell phones and texting. When their kids first got their phones 12 years ago, she saw her daughter texting feverishly with someone. To her surprise, she was messaging her friend who was sitting on the sofa right beside her, giggling in silence. Her husband thought that this was not normal and tried to say something like; "hey maybe you want to put down the phone and communicate face-to-face like a real human!" His wife then defended her daughter saying that she still knew how to communicate like humans. But they preferred using phones to connect with each other and were much better at it than us. I found this very disturbing, intriguing, and interesting. Her husband, like myself, has worked with youth for the last few decades and has seen massive changes, especially in the last 3 to 5 years. We have boots on the ground, evidence-based knowledge about the changes and how disruptive and dangerous these behaviors are, identifying the problems, and trying to offer solutions. But we were constantly being shut down by his wife with her trying to downplay the urgency and the seriousness of the problems this generation has. As I've written in the chapter about societal conditioning, if parents do not acknowledge that we fucked up and start making immediate changes, the youth will have no chance because in their minds, they're not flawed or lacking in any sort of skills that are important in everyday life. The wife agreed that modern society lacks humanity, yet she can't acknowledge or understand that her mindset, which is the prevailing mindset for a lot of middle-aged decision makers, is causing a lot of the aforementioned problems. Her stubbornness to have an open discussion is downright scary. If we have decision makers condone, normalize and say that all generations had these problems, we may never be able to climb out of this very deep hole that we're in right now. The ironic thing and frightening thing is that when I speak to people like his wife last night, I see the fear, regret and shame in their eyes but also their stubbornness to not want to admit that they have had a hand in the current problems plaguing society today. It's like the sunk cost fallacy. We've invested so much time, effort, research, money to try to make positive changes in society but because we're so fully invested in the changes, if we see problems arise, we ignore them because we feel like we're too deeply invested to change course. But as wise businesspeople through time have said, we should never be too emotionally invested in our investments and if we see the signs that it's a bad investment, we should be able to walk away and be willing to lose what we invested so that we don't end up losing even more money, time and effort into a no-win, sinking ship. Too many people are emotionally invested and want to see this modern utopian idea succeed. But the reality is that all signs point to a lost generation, that all of us have had a hand in destroying. I have had a hand in this but instead of staying silent and being afraid to admit my mistakes and the mistakes that my generation has made, I'm being proactive and trying to do something to reverse the damage that we have all caused this younger generation.

There's hope

It's late September 2023. I spoke with my publisher this afternoon about my book. There's no turning back now, here we go! Yesterday, I was playing tennis at the hill with Jim and the rest of the crew. Jim's been going to the hill for the last 40 years. He's in his mid '50s, married, with a daughter in grade 5. He's a classic liberal that spends a lot of time in California. A couple of years ago when I first started writing my book, Jim and I had very little in common when it came to politics. Fast forward to 2023, now he's freaking out. Every day since the start of the school year, I could see him preoccupied, he's always on his phone on the court. So, when we started hitting this afternoon, all he could talk about was the parents march that happened all over Canada. Concerned parents around the country came together to raise awareness about gender ideology curriculums in schools. Jim, who two or three years ago would have supported a lot of these liberal ideas, has now flipped. He's seen what the schools and leaders are promoting in schools and because his kid is exactly in that age range between 8 to 15, he's very concerned. Equally concerned are the vast majority of the parents in his daughter's school. Though they don't openly discuss this topic, for fear of losing their jobs or being "canceled", my friend is part of a group on WhatsApp of roughly 200 other parents that feel very strongly and have many similar opinions and ideas about the current state of indoctrination in schools. My friend is frustrated that his daughter's school "is filled with rainbow flags." In every classroom, in every textbook, every note on the blackboard.

There's a day for inclusion, there's a month for LGTBQ rights, there's a year for everything. There's nowhere his daughter can turn to without seeing this messaging in school. He's at wits end and almost thinking about pulling his daughter out of her elementary school. In the US and elsewhere, more parents are pulling their kids out of public school and looking for schools that don't indoctrinate but give them a free platform to think. More and more parents are homeschooling their kids. It just seems like parents right now are being forced to accept this with very little say how to parent their kids in gender ideology. As my friend has stated many times now, I can't believe they're promoting kids as young as five or ten "to cut off their dicks or breasts!" This was the last straw for my classic liberal friend who only two or three years ago supported many of the ideals that now have gone so extreme. As he states, about 80% of the parents also agree with this sentiment. There is hope that eventually, when push comes to shove and the parents see what's happening to their kids, that eventually they can admit when it's gone too far and start to make meaningful change. This is also what I talked about in my other chapters, society's going to have to make a choice about young men. My friend is worried that:

1. His daughter will become confused about her gender because of the school's curriculum and choose a permanent life altering surgery.

2. When his daughter is older, there will not be many men that will want to start families and have babies with her.

Recently, I was teaching a 16-year-old hockey goalie. He's in a hockey academy, but his friends are in normal public school. They have told him how bad it is in their schools. His friends estimate that between 60 to 70% of the guys now identify as gay or trans in public high schools.

Jim posed the question "should kids be able to receive life altering surgical and pharmaceutical treatment for gender issues without parental consent?" This was the main theme for the protest about parents' rights that happened in September. Then Jim thought about the question, reevaluated and changed the question to "should kids be able to receive life altering pharmaceutical and surgical treatment?" And he and most of the other parents agreed. No!!!! It should not be allowed with or without parental consent! This is life altering surgery and should only become an option for adults 18 +.

As Jim says, "I will do anything for my kids!" Jim has always voted and supported blue states policies. He believes strongly in universal healthcare, is against gun rights and will generally oppose most policies that conservative red states pass. He calls these places extreme and radical. But with all that, because he loves his daughter and "will do anything for her" he will not only side with these "red" states, he's all in, even with all their other faults, to protect his daughter. This is what's needed in society to balance out gender ideology, for parents to take a stand.

Margaret

I recently finished lessons with Margaret. Originally from Europe, her family moved to Canada a few years back. She emailed requesting lessons, and mentioned that she was a little nervous about driving but wanted to eventually get her license. In lesson 1, we discussed what her goals were. She was expecting to do lessons for several months and hopefully be ready for the road test. I could see that she was really nervous about driving and the dangers it posed for her and others on the road. The other thing I saw was her silent inner strength and resiliency to achieve her goal of getting her license. Finally, I said to Margaret that we adhere to one basic rule in the car which I call rule #1, to get from point A to B without hitting anything or getting hit irrespective of all the other road rules or courtesies that affect driving. It simplifies driving for my students and lets them see the big picture instead of obsessing about all the small details usually associated with taking and passing the road test. I'm still teaching all the rules and regulations for the test as set out by the DMV, I'm just doing it in a different method than what most people usually expect or comprehend. The theorem I follow is called Occam's Razor, it states that the simplest answer or solution to a problem is generally the most preferred. Why over complicate driving when it is so fucking simple? Try to not hit anything or get hit! ICBC, which is the DMV agency in the province, recommends new drivers to follow a simple way of thinking, See/Think/Do. Unfortunately, they then try to explain all the rules and regulations in such a linear and fact based way that most new drivers are overwhelmed with trying to remember everything. My students get overwhelmed thinking about when to scan, shoulder check, look in the mirrors, and all the other rules that they think they need for their test. All of these are correct, and drivers should do all of them. The problem is that students preparing for their road tests put too much emphasis on the rules and not enough on just driving without crashing.

Margaret and I get into the car, I ask her to adjust her seat and mirrors, then start the car. I have dual gas and brakes on my side, and under emergency situations, I am able to drive us out of danger by grabbing her steering wheel and driving the car. I have on numerous occasions been in life and death situations where either my students are driving into oncoming traffic, or we have oncoming traffic barreling towards us. I must be fucking nuts doing this job but actually, I love helping my students and I really care about all of them!

As Margaret starts driving, I notice her hands trembling and that she had a lead foot. I also noticed that she's had lots of road time. She had driven a lot with her parents, but was extremely nervous on our initial drive. When students exhibit this, they have built up some negative episodic and procedural memory that they default to when driving. If in the past, she had negative experiences about cars behind her, busy intersections or near-crash scenarios, her nervous behavior will manifest over and over again unless we break those memories. It is important to replace those memories with more positive ones that she will associate with driving in the present and future. With this in mind, I play some jazz in the car and talk about everything with her other than driving. I observe her strengths, weaknesses and create a long-term lesson plan. I recommend eight lessons and the road test package. Margaret had good technique but had a lot of negative driving memories. If I could replace these memories, I was confident that she would be ready for the test. I also told her to rethink her timeline and look for a test within 1-2 months instead of 6-8 that she envisioned. I had her think about my recommendations and contact me when she had decided on what she wanted to do. This is the most crucial moment of the lessons, when my students trust and buy into the process. If they buy in, the rest of the lessons will flow like water. Luckily, she was enthused by my teaching style and was excited to book the next lesson. In our lessons, we chatted about food, music, and current events. After each lesson, I saw steady improvement and by lesson four, Margaret became very comfortable and confident behind the wheel. It was great to see her smile happily instead of the frown she had on our first lesson. At this point, we started working on prepping for her road test. She easily passed, and I was so happy for her! Margaret was able to conquer her anxiety, and is now a very confident driver!

What's your type?

Last year, I started lessons with a girl named Lauren. On her 16th birthday, she got her license and was really excited to start driving. Her dad phoned me up, and we set up a series of eight lessons to start. I meet her and her dad, do my introduction, then, we get into the car. Lauren was exuberant, carefree, sweet and a very nice young woman. She went to a public school, had lots of friends, and worked as a host at a local steakhouse. Immediately, she was able to control the car, make turns in intersections, and had amazing observation skills that most new drivers do not possess. She also had solid communication skills. I started to get to know her pretty well and asked about her plans in college. We did lessons throughout the year, with her driving rapidly improving. I felt very comfortable and I rarely had to intervene to avoid a potential bad situation. All she required now was parking and road test details. In lesson 7, I noticed that she had dyed her hair slightly and she was a little bit more reserved. It was very subtle, but I noticed something slightly different in her driving. I asked her what was up. She said everything was okay, so I let it go. Later in the lesson, her driving was still off so I asked her again. She confided that it was a relationship issue. She comes out and tells me that she likes girls. To her surprise, my reaction and facial expressions did not change. I was not phased at all and because I've seen more than people can imagine, if a 16-year-old says that she likes girls, I'm very happy for her.

Normally when she comes out to people, they start acting awkwardly and treat her differently. They try to be extra nice and supportive of her coming out. I was the first person that she came out to that remained the same and treated her the exact same whether she was gay or not. This instantly relieved her tension and anxiety. It seemed to put her at ease and she began driving much better. Now that her driving was back to normal, my next question was; "what's your type?" She had a puzzled look on her face and said "I've never been asked that by anyone!" I said to Lauren, "None of your friends have ever asked you what your type was?" in the most confused way. Then I asked her if she likes tall girls, short girls, blondes, brunettes, Asians, Caucasians, blacks or if it was more of an emotional connection. When we finished the lesson, she thanked me so much for being so open-minded, even if I was a 49-year-old Catholic, Filipino dude. She had the biggest smile on her face when she got out of the car and had a pep in her step. Two weeks later, during lesson eight, she told me what her type was. She likes feminine girls with long straight hair that smell really good. I was happy for her! I said that if I ever run across somebody that would be her type, I'll link them on social media. After a year since coming out, she was finding it extremely difficult to find a partner. My last advice for her was just because she was gay, not to necessarily change her appearance to suit the modern narrative of what a gay person should be and how they should look. She should just be authentic, if she still wants to be feminine and girly, do it. If she wants to change her hairstyle or become more masculine, that's her choice too. Tats, piercings, do as you please! The only thing she can't do is follow what people think or perceive is best for her. At that point Lauren is not herself anymore, but just an avatar that society paints her to be. This is a really good life lesson for everybody, all genders and orientations: it doesn't matter what you think people will like about you. You still need to be yourself and if people don't like you for who you are, they can go fuck themselves! Change and improving yourself is always good, but it should be for your improvement not for anyone else or specifically to attract a mate. My Mexican tennis buddy, Jorge, recounted a very famous song "*No somos monedita de oro*" (we are not golden coins) which loosely translates to; I know not everyone is going to like me, so why am I trying so hard to please everyone. I will be myself, and those that will like me for who I am are the only ones that are truly important!

I may have butchered the translation but that's the gist of what Jorge was saying about the song.

Trans students

Over the years, I've had a few trans students do lessons with me. Though I have had no previous experience with trans students, I was looking forward to our lessons and to try my best. I thought the most ideal way to teach them was for me to just be me and see how it goes. A few years ago, I had two trans students take lessons at the same time. They were both biological females that were transitioning to become trans male by doing hormone therapy. Both were in their teens, one played hockey and the other was a music producer. I noticed how unsure both my students were around me so I just tried to be myself. We talked about food, music, concerts, and their present relationships. One was going out with a lesbian and the other was going out with a homosexual male. They taught me a lot about their psyche, how they ticked, and what made them anxious in today's world. It was a very complex situation and I hope I was able to help them. Both got their licenses, and one works in construction while the other performs as a drag queen and produces music.

When my first trans student went for his road test, his license still had his biological female name, Katherine (not the real name.) Steve, the examiner, was an old school fellow and extremely nice guy. He kept calling my student by his biological name. I whispered to Steve that his name was now Cal. Steve understood and they drove out of the DMV. After 30 minutes, Cal passed with flying colors. He was so thankful that I helped him get his license and how I handled that situation with Steve. My learning moment here is to be myself around anybody. I'm not trying to be offensive or old-fashioned, but I think if I try too hard to be nice it comes off as artificial and insincere.

Recently, I started lessons with Heather, another trans woman. Her family moved from the US a couple of years ago. Heather is a serious bass player and drummer. We chatted for a few minutes, and I noticed that she was hesitant and afraid to start. She had anxiety about getting into a deadly crash. After 25 minutes of getting to know each other, we start driving. Her initial drive was rough and tentative. I put on Lee Ritenour's French Roast, a furious mix of jazz and rock featuring all-time great Steve Gadd on drums and Lee Ritenour on electric guitar. We get on a long road just in time for Ritenour and Gadd to do their solos. Heather starts to relax as we immerse ourselves into this amazing jazz fusion song. At this moment, there were no labels, barriers, constructs, just the amazing sound of 80's jazz fusion. Two people jamming like we were at a smoky jazz bar in NYC. I then put on Young and Fine by Weather Report with an all-star lineup with Joe Zawinul on piano, Wayne shorter playing sax, Alex Acuna on drums and the great Jaco Pastorius, considered by many hardcore musicians as one of the best electric bass players ever, he was credited with inventing the fretless bass. Young and Fine (Live in Offenbach 1978 version) is perfect cruising music, fast, with deep bass cuts and a sax solo that pierces straight in your soul. Next, I play Crash of Rhinos, an alternative band that my son Alex would blast on our way to his school 10 years ago. Heather loves it and says it's Midwest emo. Courage My Love is another pop punk band we had on the playlist. Now I'm mind fucked cuz of Heather's expansive musical knowledge. I feel her confidence and belief growing exponentially. When the lesson finishes, we fist bump, and she almost breaks my hand! Heather's fists are like Mike Tyson's! The following week, Heather was so excited and surprised me with a playlist to listen to during our lesson. The music, shall I say, was diverse, edgy, and dark.

Again, she was ecstatic with the lesson. We fist bump again but this time, I used my left hand. She lightly taps my wrist, laughing from almost breaking my hand the previous lesson.

I believe that it is important to be authentic and be yourself in every situation. Heather and I were two people vibing and having a good time with no labels, period.

Best prize ever

By the time I was 17, I had played and competed in multiple sports, from little league baseball, basketball, tennis, bowling, volleyball, football. I had won many trophies and medals and even represented the Vancouver region, in the BC Summer Games for tennis. In baseball, I was an all-star pitcher, in basketball, an all-star point guard, and a junior tennis champion. But I want to share the best prize that I have ever won. From 1988-1990, I attended Brent International School Manila in the Philippines. The school was very exclusive and had an International Baccalaureate program. Students came from the top Filipino families as well the expat kids. Though I went to this posh school, I wasn't rich and still lived in our original town of Malabon. I had friends from both the richest and poorest families in the Philippines. On weekdays, I played on the Brent Team and on the weekends, I would play with the neighborhood kids. It was a blast hooping in my backyard. I would trade my basketball kicks for beach slippers and be one of the boys. We would play all day long and the camaraderie was amazing. Anyone who has played in slippers knows how dangerous and difficult it is to run and jump in them. You had to adapt your footwork by shuffling your feet close to the ground and cushioning the landing of your jumps. To this day, I'm not sure how I didn't break my ankles on the hard, slippery cement basketball courts that we played on. Our neighborhood team would travel to different barangays (neighborhoods) and challenge the other teams. We would place a wager on the game. The Philippines is a very hot and humid country and, was extremely poor. Water quality was iffy due to the aging pipes and lack of filtration. We take our crisp, clean, perfectly safe, drinking water in Vancouver for granted, and played Russian roulette with every sip of water in Malabon. People could get cholera and other water-borne illnesses instantly.

The bet with the opposing teams was for ice-cold, bagged tap water. In the stores beside the court, vendors would sell the coldest, most refreshing water in small plastic bags. After a hard-fought battle, this was the ultimate prize, to drink this liquid gold. It's hard to describe how good that bagged water tasted in the tropical heat, with sweat beading out of every pore in your body!

I've won trophies and awards in multiple sports, but that water was hands down, the best prize I have ever won in my life!

Contentment

This past couple of years, I've been out and about town more than probably any time in my life. From playing tennis five times a week, pick-up basketball at Crystal pool, Wednesday Volleyball with Lee, Donnie and the boys, golfing, talking to my students and hanging out with my buddies at the Beagle, it's been quite an experience. I've talked to A LOT of people and have gotten to know them really well. After the Covid lockdowns, there has been an heightened dependence with technology, in our daily lives. People spent more time indoors gaming, and using social media apps like YouTube, Snapchat, IG, and Tik Tok. With the increased use of social media, people are seeing their friends pages and random accounts more often. It's a great way to connect globally, but there is a catch: many times, we're comparing our lives to our friends online and even worse, social media influencers. With the Paris Hilton, Kim Kardashian phenomenon, the role and importance of the influencer profession has exploded. Before then, there wasn't really a way for normal people to compare and see the lives of others on a daily basis except through traditional media like magazines, TV or newspapers. The one thing most people don't realize about social media, is that they are showing the best parts of their lives. If there's something negative that happens, they can edit it out in post-production using filters and Photoshop, or just not post a certain picture or video. It leads to an almost unrealistic expectation when looking at social media pages. Most times, what's posted is the very best version of the situation but not as genuine and authentic as a raw photo or video. Therefore, when an average person sees this, they tend to feel inadequate when they compare their lives to what they're seeing on social media. This leads to a lack of contentment and happiness. One thing I notice about most of the people that I surround myself with, whether they're my really good friends or just acquaintances or random strangers, is that most of them are really insecure and unhappy about themselves. This insecurity about not being good enough leads people to strive for more and more but they end up not being happy with their current situation. Here's an example: I have a lot of students and friends that go to the gym to work out. When they first go to the gym, they have goals in mind; to be healthier and to look better. They may be flabby, overweight, scrawny, they want to sculpt their bodies. After getting a training regimen, people will start going to the gym. Over the next few months of hard work, they will see the positive changes in their bodies. This is where the problem lies. Once they've achieved that initial goal, they start to feel like they should need to improve another aspect of their physique instead of being content with the original goal of, say, getting fitter or toner. It becomes more of an obsession to keep trying to improve instead of feeling satisfied. There's no contentment and people will feel inadequate even though, to an outsider, that person will look amazing. I see gym people that look like "eights" or "nines", but they see themselves more like "twos" or "threes". The more I witnessed this, the more I was fascinated but also disturbed because people were not content or happy with themselves and instead had this need or obsession to keep sculpting while feeling that they were never good enough. This goes back to comparing yourselves in your daily lives on social media with influencers that always have a perfect photo, video or backdrop.

It's really interesting to see how this affects the modern dating scene. In one family gathering that we had recently, my younger nieces who are in their late teens and early twenties, were showing Maria Tinder and how it worked. A couple of them were single and looking through tinder for prospective dates. They scoured through bios, first looking at height. If the guys were under 6 ft, they swiped to the next picture. If the guy was over 6 ft, but his photo was meh, they would swipe to the next picture. Next, they looked at the bio and if the person didn't play sports, they would swipe to the next picture. If they looked at the bio and the guy didn't have very many female friends, they would swipe to the next picture. If the guy had too many male friends and too many female friends, they would swipe to the next picture. My wife found this so confusing and mentioned that my nieces were looking for a perfect tinder date which probably didn't exist. Or if he did exist, he would only be 5%-10% of the available tinder males on the site! This phenomenon again relates to real life. I know so many people that are in their twenties, thirties, and forties that are single. They're nice, attractive, have great jobs and stability, but are having a heck of a time meeting other people. Even if they do meet somebody, and they go on a date, the chances of a more serious relationship developing are remote because of contentment. They will see a flaw in this person, and because of the ease of tinder and other means of social dating, they will swipe to the next person. There are a lot of single people looking for that perfect partner but if their standards are too high, they may never meet a partner or if they do have a partner, this union will become brittle because of that unattainable bar set by society. It all boils down again to contentment and being happy with less than perfect. This is so hard for people to grasp, but as I've written in my other chapters, imperfection is what makes humans perfect or, in other words, imperfection is the beauty of humanity.

Various religions and beliefs have advocated for the practice of humility in ourselves and to not be envious of our neighbor's lives and accomplishments. I fear that in modern times, we're doing the exact opposite when we're trying to compete in this invisible rat race and always comparing ourselves to others which is resulting in people becoming very envious of one another. The irony of all this, is that these social media influencers and YouTubers eventually burn-out by having to keep pushing themselves to get more views and likes. They are never content with their current level, even though they're seen as very successful by most of their fans and followers. People are stuck in a feedback loop or an echo chamber that is increasingly and exponentially making people less content and more envious. This cycle just keeps accelerating which is causing most of the problems we have in society today.

CHAPTER 7: REDISCOVERING REAL CONNECTIONS

How to meet someone organically

After spending months observing and immersing myself in the community, I have come to the conclusion that couples meeting organically seem to have much stronger, deeper relationships than those meeting online through dating apps. I'm always asked how to meet someone organically, people tell how hard it is. We're in a really tricky situation because of social norms, and boundaries. Many people today struggle to initiate and carry a seemingly normal conversation.

I have many friends and acquaintances that are single. Universally, everyone says that the dating scene today sucks! Not only is it hard to set up a date, once they go on a date, it rarely works out. It's the boundaries that people exist in today. People will have different personalities and roles depending if they are at work, school, in public or on a dating app. It's rare to meet people that are authentic and themselves most of or all the time. Society simply makes this almost impossible to do. Many times, I see people meet and hook up at different clubs. Purely physical by nature, this will rarely lead to anything more serious . If they do have a spark but don't hook up, they will exchange IG or Snapchat information. If the guy DMs and asks her to go for coffee, it becomes a much bigger deal, and most times will not happen. There may be several reasons for this, but people aren't as open or used to meeting people in person. Having coffee has become a bigger deal due to the intimate, personal setting than just hooking up physically for the night. People use dating apps if they are in dating mode or hook up at clubs because they are in hooking up mode.

An example of these boundaries happened today. A couple of months back, I was watching OK Charlie band at Irish times. I'm pretty tight with Mitch, the guitarist and lead singer, Dustin who plays bass/keyboard and Graham, the drummer. They are a killer band with a loyal following. I ran into a musician buddy hanging out with a female friend. We exchanged IG and she started following my posts and stories. Last week, she had a book publishing event on her story, and I asked her about it. I told her about my book, she gave me her email and asked me to connect with her by email. The following morning, I Dmd and emailed her and she responded to both by sending publishing information by email. I replied and her next dm shocked me. She asked if we could communicate by email only for the book and separate it from IG dm. I never even thought of the distinction or separation as she had used her IG to highlight the publishing event. It gave me perspective on how she separated IG and work email. The different roles for public vs private.

Societal barriers are making natural ways to meet people almost impossible because most times, people are not in dating mode but instead in work mode, sports mode, dance mode or meditation mode. In the past, since people had less barriers, organic meetups happened more often. It now makes sense why people can only really meet and date on these apps because that's the only time they are in dating mode.

It's the first week of November in 2023. While visiting my mom for a couple of nights in Vancouver, I decided to go out and see how the dating scene was in town. The first night, I went to Guilt and Company, it is an upscale jazz bar in Gastown. I've been there before, and I've always had a great time listening to amazing musicians! Last night, I was floored by Krystle Dos Santos and her band. They sounded like they should be playing in the Blue Note in New York City! It was a packed house and I moved around while I was filming. From time to time, I would ask the people in the other tables if I could sit or film around them. They usually said yes but seemed a little uncomfortable with me going up to them. The next night, I was trying to find a place for dinner. Since I was by myself and Maria was home in Victoria, I went to do some more research. First up was Browns Social House. It's a chain restaurant that has locations across Canada including a couple in Victoria. I sat down at the bar and ordered a vodka tonic. It was dead so I asked for my bill. The bartender was a woman in her early 30s, very attractive and extremely friendly. I asked her if she knew any bars in Vancouver she could recommend where people still met organically? I told her about my book and the research I was doing. She was very helpful and spent 10 minutes giving me lots of great information. Being an older millennial, she has both met people organically and has also used dating apps. But nowadays, she's noticed that most of her friends only date using apps. Organic relationships only happen at school, workplaces, or through friends setting them up. Other than that, she said that it was extremely hard and rare to meet someone organically in 2023. She met her husband while both were working in a restaurant. She also said that women were much more open to meeting guys. Guys on the other hand, with a fear of rejection, are simply not stepping up trying to meet someone face to face. They prefer to text or use social media because as she said, if they get rejected, they don't have the burden of a face-to-face rejection. It goes both ways and it's also easier for women for the exact same reason! And if it doesn't work out, they can just ghost the other person and call them an asshole or a bitch. She wished me luck with my research but couldn't really recommend a place. I used Google to search up other places and found Craft Brew House. It's another chain bar restaurant, we have a location in Victoria managed by my tennis buddy Corey. When I arrive at Craft, I'm seated at the bar beside three young women in their mid-20s. The place seems cold and the people very disconnected from each other. It's probably as unfriendly a spot as I've been to in a while! It takes the bartender a few minutes before taking my order. She's also very frigid. After 15 minutes, I ordered salt and pepper wings with blue cheese and a lager. As I'm waiting, I say excuse me to the three ladies beside me. We started talking and

I asked them about online versus organic dating in Vancouver. I asked if it was still possible to meet people organically? They said that it was pretty hard and normally, the only place you can meet them is at school or work. Because of modern social norms, they said it was awkward and a little creepy for strangers to approach them. When they were in Edmonton, a smaller city in Alberta, it was much more common for strangers to come up and say hello but in the bigger city like Vancouver, people were just more guarded in meeting organically. They said that they were okay with meeting strangers but they weren't really open to the idea! I didn't want to push them so I said thank you for their input and went back to devour my wings! As I was leaving, I thanked them again, and they gave me a really warm smile. I stepped into another bar beside Craft. It was dead with 2 tables of older couples and not much else. The hostess at the door was a really nice young woman in her early 20's. Her name was Vikki from Mexico City, she was finishing her business degree at UBC. I asked her if she knew places in Vancouver where people could meet organically? We talked about the dating challenges in the city. When I brought up dating apps, she rolled her eyes and we both started laughing! She told me how hard it was to meet people because everyone seems so awkward, especially the guys! She had bad experiences with dating apps because as she said, it's almost like she's expected to do something and getting to know the person was so programmed and pre-planned. There wasn't the exploration and getting to know phase as you would in a more random and natural meetup. She told me that there weren't a lot of places to bring someone on a first date in Vancouver and most of the places were cliche like beaches and parks. I suggested mini golf or bowling and she screamed with excitement and joy! She said that she wasn't interested in dating now because the dating scene is horrible! I asked her if she listened to music and if she wanted to follow me on Instagram, she did. I would have stayed longer but because she was working, I said, "*adios*" and left. We had a nice chuckle with my terrible Spanish!

From all the women I spoke to the last couple of days, they seem resigned and apathetic to the idea of meeting someone organically in Vancouver. Impossible and terrible are words they used to describe the dating scene!

A solution is to start opening-up and slowly lowering the barriers people have. This will widen the opportunity window to meet people in more situations, increasing the likelihood of creating that spark or buzz that used to happen more regularly in the past. Obviously, there's a big risk to lowering your boundaries. It makes you more vulnerable which may be the reason why people don't do it. They don't want to get hurt, but this is a risk/reward scenario. The more risk people are willing to take, the bigger the reward that is possible. But if things go awry, the harder and more painful the fall will be. That choice is yours!

Ways to Attract a Woman

This is a very interesting and tricky question. On the one hand, I am trying to reignite strength and masculinity. On the other hand, that level of assertiveness is sometimes too intense for this generation. What I have observed is that a mix of traditional strength with finesse and a low-key approach seem to work best. With the push for equality, modern women are becoming increasingly more aggressive. Therefore, the key for the guys is to become more masculine but understand and be comfortable with sometimes being more patient in the initial attraction process. Let the ladies come to you, show some initial interest but don't push so hard. A natural ebb and flow is the desired outcome with both parties equally slowly building the attraction. Shoot your shot but be more subtle and not be so over the top!

Two years after writing this chapter, I witnessed an amazing encounter happen this morning!

My publisher gave me a hard deadline of November 4, 2024 for final submission for my manuscript. The process for my book publishing will take 3 weeks with the published copies available for the end of the month! I have been feverishly cleaning up the manuscript, doing one last read through, while they are formatting the book.

I'm at JJ Bean, the same cafe that Marie and I reconnected after 36 years. There is a long worktable that patrons set up their laptops with me positioned, at the very end. A lady in her 30s, sits down right in front me. Seconds later, a man in his 40s, asks her if he could sit beside her. In the most casual way, he starts to chat with her. She looks relaxed and engages in the conversation. Half an hour in, they are laughing and talking about her dog and hobbies she likes. I was so happy for them both! It's so refreshing to see a couple meet organically these days. These types of connections used to happen all the time, and after witnessing them meet in person, it gives me hope for the future!

Smokey Mountain

Back in 1988, Metro Manila, which was a bustling metropolis of about 15 million people, had one place where the city would dump all of its garbage. It was called Smokey Mountain, and it got its name due to the amount of garbage dumped there forming a large mound. The local government at the time was in total chaos and in a state of flux. The dictator, President Marcos, had just been deposed in 1986 and the city's infrastructure was crumbling due to the lack of resources caused by the rampant corruption that was embedded in all levels of government. To try to alleviate the problem, city workers burned the garbage by open air incineration hence the name Smokey Mountain. Driving near this smoldering mound even a mile away, the stench and smell was so putrid that it would seep into your car even with all the windows closed. That awful smell would remain inside your car for at least a couple of days.

The Philippines in 1988 was a very poor country, so poor in fact that there were thousands of families and people that lived on Smokey Mountain in small wooden shacks. People would find scraps of wood, and other materials that they could build into a temporary shelter. Families would scavenge together for anything from leftover food, old clothes, household items like old tables and chairs, old radios, or children's toys to resell for money. The people were so resourceful that nothing was wasted, and everything recycled. The modern recycling generation we have right now would be so amazed and proud of how resourceful these people were to not waste anything all the while existing in the most inhumane and destitute situation. The other thing is that these people by and large were very happy. They had nothing. They struggled every day to find something to eat, but their level of happiness was surprisingly high. The people in Smokey Mountain were extremely poor and just made enough money to feed their families day to day. They would always have a smile on their face as they would respectfully ask for money, food, or any sort of assistance that you could give them. If you gave these families some bread, a can of sardines, and a bottle of rum, they would be the happiest people on earth. They would be smiling and be so grateful for that small blessing that they had been given that day. I compare that to people here in Victoria or in the Western World. We are blessed with so much; good education, housing, and an over abundance of food, but with all of this, unfortunately, the level of happiness that I see is so low and their threshold of happiness is so high that it shocks me how fucking miserable everyone is and how entitled they are! If all the boxes are not checked materially, experientially, educationally or in other aspects of life, the people are so miserable. It's rare to find people that are content and happy in this town. We're always looking for perfection because of social media, social influencers, and expectations. What may be required is a reset of our priorities, self-reflect, go back to basics, and figure out what is important in our lives, and what will truly make us happy.

Vegan Food

A close friend of mine recently introduced me to vegan food. She had been a vegan for a few years and touted the benefits of it. I'm a voracious carnivore and, as stated earlier, I will try anything anywhere, anytime at least once. One day, I went to Bunny's Restaurant for lunch. They had both vegan and non-vegan menu items, so I ordered a vegan burrito. When I took my first bite, to my surprise, it tasted okay. After a couple of more bites and a splash of homemade hot sauce, it started tasting better and better. By the end of the meal, I had an unusual and unexpected umami experience. My friend was very happy that I enjoyed her recommendation. 2 weeks later, one of my friends took me out for lunch at Bunny's. She ordered a breakfast sandwich for me, and a vegan bowl for her, plus 2 black coffees. Now knowing how good the food was, I had higher expectations for my brekky sandwich. It came on a nice, toasted gourmet brioche burger bun, a homemade vegetarian patty with simulated eggs made from tofu, vegan cheese, lettuce, tomatoes, greens, and vegan house dressing. I took a massive bite and an umami explosion happened in my mouth similar to my first Big Mac at age 6. It was orgasmic!

I have no plans on going vegan, but I would have no qualms eating at Bunny's again. After the meal, the owner passed by and was floored by how much I enjoyed her food. She looked so happy to see the pure joy that I had and her face was beaming. We should never judge a book by its cover and always have an open mind when trying new things or activities. Even a prolific meat eater like me is open to anything and looking forward to my next vegan experience.

Sports injuries

Injuries are a big part of sports. Sooner or later, an athlete will deal with injuries ranging from bruises and bumps to more serious, long-term, season ending ones. As a kid, I suffered numerous injuries playing all the different sports starting at age 13. Before then, I really didn't feel anything hurt or if it did, I just ignored it. In Basketball, I jumped pretty high, being able to touch the rim even though I'm only 5'10". When I played on the Varsity team, I played the middle of the zone on defense which normally is the position for the much taller players. A Center's average height is over 6 feet and I remember going up against guys that were 6'4 to 6' 6. I had to use my body and wide ass as leverage, to box out while rebounding, then jump like a cat to snatch the ball from these giants. From time to time, I would land on someone's foot and roll my ankles. In one particular game, I soared high like an eagle for a rebound but landed on my opponent's foot. My ankle twisted in a way that it shouldn't have! I screamed, while feeling the most excruciating pain I have ever felt on the court. Again, this is 1988, we did not wait to get carried off the floor, so I got up by myself, and tried to walk it off. I couldn't put any weight on my foot, so I hobbled off to the bench by myself. Mr. Clark came over to see how I was doing, I said that I was fine but my foot was really hurting. After five minutes, I felt a jolt of adrenaline which temporarily masked the pain. I told Mr. Clark that I was good. He put me back into the game and I finished playing, helping the team win. In the locker room after the game, I tried to take off my shoe but I couldn't because of the intense pain that appeared. The adrenaline had worn off and my foot was 1 ½ times its normal size. Mr. Clark cut the laces to take off my shoe, and iced it to get the swelling down. To this day, I'm not sure if I had fractured or broken a bone in my ankle but I was at practice 2 days later with my foot fully taped.

My son Alex was in HS doing weights at the gym. Some teenage boys try to squat more weight than they should. All of a sudden, he felt an explosion in his back. When he came home, Alex was barely able to stand up straight. He did physiotherapy to strengthen and rehabilitate his back. Alex couldn't swing or play golf for 6 months and, after rehab, his game suffered, and was not the same. He felt miserable, and his injury started to affect his grades. He doubted everything and would often have bouts of depression and self-talk. I told him to be patient and stick with the process of rehab and practice, but this is not the advice a 16-year-old wants to hear. After 18 months, his game slowly started coming back and because of all the adversity Alex endured, he seemed more mature and not as emotional about his golf game. He plummeted to the lowest lows of despair but with determination and belief, he was able to climb out of the funk to where he is today, a collegiate golfer with a +1 handicap. Alex has grown up a lot going through all his adversity and this has helped him become a much more confident dude.

Seve suffered more injuries on his lacrosse journey. Because he worked so hard on his fitness, Seve sustained minor and major injuries. His first serious injury happened while doing track. He pulled a hamstring running 100m sprints and was advised to rest it 3 months until it fully healed. He did not follow the advice and he tried to push through pain like I did with my ankle. It wasn't fully healed but he kept playing. That summer, Seve struggled and had a poor season. The following spring at Georgetown Prep, he severely sprained his ankle and was in a walking boot for a couple of weeks. When he was cleared to play, he was only 75%. Then that fall, at a Halloween dance while dancing, he jumped and landed on a cellphone, fracturing his foot. He was in a cast for 6 weeks. A common theme for Seve is that even when injured, he will still practice lacrosse and his stick skills. The day after he broke his foot, he was back doing wall ball drills by sitting on the floor of the squash court, with his cast leg laying flat on the floor. His coaches and teammates, had rarely seen such determination, and thought that Seve was crazy. He would not be able to play for another 6 months but he was back practicing with a broken foot sitting on a squash court by himself for hours the day after breaking his foot. This is the ultimate example of delayed gratification as there was no immediate benefit for the practice. Because of all his work while injured, Seve's stick skills are at an expert level. Control the controllables. There are no excuses even if you are tired, if you don't have time, or if you're injured. Driven people utilize every moment they have to get better.

Carpe Diem!

Authenticity

Before COVID and the lockdowns, I noticed that day to day human interactions both directly and indirectly started to slowly change. I began to hear speech patterns and verbiage used were very similar in a variety of places and settings. It seemed as though people had a different persona in public and private. More and more people were afraid to be themselves and often would say or act on how they thought the other person wanted them to. I remember about 20 years ago; I was still in the golf business and started hearing this term called "optics". In business, we practiced optics to show your very best self to look good for others. A similar term would be "simping", which means being nice to achieve a goal or objective without actually believing in the action performed. The term optics or simping has morphed into a more an uncontrollable duplicitous persona. In the past, people could act one way to show the very best but still knew who they were. What I have observed these days is that people's optics have become their persona. Where, in the past, people knew who they were and could switch on and off, today people have a harder time separating these. Therefore, a growing number of people are developing an identity crisis and are struggling to know who they are and what they really believe in. People start to become duplicates of society (NPCs,) and it is very hard for a person to act or speak independently in public. I often hear from my friends, acquaintances, or students that they are very afraid to walk or speak outside the strict boundaries of society. Therefore, most people play it safe and will just speak talking points without really sharing or believing in their own ideas. When I meet strangers in public, I'm very friendly and will talk about anything. I'll ask them about their lives, if they're in school, what they do for work and what activities they enjoy. In the beginning, they're very friendly but are taken aback by how honest and raw my conversations are with them. They are not used to somebody speaking with the depth and authenticity that I do. Our conversations will hit a wall because the person I'm speaking with struggle with transparency and will try to shut it down. I'll meet people everywhere, and when we talk about their lives, they try to change the subject to a more neutral topic. Generally, the more educated the person I'm speaking with is, the more guarded they are about their lives. My buddy, Paul is doing a PhD. He recently had his birthday at Beacon Hill Park and invited several friends over for drinks and appetizers. We have gotten pretty tight even though our views, and perspectives are quite different. On the day of his birthday, he asked me to play tennis. He wanted to chat about his friends who were also doing PhDs and master's. Paul was scared that they would be intimidated by my openness and transparency. He asked if I could be more mindful about how I speak with his friends, especially his female friends. I mentioned to Paul that I have met many thousands of people and have rarely had any issues when it comes to making women feel uncomfortable. I'm very real and authentic when it comes to everybody. I just try to be myself. With that said, I promised Paul that I would be respectful. After tennis, I meet his friends sitting on the grass beside the cricket pitch. Everything goes without a hitch, and I really enjoyed meeting all of them. I was able to say hello to some people, but I noticed how reserved most were.

Their conversations were generally polite, calm, and neutral, respectful but guarded. I noticed that the girls in the group kept to themselves and didn't really open up to people they didn't know.

This feels so different when I'm around blue-collar people. In lacrosse, most people are in trades; like carpenters, electricians, plumbers and contractors. They are friendlier, louder, and more easy-going. People have booming loud voices and will typically be more raucous, rambunctious and be less politically correct. It is interesting to see the direct correlation between people's educational backgrounds and their behavior.

A few years ago Maria, Seve and I drove from Atlanta to Washington DC visiting several boarding schools. Driving through the Eastern Seaboard, we met people from different socio-economic backgrounds and demographics. It was eye-opening how different people were. As we were driving over a mountain in North Carolina, I felt sleepy and decided to stop by a Waffle House to grab a coffee. The restaurant was empty except for the cook and waitress standing outside having a cigarette . The cook asked us where we were from? I said that we drove from the other side of the mountain from Atlanta. The cook, in the most serious tone, said "I've never been over the other side of the mountain!" That surprised the fuck out of me, that this guy in his thirties, has never been over the mountain range and has stayed in this little town his whole life. The cook and waitress were extremely nice people. It was an authentic interaction which I found in most small towns that we have been to in the US. I noticed that as we got into the bigger cities, the people became less friendly. Victoria is becoming a medium size city. It's a very well-educated town with lots of money and the one thing that is becoming apparent is that people are becoming very bougie. When I meet transplants who come to Victoria for work or school, I ask them if they're from a small town. Generally, I will tend to get along with these people more so than the bougier elites. It all goes back again to authenticity, which is one of the main themes in my book.

The Atomic Bomb

I started writing this book in March 2021 but hit my first writer's block moment after a few months! It's now February 2022 and I have renewed energy and motivation to complete this masterpiece. The bonus of my extended writing break was the chance to experience and observe more real-life examples to add to my book.

Our local government halted in-car lessons for 2 months, back in February 2020. We were able to restart teaching April 2020. I began to notice the massive impact on my students due to the Covid lockdowns. After being home for months, my students started to exhibit both subtle and more obvious behavioral changes. It seems as though an atomic bomb was detonated, and it wiped out most of the masculinity from the guys in town. When I described this to my female students, the vast majority not only agreed with this assessment, but they too started to experience changes in their own behavior. They said that there are "no guys" in their school, work, or generation. What's interesting is that even my student's 44-year-old single mom echoed the same thing and shared her own frustration with her recent dating experiences. She would try to date men but she found all the men seemed to only want non-committal sex and most acted like jerks. When I asked her if she considered younger men, she said found them to be too immature. I gave her some advice, try dating younger guys and teach them the ways. We had a good chuckle with that one! As for my younger female students, they shared a more alarming situation. Most were in HS and University. They complained that there were no guys and that about 9 in 10 guys displayed minimal masculinity with only a handful that still retained traditional male masculinity. One of my students worked at McDonald's. Her manager was in his mid-30s; she and her female co-workers would constantly flirt with him. All the girls were in their teens with some younger than 18. Another story is from a 17-year-old student. Her dad was in his late 40's who played multiple sports and was very masculine. Her friends would always gush and tell her how hot her dad was and when they would go out for food, younger women would always flirt with him openly.

In school, girls would have territorial fights over the limited number of "good guys!" They would get very protective and extremely jealous of other girls poaching their dudes.

From a teaching perspective, I have noticed a shift in confidence pre covid to today. For most guys pre-COVID, 60% not confident and 40% confident. Today, about 85% are not confident and 15% are confident! Even guys that are traditionally confident are having self-talk and self-doubt issues. I found this to be the most alarming! Speaking with one of my volleyball buddies Steph, she shared with me her frustration with guys in Victoria. She had come from a small town in Ontario, moved around to different cities and ended up in Victoria. She noticed that the guys back home were much more aggressive, masculine, and bigger in stature than the guys in Victoria. Since moving here, she's had a hard time meeting guys because as she says, most of the guys here are scrawny and weak. Steph is not the only woman that has shared this with me. Maybe this is just a West Coast thing but most girls I talk to here have the same problem about meeting strong masculine guys.

What we need is a massive nuclear bomb to detonate and explode over the city and radiate all the men with testosterone, reigniting their masculinity!

CHAPTER 8 MODERN MASCULINITY AND THE QUEST FOR GENUINE RELATIONSHIPS

Dudes today are so boring

The biggest change I've observed from pre-COVID to post-COVID are the number of guys I see around town. Whether it's at the mall, park, tennis court, bars, restaurants, or clubs. There seems to be less guys hanging out. Usually, I see a lot more girls in pairs or big groups. The possible exception is the gym. But more and more, I have noticed firsthand, and from talking to people, that most guys would rather chill at home alone or with buddies, playing Xbox and chatting online. Their nights would normally include some weed, shrooms, booze, Uber eats and hours of gaming. Guys would do this in varying degrees but it's having a huge effect on their maturity levels, interpersonal skills and personality. Most young women complain to me that they have a hard time having a normal conversation with guys their age. The girls find the guys so boring and lacking any sort of depth or range! It's resulting in more young women dating older men to match their maturity level. In high school, a few grade 11 & 12's will date college guys. And in college, the gap increases and I start seeing 20-year-olds dating guys 30+. I know a few women where the relationship gap is 20+years.

In clubs, I see this play out on the dance floor. I will see groups of girls in the middle of the dance floor while the guys are spread out on the outside. There are a few alpha guys smattered in the middle but with a lot of the COVID babies lacking rizz, most of the younger guys are scared to interact with the beautiful ladies in the middle of the dance floor. Therefore, the older, more confident guys swoop in and pull the younger women. For all you guys gaming every day, maybe drop your controller, go outside for some sun, and enroll in some coed sports like volleyball, pickleball, tennis, or ultimate.

While in line outside the club to get in, I asked a 27-year-old waiting for her guy friends what her thoughts were. She had good insight and thought that guys would have a lot of acquaintances but would only talk about surface level topics. Anything deeper, guys would deflect and try to end the conversation while she and her friends would be able to talk about everything. She agreed that the guys' maturity levels were not on par with the girls by a large margin. I suggest that dudes try to talk to women and learn about the world so that you have more to talk about than just the new game coming out next week!

Looking for a G (gentleman)

It's February 2024, I'm trying to figure out how I'm going to get my book published, but pretty much, all my thoughts are done. For whatever reason, the book still felt incomplete! I haven't opened it in 3 months and I'm not sure why? This doesn't feel like all the other times that I had writer's block, but it seemed that I was a rudderless boat lost in the middle of the sea.

I was visiting my mom in Vancouver and decided to go out again like last November. Though I grew up in the city, it's been three decades since I've been to Granville St. I wanted to check out the vibe at night. The scene has a much colder, more disconnected feel than Victoria with people seeming to be more aloof. While doing research, many people shared their dating experiences and just how awful it truly was. Most use dating apps and say that it's next to impossible to meet people organically. I went to a small restaurant to grab a light snack and a beer around 9:00 p.m. It was a low-key place and had several tables of women busy chatting. At the bar were solo dudes. As I was observing the room, all the women seemed sophisticated, confident, and having a good time. Conversely, all the guys were keeping to themselves with their heads down, less confident than their female counterparts who were having a blast. One of the tables had six women in their mid to late 20s. They seemed to be vibrant and outgoing. I decided to ask them about their dating experiences in Vancouver and what they were looking for in guys. The lady at the end was a blonde. She was excited to share her perspective. Her name was

Emily and what she said was extremely profound. She's looking for guys that are confident, obviously, but are also chivalrous. She kept stressing the importance of a guy with manners who would open the door for her, and if they lacked confidence, they should fake it till they make it! Essentially, she said that most guys now are lacking basic morals and values that my generation took for granted 35 years ago. She kept going on and on about the importance of traditional values. For context, Emily was a very successful, beautiful, young woman. Yet all she's looking for in a guy is to be a gentleman, looks and wealth be damned! She just wants a guy to be polite, kind, with good manners that will act like a gentleman, a true gentleman. So, for all you dudes out there that think that you have to go to the gym 6 hours a day to get jacked and shredded, take it from these beautiful women sitting in the booth.

It's far more important for you to work on the inside, than it is to obsess about what's on the outside.

Caroline

On our last week of League matches, I was warming up at the hill. In the parking lot, I saw this young lady looking at her phone seemingly lost so I asked if I could help. She was there for her League match at 6:00 p.m. but looked confused, so she asked me if she was at the right tennis courts. I assured her that she was, and that the ladies would be coming shortly. I asked her where she was from because she did not look like a local. Her name was Caroline, she was a DIII tennis player from the East Coast. Her family just moved into town for work and, I suspected, for the peace, tranquility and beauty of Victoria. Serendipitously, she went to school 15 minutes away from Seve's boarding school in Hartford. When I told her that, she started freaking out and was so happy to meet somebody that knew where she was from. I had to leave for my match on the other side of town. She asked if I wanted to go for a hit sometime, so we scheduled a singles match the following day. We met at a court near her house, rallied for a little bit then played a set. Maybe she was rusty because she hadn't touched a racket in a month, but in the first set I steamrolled her and won 6-1. She was a little bit shell-shocked. The next set was a lot tighter, but in the end, I won 7-5 in a slugfest. We headed to Township Coffee where I hung out a lot and know the owner, Eric. She buys me a latte, which I won from our match, and we start chatting. Caroline was born in Eastern Europe, moved to Florida as a toddler, then went to high school in Boston. She was a diehard Red Sox, and New York Ranger fan. I told her about my book. She started freaking out and wanted to know more about it. Being a

20-year-old woman, she was experiencing the dating woes in real time! Her problem was meeting good guys. She said that most of the guys on the east coast were awful and just wanted to hook up. I said to her that guys in Victoria were different, kinder, gentler but had their own set of problems. She was curious about what I meant. Her summer was eventful meeting a lot of guys. She would go out for drinks, dinner and dancing and would dm me every day complaining about her dates and hookups. She found the dating scene here was absolutely awful with the endless mind games being played and the lack of commitment. There were numerous guys available, but the city is sorely lacking good men! I wish I could have given Caroline better news but unfortunately, I have none!

I almost died from pneumonia

I thought that being so active in sports, that I could eat and live like a 25-year-old! For the last year, my diet consisted of wings with blue cheese dip, and a bag of Lay's ketchup chips every other night. I loved mixing clamato in my beer and drinking the occasional Sunday Caesar. Chinese food and Vietnamese Pho were my food staples in the colder months. I drank and ate with no fear because I was playing sports 6x a week. Boy was I wrong. God struck me down with his lightning bolt and because I was eating so much salt, my body retained excessive water which then seeped into my lungs causing pneumonia. The first symptoms happened a few weeks ago. On a Sunday morning at 5:00 a.m., I woke up, coughed for 2 hours straight, and had difficulty breathing, but I didn't really think too much of it, being this OG, hardcore, crazy, '70s baby. I thought that I could get better with no meds and I didn't think I needed to see my doctor. With every cough, I spit out a little bit of blood mixed with my phlegm. I was so fatigued that I slept for a few hours in the afternoon. When I woke up, I was still experiencing shortness of breath. Again, I still didn't think anything of it. The following day I rested, then worked in the afternoon. For the next two days, I was still struggling to breathe but I slowly started feeling better. Unbelievably, I started playing tennis after two days and though I was out of breath after each point, I was feeling okay. The following week, I played a singles match in our citywide Corona open. Uncharacteristically, I lost 6-0 6-4. At that moment, I knew that something was really wrong with my body! I went to my doctor for a full check-up. He ordered a blood test and an EKG. Everything turned out negative except for an infection. Dr. G. said that if it got worse, to come back and see him. I had an amazing weekend of tennis. I played 15 sets and won a doubles tournament with my Filipino buddy, Jun. That weekend, I had four Caesars and nachos at the Beagle. The next day, I bought three bags of chips. Around 10 p.m., I smashed a bag of old Dutch chips, *au gratin* flavor. Thirty minutes later, I started to have a hard time breathing but ignored the symptoms. After another hour, my condition worsened and this time, I knew it was serious. I decided to drive myself to emergency. What a terrible idea because on the drive there, I almost fainted twice before finally arriving at the hospital. I stumbled to the front entrance and barely had enough oxygen to press the button to open the door. I hobbled over and checked in with the nurse admitting patients. She was a middle aged, Asian dragon lady. Even though she saw that I was in distress, she ordered me to wait in the waiting room until I was called back to the desk. But because I really couldn't breathe, I came back to the desk gasping, "I really can't breathe!" At that point, the nurses started to panic and immediately admitted me to emergency. Luckily, I went to the hospital because my condition was serious, and I was actually dying! Fortunately, the head nurse, looking after me immediately identified my symptoms and gave me antibiotics and a water pill. After a couple of hours, peeing four liters of water, I started to feel a bit better and was able to breathe again with the help of an oxygen tank. She also gave me a couple of inhalers which loosened up my lungs. I was in emergency for eight hours. As my condition slowly improved, I was moved upstairs to the cardiac ward. On my way up to the 4th floor, I see Geoff, my tennis amigo and one of the top players at the hill. He was so surprised to see me lying on the stretcher 'cuz we had just played an intense match two days ago!

What an awful and scary experience but also very eye-opening about my mortality and how fleeting and precious life is. It's given me a whole new appreciation for life and most importantly, the motivation to finish this book. While I was at the hospital for a day and a half, I noticed that most of the female nurses, doctors, and staff were extremely confident and strong. Conversely, most of the males were much weaker and more subservient. That time gave me an opportunity to reflect and think about everything in my book. Being at a place that I haven't been to in a decade, I saw the massive changes inside the hospital and how it is a miniature replica of modern society. The interactions, the social dynamics, and the overall lack of real men was eye opening and frightening.

What women want

It's September 2023, I'm at the home stretch of finishing this fucking book! After more than two and a half years and multiple writers block moments, I'm nearing the end. Maria and I have been fighting for the last few months because of this book. After she found out about my research, she was very upset. I hit the last and longest period of my writer's block moments because of our daily fights. She was pissed that I went undercover going to clubs, meeting people around town and about my Instagram page, @ alexlovesjazz. This weekend, I finally decided to take a stand and go out anyway, without any fear or inhibitions worrying about Maria. If she was going nuclear, so be it, it can't stop me finishing this fucking book. It is just too important not to be completed!

I have learned so much about young men, the dating scene and modern society. With this knowledge acquired, I wanted to put all of these learned skills to the test and see if they could pass the scrutiny needed to make sure that the stuff I'm writing isn't just a bunch of bullshit.

So many women of all ages have shared with me the complete and utter despair they are feeling with the drought of men. These women keep complaining that there's not that many guys available or that are dateable. I've touched on these topics in my earlier chapters. Whether it's social media, dating apps, video games, or men not having the confidence or motivation to date, there are not that many guys hanging out around town. And with the push to confuse men about their gender and their self-identity, there are less men available in the dating pool. So, with that in mind, I wanted to see and experience meeting people organically. I'm 51 now, reasonably fit and play lots of sports.

Women in 2023 are demanding and starving for men with substance, strength, and personality. Basically, what guys used to be 35 years ago. So, with that in mind, I set out to try to test out my theories.

Obviously, I could talk to all the people I wanted to and listen to their stories but without observing all these different ideas myself, my book and its contents are just theories. I know Maria is going to kill me for this once she finds out, but I had to scrutinize and experiment all the different things about this book and how to talk to women. Within the last year of going out, I've had a lot of interactions with women. These interactions range from saying hello in the coffee shop to meeting them at volleyball, at the Beagle or while out filming live music at different locations around town. Even at the hospital when I was dying from pneumonia, I chatting with the nurses! I started to get a better picture of the social dynamics at play today. What I found is that there are a whole lot of women compared to the dwindling number of guys. There are guys, but they're at home gaming, ordering Uber eats in the basement or many are identifying as they/them instead of he/him. Therefore, all the strong, independent confident women are left scrambling for a smaller pool of normal guys. Even at 51, I am able to meet women organically when I'm walking around town. And I'm not sure why but a lot of my buddies tell me that it's my personality, confidence and energy.

So, if that's the case, guys don't need to spend as much time in the gym or come up with cheesy pick-up lines but instead to work on themselves interpersonally, learn how to communicate and talk. Learn to look women in the eye without being creepy. And be less sensitive! Working out and playing sports are very important but if the choice is between shredded abs or a guy that can make a woman laugh, it's surprising to hear from many women that the latter is more in demand than the perfect six-pack! Having both would be the ultimate but if you could only have one, having a great overall personality is the better option.

But be careful because you could become too overconfident and end up being a douche and a fuckboy!

To finish this book, I started to take action. Being new to Instagram, I'm not really an expert in how it works. That's a bonus for me because I have no hesitation or qualms about communicating with people. Some of my younger friends rarely DM girls or if they do, send the most bombastic messages. But they have a hard time just sending a normal text. They're amazed at how easy it was for me to just reply to a story, to say hello, and to speak my mind. For them, sending something requires so much thought that they spend a lot of time overthinking and trying to curate the perfect message to send. In the end it becomes inauthentic and very unsure.

A few months back, the boys and I were playing tennis at the hill. Most of the time, it's just us playing tennis but that afternoon, two attractive ladies started warming up on court three. All the single guys hesitated to approach them, which is standard here in Victoria. Looking like out of towners, I was curious and asked where they were from? One was from the east coast and the other from the UK. In their mid-20s, the ladies looked very successful and super confident! After chatting for a minute, I went back to the boys. As they left, they said that "it was nice to meet me and hopefully we'll see each other again in the future." A month later, the ladies drop by to play again. I was hanging out behind the fence and said "hello", but I didn't really want talk to them because I was too busy bullshitting with the players on court one. After a few minutes, I turned around and asked how their summer was going? We had a nice, friendly exchange and before leaving for work, I showed them my Instagram page. Both ladies gave me a follow. I post a lot of content and share about five or six stories every day. These two ladies started to follow my stories regularly. When they post their own stories, I would sometimes reply with a very simple message like "great view", "that dish looks awesome", "hope you guys are having a great weekend!" Last week, one of them was back from New York and posted a story of a coffee shop. I asked her if she was back in town. She replied that, yes indeed, she was home and was going for dinner and drinks with her two girlfriends.

That weekend, I went out with my buddy Zach. The Pickups were playing at Irish, but we only stayed half an hour because the room was dead. We headed over to Darcy's. My boys, Ok Charlie band were playing. Friday night at Darcys is dope. It's about 10:00 p.m. and I get a text from the girls. They invited me to join them at a tapa bar next door. I told Zach that I'd be back in an hour so that I could talk with them and get some more research done for my book. On my way to the tapa bar, I saw Caroline, my 20-year-old tennis buddy taking money out of the ATM. My tennis buddy asked where I was going and what I was doing. I didn't really want to tell her, but she was very persistent, so I relented and told her I was meeting three ladies next door. She started to go off on me and said that I was married, and I shouldn't be meeting with three ladies! While we were talking, two ladies behind her in line joined our conversation. I wasn't really minding them but apparently, they were intrigued and asked me how old I was? The two ladies guessed 33 or 35, and with the most sheepish grin I said "51" and ran off to go see the three ladies at the tapa bar! The bar was closing soon, I sat down with them and ordered a vodka tonic. The room was pretty dead with only a few people inside. We only had a few minutes to chat, so I start asking them questions about their dating lives.

They said that it was hard for them to find guys right now. It's crazy because these ladies were smart, vibrant and attractive but they were having a hard time meeting guys. But maybe it wasn't the meeting guys, but meeting guys with substance. The British woman said that back in the UK, there were a lot more guys compared to here in Canada! She said that she's looking for guys that would ask her out, look her in the eye, be able to talk and carry a conversation longer than 30 seconds and to be a gentleman, treating her like a lady and paying for her dinner. Not that she wasn't able to afford her own but she was looking for a more traditional man. Unfortunately, because of equality and the eradication of masculinity, men like this are almost extinct.

In the summer, during one of our Wednesday volleyball nights, I had a long chat with Steph. Originally from Victoria, she went away for school and worked in the US for 8 years as a nurse before coming back home last summer. Steph had been in two long term relationships and thought that she had found the one a few years back. Unfortunately, it didn't work out because her boyfriend was not ready to settle down. They eventually broke up.

Straight up, the number one thing Steph is looking for is an alpha male that she says, "will be the protector, provider and rock!" Her dream would be to live on a farm. Her husband, working the whole day outside, and her being the nurturer, taking care of the house. Basically, how men's and women's roles have been for the last 199,950 years. Steph is a very strong, independent, modern woman but even with that, her maternal instincts are too powerful. Her need to reproduce is attracting Steph to men possessing more traditional traits. She wants to start a family with kids. Steph believes in roles for men and women and sees them as positives. As she says, "men and women are definitely different and I want a guy that will chop wood and get his hands dirty, while I take care of the house and kids."

With the push for equality, modern feminism has destroyed the patriarchy. It has been eroded so much that it has left many women searching for a father figure type leaving many with severe *daddy issues*. She fears that "it's so hard to find a guy like that right now!"

Last night, I grabbed a drink with Steph and her friend Crystal. They have been friends since high school. When we were alone, Steph shared a secret about Crystal. She is a lesbian and had been in a 5-year relationship with a woman but they had recently broken up. Crystal's maternal instincts had woken up. She wants to start a family and have kids and even though it's possible a gay couple to do this, she wants to do this in a more traditional patriarchal family.

And over and over again from many of the women I've talked to, they complain that there's no guys. I was watching a podcast last week about a study conducted in the US. In it, 45% of men aged 18-25 have never approached a woman in person in the last year. The podcaster was shocked to see such a high percentage and theorized that it was a component of the "me too movement" and wokeness. He asked, "how do you meet people?" Because of modern social norms and fear of getting canceled, guys are relying too much on dating apps to meet women. Dudes have lost most of their mating and dating instincts.

They don't know how to flirt! It's not even sexual but to be able to give a mischievous smile, a look, a suggestive pose. To look her in the eyes and want her. A lot of women I talk to are looking for this but can't find it because the men are too afraid to look at them and to flirt with them fearing a "me too" reaction. Therefore, these women are left feeling frustrated and desperate to find a man with confidence, authenticity, genuineness, ruggedness, and sex appeal, and who are not afraid to be themselves. A man that will want them fully with no reservation or hesitation. To want to spend time with them, hold them, caress them, ravage them, and take care of them. This is the man they want but can't find. What a sad state we find ourselves in, when the man that they're looking for is almost extinct. But as with modern science, we can find solutions to revive them again and hopefully this book can in small part contribute to this revival and rebirth of man!

Rizz

One of the benefits of being around so many Gen Z students is that I get to talk to them, vibe with them and by osmosis, start to learn some of their vocabulary. Ten years ago, most of my students were millennials but, recently, most are Gen Z. It's been great to be around them. I always joke that I absorb and take three days of their youth like a vampire having a midlife crisis! Because they're so young, three days is nothing for them but for me, it's massive. The accumulation has essentially made my life force younger by fifteen or twenty years, if not more. The main positive is that I can connect to my students more on their level. It fosters a much better learning environment. My students can be themselves not seeing me as an older teacher. Instead, we have a more peer-to-peer dynamic and I can teach them in divergent learning style. I ask a lot of open-ended questions, and I give my students the space to answer authentically and be themselves. This has really helped me understand them on a deeper level. As a bonus, I've picked up some slang from my younger Gen Z students. My family, especially my kids, cringe every time I say "no cap, what up, let's go, bussin" and all the other terms that younger kids use. It just comes out. When I'm with them, I subconsciously start mirroring their speech.

One word I hear often is "rizz". Rizz is short for charisma. The first time I heard it, I thought it meant an excess amount of semen! But it actually means a guy's charisma when it comes to girls or people in general. The more rizz someone has, the more they're able to chill and be themselves in the random setting or with a group of friends. This is a very important trait that seemingly, only 5-15%% of the guys have left. The other 85-95% have no rizz. It's a big problem because they become socially awkward, don't develop self-confidence to be free and authentic and it affects everything in their lives. And this is one of the reasons why so many guys have problems interacting with or speaking with girls. Last year, I was watching a podcast, and they were mentioning a university study done in the US about men aged 18 to 25. In the study, they found that 45% of this group has not voluntarily talked or interacted with a woman in the past year! In other words, their only interaction would be at work or in a formal way. But the study found that these men are not developing the social skills or rizz to be able to carry a normal conversation with girls. This is actually quite scary because it's leading to isolation and social awkwardness. I see this a lot when I'm out and about town watching live music, dancing or I'm writing my book in a coffee shop and observing how people act in public. Back in the day, if guys didn't have rizz, it would have been almost impossible to meet a woman. Guys had to put themselves out there and take a chance. Rejection from a woman was real and through failure, they would either learn to adapt and become better or they would ask for help from older male role models and mentors. But these days, because of technology and social norms, these men are struggling to improve themselves and instead, feel more isolated. I've heard many instances of guys watching excessive amounts of porn and the rapid explosion of Only Fans and other social media sites. These aren't real human interactions, but they have replaced the real connections between males and females. Due to loneliness, more and more guys are turning to technology to fulfill that void for love and companionship. It's gotten to such a dystopian point that I've heard of many guys having AI girlfriends, but what's more frightening is the robots or sex robots. I can foresee the day very soon that they will be able to program the sex robots with AI and when that happens, the world will get into a pretty dark place. I'm not trying to be conspiratorial or negative, but we're already seeing the early signs for this upcoming apocalypse. So that's why it is so important for guys to read this book and choose the path they want to take. Do they want to take the red pill and free themselves from the matrix or take the blue pill and keep living in this dystopian fantasy world? The choice is yours.

Toxic masculinity

I moved to Canada in 1979. The men at the time had a lot of similar traits and characteristics worldwide. Most valued competition, sports, and providing for their families. They had activities like men's night in golf, all male clubhouses and golf clubs, various different men's groups, poker nights in the basement, and the boy's night out. These were places where men would blow off steam with other men after a hard day's work. In many countries, there would be rituals and traditions exclusively for men. Again, around the early to mid-1980s, with the rise of feminism and female empowerment, many of these traditions and institutions were called out and changed one by one. Whether it was admitting the first female member at Augusta National, the creation of Ladies night on another night of the week for women, legislative bans on single gender clubs or events, and the overall negative perception of "boys being boys." Toxic masculinity definitely existed leading to a natural desire to curb these traits that were sought out by society. I searched up the definition of toxic masculinity in the Oxford English dictionary, and it's described as "a set of attitudes and ways of behaving stereotypically expected of men, regarded as having a negative impact on men and on society as a whole."

The traditional meaning of toxic masculinity is slowly being changed with the more progressive ideas of today. Before, the goal was to lessen and ultimately eradicate violence against women whether physical, emotional, sexual. Nowadays the definition of toxic masculinity has been expanded to include many forms of traditional masculine traits but don't necessarily promote or propagate direct violence against women but that these traits may lead to violence against women. In other words, the change in definition of toxicity has created many policies in society that are punishing the vast majority of normal men. I was recently watching a YouTube podcast that redefined the version of toxic masculinity and it was so radical that competition, physical strength, and ambition were all considered to be toxic masculinity. These traits by itself, don't lead to violence against women, but if modern males compete in sports, try to do well in school, in academics, or have grand ambitions in life, they are immediately branded by more progressives as toxic males. No wonder that most of my young male students are more docile, afraid, not motivated to excel in school, sports, and are not interested in exercising, competing and going to the gym! I was shocked by this most recent change in definition of toxic masculinity. I've been in writer's block the last few months not understanding why I couldn't finish the last couple of chapters of this book. It is now all making sense to me. The reason that I've had a hard time finishing the book is because I needed to fully understand the change in definition of toxic masculinity and how everything that I've written can be fully attributed to the societal changes in how we both view men and how we are conditioning these men to act in a very weak, docile and uncompetitive way. When I'm out and about in town and I meet random young men, I notice that they would be very uneasy just being around me. My natural masculinity, competitiveness and overall physicality intimidates a lot of these docile and weak young men. A lot of them find me so abrasive and confrontational and like an alpha dog being around other dogs. The first chance that these young men have to get away or not look at me in the eye, they take it. I also noticed that I have a very similar effect on other men but that they take an instant connection with me. These men have been seeking guidance, inspiration, and validation. Whether it's bouncers in a club, servers, musicians, young guys I play sports with, in tennis, basketball, or volleyball, these young men look at me like I'm a guru, a mentor, an older brother or a father figure. They've been seeking answers to their questions about their own masculinity and why what they're feeling instinctually doesn't match or is in line with modern societal expectations of them. We now face a fork in the road for our society. What do we do? Try to change all the men to a more modern acceptable way but create a vast majority of weak men that are unmotivated, apathetic, and are found to be unattractive by a large majority of the more modern strong independent females? Or should society accept that there are many positives with strong, independent, motivated and ambitious young men who are chivalrous and act like gentlemen? With the latter, there will be outliers of toxic men and for these males, there should be repercussions. With that said, this is the choice that modern society will have to make. When I first started writing this book two years ago, I was merely a guy to reignite some traditional values in males. Two years later it is becoming more apparent that society's time is running out to make this choice because if the trend continues with this conditioning, it may be too late to save a number of countries from a population, nuclear wasteland. This is pretty frightening for me. When I'm around a lot of people, and we talk about topics like this, I ask them two basic questions;

1. Do they want kids? An overwhelming majority say, "NO!" Most young people have been conditioned to think that having kids is extremely negative.

2. If Canada was invaded by a foreign country, would the young men sign up and take up arms to protect this country? The overall consensus from all the people I talk to, whether young or old, is that males younger than 42 are unlikely to fight for this country and the vast majority of males that will fight for this country are older males. That is not a winning strategy when it comes to an emergency or social crisis. We cannot count on old males to protect society. As patriarchal as this sounds, in times of war it is men and young men that should be fighting it and when these young men don't want to fight, it's game over for all of us!

Controlled aggression

During one of our Tuesday morning practice sessions, our head coach Glen was off to a tournament down in Palm springs. John, our fitness coach, led the drills for the morning. I arrived late and missed the fitness part of the training by design! After some light stretches, I was ready for the first drill. John had us do a cross-court rally but instead of just hitting the ball in the court, he wanted us to hit it harder to get more of a workout in. My drill partner, Colin and I, had some great rallies and we pushed ourselves to the max. The ball was humming, and we could really feel with each ground stroke, the aggression of wanting to hit the ball through your opponent. Being high-level players, we couldn't just hit a ball and expect to hit a winner and end the point quickly. Instead, we had grueling rallies, lots of grunting and a couple of f-bombs! On our water break, we chatted about the drill. I realized the goal for us was learn how to play with controlled aggression. It is rare today for guys to be able to use that level of aggression. It seems like in most situations, whether workplaces, school, dating, and sports, society is purposely or inadvertently trying to tame the aggression out of males. As an example, in the NHL, there used to be a lot more fighting. When old time players are asked why they fought, they would have several reasons why. The number one reason was for the players to police themselves on the ice. If somebody got out of line, it would be taken care of on the ice without any punishment from the referee or the league. Veteran players that played up to about 25 years ago would always say that there was a code in hockey. If you ran around acting like an idiot, on your very next shift, you would have to answer the bell and fight. It was an understood and accepted part of the game. Generally, most of the players then had more honor and would not purposely hurt players on the other team. If it was a clean hit and a solid check shoulder to shoulder or from the front, there would not be any retribution but if it was a dirty play like a spear, high stick or if someone ran you into the boards from behind, you would get pummeled and pay the price for your indiscretion. When the NHL started to clean up fighting, they did so, to reduce concussions and CTE. Another reason was to increase the skill level in the game, theorizing that, increased scoring, would attract more mainstream fans in the USA. Yes, the game is a lot more skilled these days but there's also a lot more dirty players than before. A player like Brad Marchand from the Boston Bruins is a prime example. If Marchand had played in the '70s or '80s, he might not have been as effective as he is now because he would have been policed by the opposing players or his own teammates. But today unfortunately, he's allowed to play like a rat and be less disciplined without the self-policing and the unspoken code in hockey. This example has parallels to modern society, hockey is a very brutal sport but if you speak with players of the past, they just had a different value system. I could make the same argument for golfers, tennis players and basketball players. I've played all these sports from the 1970s, '80s, '90s, up to today. I've noticed massive changes in athlete's behavior throughout the years and because I still play at a high level at 51, I'm able to relate to and compare the different eras. Back in the '80s I played streetball at Kits beach. If someone acted a fool and ran their mouths, some OG would lay them on their ass on the very next play! If they tried to do anything, they would have gotten beaten up. So, players in the past learned to play extremely hard but were more in control of themselves and their emotions.

These examples lead back to controlled aggression where athletes in previous eras would be able to play sports pushing the limits and the aggression levels. No one wanted to lose but the majority of the athletes in the past were able to play within the rules with maximum effort, tenacity, competitiveness without doing so in a negative way. These days, you still have athletes that get to this state of aggression but due to their lower competition skills or because of fractured masculinity, the athletes aren't able to stay in control. If they play with that level of aggression, they don't have the ability to pull back and say good match or good game after a tough loss or to shake someone's hand and say my bad. It is imperative that we reignite and reintroduce sports and activities that can develop controlled aggression in young males. For these males to be able to have an outlet for their masculinity/testosterone and to learn how to control and be disciplined with it.

For the next drill, John had one person serving and the other one returning. His instructions were that the server would serve, the returner would try to hit one hard, the server would then volley and try to finish the point.

What's interesting is that John is around 30. We've had some minor conversations about coaching in the past and he seemed to be more modern with his philosophies. That's why I was happy and pleasantly surprised about the drills that he had for us today. Thirty years ago, coaches would try to have us work more on our consistency and lengthening points. Maybe our games were too aggressive in the past but it's interesting that now, we're trying to reintroduce aggression in the modern game. It's just funny to see the contrast. We may have had an issue with too much aggression in the past, but we have a bigger issue with the absence of controlled aggression today. The key to John's drills was that with the display and release of the aggression, regardless of whether we lose the point or drill, we can ACCEPT the result with minimal anger, frustration, or spite with our opponents or ourselves. To be able to be super aggressive but play within the rules showing sportsmanship and class. Whether we win or lose, learning to accept the results without the toxic emotions and behaviors.

Many modern males are conditioned to lessen of their aggression with the goal to reduce toxic behavior. From the way they play sports, how they conduct themselves in real life, and in dating. The problem is that, instinctually, the aggression is still inside the modern male. But since they have not learned to control it through sports, when they are experiencing this sudden rush of aggression, they lack the skills be able to handle the situation in a disciplined or controlled manner. Unfortunately, the toxicity still exists and is far worse for the modern male.

Too much testosterone

During our Sunday night doubles last week, I was amped up. I have played extremely well over the past month and felt invincible on court. The big guns were all there; Octavio, Niu, Yudi, Robert and the rest of the gang. I wanted to go up against the strongest possible team, so Yudi and I took on Octavio and Niu. Octavio, from Mexico, has played in their junior Olympics while Niu was a collegiate player from back east. We were in tough even though Yudi was a two-time city champ and a very solid player himself. I love to compete, so even as underdogs, I wanted this matchup! My juices were flowing, and in the warmup, I was hitting the ball pure and moving extremely well. We started the set with some explosive points. I got even more aggressive and could feel myself really grinding and pushing hard. Unfortunately, that would prove to be our undoing as; despite hitting some supernatural shots, I made too many errors! I am known for having smooth, fluid strokes like Roger Federer. That day, I was playing more like Rafael Nadal, grunting and diving. Because I was producing and using too much testosterone, I lost my controlled aggression and instead played recklessly and out of control. This was so out of character for me. We ended up losing and after the match, Yudi talked to me about how crazy I played. He noticed me panting and thought that I was going to collapse on the court! No one is immune to excessive testosterone. But the ability to reflect and change, is key to be better in the future. I am inspiring dudes to be more competitive, but they must learn how to regulate and control their aggression and make sure stay in control.

Why we're here

Last night, the Pick Ups were playing at Irish Times. The place was kinda busy, with a mix of people of different ages and backgrounds. The band plays cover songs from the 1970s '80s '90s, attracting a slightly older crowd. One of the servers, Morgan, was celebrating her 22nd birthday with her friends. They were dancing, partying, and having a great time. I stepped outside to get some fresh air. Suddenly, Morgan runs outside and looks for Mike, the bouncer. She tells him that there's this old creep on the dance floor touching multiple girls inappropriately and without any consent. He rushes over to confront him. Mike's an old-school, no-nonsense Alberta kid, conservative as they come and the ultimate protector. If I was going into war, I would want him right beside me. The guy starts arguing with Mike but to no avail. Mike escorts the older guy, in his late 60s, out of the bar. He tells him that he's crossed the line and can't touch any of the patrons, especially the young girls, without their consent. This behavior should never be tolerated! Due to a small number of toxic males, society has tried hard to change and redefine masculinity which has affected the rest of the normal males that are not toxic. In trying to eliminate toxic behavior, society has unintentionally almost killed healthy, traditional masculinity. I do not and will not ever condone this type of behavior, this is not masculinity but depravity and one of the worst parts of humanity. Men should never ever do this under any circumstances. This book is trying to highlight and reignite traditional, masculine strength while learning chivalry and to be a gentleman. It's unfortunate that this guy can't keep his fucking hands to himself. After being escorted out, he is still belligerent and unapologetic. I'm outside chatting with Morgan while she's vaping. He looks at her, looks at me, and for a moment, seemed like he was going to attack us. My protector instinct kicks in, and I shield Morgan from him. I would have protected her like she was my own daughter! Fortunately, he changes his mind, walks away and gets into a taxi. This experience both saddens me but also gives me hope. It saddens me because in 2023, there are men that will try to take advantage of vulnerable women. It gives me hope because, on the flip side, there are also men like Mike that will protect women at all costs!

Teaching Styles

Over the years, my teaching style has evolved. I have had extensive training as a Golf Professional and am able to employ different teaching styles from Direct Method, Student Driven, kinesthetic, and many other techniques that help teach golfers of all ages and skill levels. Through many successes and failures, I have refined my teaching method. Kinesthetic learning(hands-on) was how a lot of people learned in the past. The learner will keep practicing by themselves and learn to master a skill. It is unlimited trial and error, if you make a mistake, try again and again and again until you get it. Golfers like Ben Hogan, and Moe Norman would routinely practice hitting golf balls until their hands bled. This type of hands-on learning was a very extreme way to learn the skill, but it did teach them to be resilient and have patience in developing their skills. They felt that even under the most intense pressure of competition, their swing would hold up due to the thousands of hours of repetition that helped develop muscle memory.

Modern learning methods such as student driven, believe that teachers should adapt their lessons to fit their students ideal learning style. This method is encouraged to optimize the learning window and to be efficient with little wasted time. One drawback to learning in this way is that students are not as able to adapt to scenarios that fall outside the specific learning parameters. In other words, more modern people are masters in a specific skill, but are unable to adapt when an unexpected situation arises.

Other methods incorporate visualization, positive affirmation and a holistic approach to sync together both your mental, emotional, physiological and biomechanical capabilities.

No matter which method a student incorporates, it still is about getting the job done and hitting the golf ball!

I'm not saying that one teaching style is better than the other, what I have found is that there's room to implement multiple techniques without being polarized to just one method. Today, there is a growing resistance and war of ideologies between generations. Older generations think that younger people lack initiative and common sense. Younger people think that older generations are too harsh and just don't understand their current situations. These interactions happen every day at home, school, workplace, in a golf or driving lesson. When I first started teaching many years ago, my lessons had a much different feel than they do today. I would be very encouraging and give lots of positive reinforcement. Through the years, I have modified this by being more direct with my feedback instead of giving a false and sugar-coated assessment of their progress. Though it can come across as harsh, I have noticed better long-term results with my students when it comes to achieving their big picture goals.

In the past, the older pros would let students try and experience things by themselves, then tell them what they were doing wrong, and how to fix it. And then leave them for 15 to 30 minutes to work on and figure out the solution. Students would have to do more trial-and-error learning, develop persistence and resiliency in the face of failure or frustration. They would have time to attempt to figure things out before asking for help again.

Today, I find my students wanting me to tell them instantly what they are doing wrong and how to fix it. They do not take the time to assess, experience, re-evaluate and adapt. The way that students expect to learn these days is the biggest difference I have noticed. Students and teachers can learn to be more patient and try to not get instant results. Failure and frustration are not only part of learning, but they are essential for students to develop more grit and resiliency to become better golfers, drivers and people, overall!

I make students cry

Though I try and make the learning environment pleasant, I will sometimes push students to their limits and point of frustration. Last year, I started teaching a 17-year-old student named Sam. My first impression of Sam was that he was a cocky and aloof but after a couple of lessons, I saw something different. In lesson one, he drove well but he kept saying how afraid he was of driving, and this made me curious why.

Sam is a gamer and friends with my other students, Nick, David, and Lee. During the lesson, Sam wasn't friendly. He seemed to not care and throughout our drive, did not enjoy it. I took him home and told him to have his mom contact me if he wanted to do any more lessons. I didn't hear from them for 2 months. Meanwhile his buddy David and I started lessons. During our lessons, I would ask him about Sam and if he was going to continue our lessons. I was sure that Sam hated my teaching style and would never come back.

David and Sam are tight, they hung out in school and gamed online all the time. David's family recently moved from Vancouver. He was very easy to talk to and though he had just started driving, his skills were very good. On our first lesson, I took David for a long windy drive through the countryside listening to some straight ahead jazz. It's very improvisational and is great for long drives where we want less thinking and more creative flow. Driving really is like jazz, improvisational and instinctual. As we drove into the city, David was in a groove and driving seemed so easy for him.

I then took him to a semi busy road. He was able to make turns and navigate with little problems. We drove home and debriefed. I was very happy with the initial lesson and recommended eight plus the road test package. His parents agreed. On lesson two, we drove downtown and started to do lots of left and right turns. I get students to do lots of repetitive turns to ingrain the skill. Turning is often under taught and taken for granted, hence most crashes occur in an intersection. I was playing some Robert Glasper hip hop jazz. His songs are great when I want to work on specific skills. It's jazz-based, infused with hip hop and R&B. I love jazz! I used to ask students what music they wanted to listen to but after multiple country song requests, I've become a playlist dictator. There are genres that I tolerate but it takes a special student for me to play their music.

David's skills are improving at a rate that I seldom see, and I tell him that I'm pleased with his progress. Lesson three, we keep doing turns but this time, I start to take him into busier intersections and different areas in the city. He struggles a little in the beginning, adapts and improves by the end of the lesson. Lesson four, we start to learn how to back up which is the base skill for all types of parking; stall, parallel, plus 2-point and 3-point turns. Backing up is a very hard lesson for students because it takes so much mental energy to drive backwards. I play some smooth jazz to lessen the strain in them. Lesson five, straight ahead jazz again, we work on all the skills and start to practice near the road test area. I firmly believe that if my students have solid skills, they would be ready to pass the road test without the need to memorize the road test routes. David is killing it and has a good chance of passing the road test. Lesson six, with the test fast approaching, I start noticing David making small mistakes like missing shoulder checks or doing forced shoulder checks. He also seems a little less friendly and more on edge. I dismiss this as him just being tired from work or school. Lesson seven, we go back around the test area. David is making even more mistakes and now is a little testy when I try to make suggestions. I know something is up and I ask if everything is, okay? He says he's worried about the test. David's technical skills are good, but he is experiencing text anxiety. He wants his license so bad but is afraid to fail his test. As they get closer to the test date, many of my students start to change the way they drive and prepare. It is more common than people realize and is the biggest obstacle that students face when trying to get their license. At this point, they now work tirelessly to perfect their technique instead of trusting the preparation and practice what we have previously done. They stop trusting their skills and instead go into panic mode. It's the difference between technical(thought) and competition(action) skills. These days, we do so much thinking (thought) that when it comes to pressure situations, we do not allow instinctual behavior (action) to kick in. People will overthink which leads to making mistakes. The more anxious my students get, the more their processing ability shuts down in their brain and this cycle may spiral out of control on the road test. Lesson eight, David has a decent last lesson. Test day arrives, he looks ready, and we have a good warm up drive. I remind him to just chill the fuck out and relax. After 30 minutes, David and the examiner come back into the lot. The last maneuver in the test is a reverse stall park. David backs up and is in the stall but a little crooked. Not satisfied, he drives forward to readjust and he backs right in the middle of the stall. David and the examiner talk in the car, but it takes longer than normal. They got out of the car with me expecting David to give me a high five or something. He's not happy and he tells me that he failed his test. When David readjusted, he did not look through the back window and do a 360-degree check. Even though he was perfectly in the middle of the stall, he committed a dangerous action and failed his road test. He is devastated! If David had just finished his original backup not worrying about being perfectly in the middle of the stall, he would have passed but because he tried to be perfect, he missed his 360-check. This is the problem with thought over action. I teach students that it's more important to look around and see the big picture than obsess to be perfect. When we got home, David was visibly pissed and almost in tears. He can't get over failing for that one thing. He does his second test on his own and successfully passes. He texts me to say thank you and how grateful he was for the lessons. I encounter this test anxiety every day and my advice for all my students is to just chill the fuck out, drive with less thought and more action!

Sam finally texts me after 6 weeks to resume the lessons. I was happy to hear from him and we booked lesson two. His skills are pretty good but he is still scared shitless about driving and crashing. I take him for a drive around the city doing turns and working on his shoulder checks. Again, he is driving well, but for whatever reason, he would have moments of panic. And, he doesn't like when I see him make a mistake like a missed scan or shoulder check. He will dismiss it and say that he did do them.

This is a recurring theme that keeps happening in the future lessons. Lesson three, we start backing up and parallel parking, no problems and he is crushing it! Lesson four, I take him downtown to experience a different area. Lesson five, preparation is spot on and he's ready for the test. Lesson six, what the fuck happened? We turn left on a busy intersection that we have done many times before. He is very hesitant to commit into the intersection, anxiously waiting behind the line. He finishes turning and we talk about how he should have moved into the intersection. Suddenly, he freaks out at me and says that I never taught him the rules for that turn. He can't admit that it was his mistake. He doubles down and starts to get very irritated. We drove away from the test area to a parking lot with a view of the city. We talk for thirty minutes as he breaks down crying. He is so afraid of making a mistake and failing the test that his processing ability has seized up and the only emotion that was present was fear. I start reading him excerpts of my book and he proceeds to say that his generation sucks! He hates how insecure, anxious and afraid he and most of his guy friends are. He knows that he was in the wrong, but he could not own up to making the mistake. He would rather try to pass it off or lie to make it disappear. I keep reading him more stories until we head back to his house. Sam's test is the next day, and I suggest that he take a long walk and get some exercise before his test. My only advice to him was less thought and more action and to chill the fuck out! Test day, I get a text, Sam passes! I texted him to say congrats and sorry for making him cry. He said it was okay. It was a combination of him having to pee and just me being so tough on him, but he understood what I was trying to do. I said I'll see him around and to make sure that if he recommends me to his friends, warn them that I'm an old school drill sergeant instructor. He's already recommended me to his friends and warned them. He looks forward to reading the rest of my book.

Nick was probably one of my favorite students ever. He stood at 5'4", thin, thick glasses and rosy cheeks. He looked like the cutest puppy in the litter and had big, round eyes. His mom is a baker at a cafe downtown. I pick Nick up from his house and we chat with his mom before the lesson. I asked what their goals were, his mom said that she wanted Nick to be a better, more confident driver. Nick didn't say much, he seemed very shy and reserved. We start the lessons, and I have some jazz on with the sunroof open as we drove around the city. Nick had good basic technique. The problem was that he seemed artificial and robotic in his driving. It was like he was doing all the proper checks and knew all the rules, but he really didn't understand what was happening on the road. He was following a script and not adapting to the changing conditions of the road. I take him back home and debrief with Nick and his mom. I shared with them what I observed and recommended six lessons. His mom agreed and I added one caveat, that if they are happy with the lessons, she would bake for me a strawberry cheesecake. I was excited because Strawberry Cheesecake is my all-time favorite dessert! Lesson two, Nick and I start talking more. He opens up and I start to really enjoy having him in the car. Nick has a dry sense of humor. We're driving around and he's starting to become less mechanical.

We stop by a busy street corner, park and get out of the car. One of the things I teach my students is the importance of communication and initiating human contact when driving. An exercise that we do is to walk across a busy intersection looking at all the cars and pedestrians trying to figure out what each road user is thinking and doing. Modern people will rarely make eye contact, and it makes it extremely difficult to judge and predict their intentions. When we walk across a crosswalk, I teach my students to freely look around with shoulders back and head up. This helps them see the big picture and communicate with everyone. It is overwhelming if you're not used to doing it. Nick starts to get what we're trying to do and on the drive home, he is chattier. Lesson three, with his driving is rapidly improving, I take him downtown to drive in a different area. I notice that his observation needs more improvement, so we do another drill. I have Nick stand on a sidewalk and try to walk across the street in-between parked cars. It simulates when we have a stop sign and must go straight without having good visibility on either side. You need to stop, creep forward and make a second stop to get a better line of sight before going. A lot of new drivers think that if they stop, they are entitled to go, and this causes a lot of dangerous situations. I have Nick look around the cars before crossing the road. Mission accomplished! Our last drill was to use my cell phone camera app. Today, we view the world mostly through our phones, tablets and monitors. We tend to look down and focus our vision on a small spot, but we don't spend enough time observing the landscape, horizon and the big picture. I had Nick look into my phone and instead of focusing on the middle of the screen, I would move the phone in a panoramic motion and have Nick follow the whole screen to simulate zooming out of fine details. This helps my students unlock their focus on specific objects and observe the landscape in a more passive way. I try to not use words like focus and instead will use terms like "observe". Even "look" can lead my students to focus on a specific quadrant and not the horizon. After the exercise, Nick drove home and instantly he sees more of everything. It's like I unlocked a blockage in his brain, and this freed up his observation and communication skills. At the start of lesson four, his mom was so pleased with Nick's progress. He has even started to talk to her more while they were practicing on their own. Nick was always been quiet but now he couldn't stop talking to his mom. She was over the moon! The following week, he got his license and I got my cheesecake. It was delicious!

But more importantly, I gained an even deeper insight on how rigid and stuck the minds of my young male students are. I'm not a neurologist but with hundreds of students that are exhibiting a common behavior, something must be up. Their behavior is so frozen that I am having to find inventive ways to be able to effect positive change in their mindset. It's getting harder and harder!

I started teaching Lee before the Covid lockdowns. I knew his family seeing them in church but recently, I have only attended mass a couple of times a year. Catholics are expected to attend mass weekly so I have to be better about this and start going more!

In lesson 1, Lee had a natural, relaxed feel for driving. He was an avid basketball player and played for his school team. He also loved music and played guitar in his spare time. Lee is a pretty good student, relatively shy but since I am a familiar face, he feels more comfortable in the car. In lesson 1, I take him to Colwood, a small municipality in the outskirts of Victoria. It's pretty rural and we get lots of continuous driving in. I take Lee home and tell his parents that we're going to be good. They signed up for 6 lessons and the road test. On lesson two, we start doing turns while listening to some jazz fusion. It's amazing cruising music.

Fun fact: when I was nineteen, while driving to the golf course, I was zipping around at 140 km/h through the city while listening to First Circle by Pat Metheny. Not recommending this to anyone, just a fun fact!

Lesson two, Lee is driving great, and I'm pleased with his progress. Lesson three, we start working on reversing and again, he is knocking it out of the park. Covid hits and we pause our lessons for a couple of months. When we resumed our lessons, Lee had gotten quieter and more distant. Lesson four, Lee is driving more hesitantly and he is not as confident. I ask him what's up and he doesn't say much. Then I ask him what he's been up to while in quarantine, and he says nothing. He was in a funk and almost looked like a zombie. I had to try to shake him out of this stasis, so I played a more aggressive style of jazz fusion. I also used profanity to snap Lee the fuck out of the funk he was in. I said that he should start to get out of the house for walks and play music on his guitar. I wanted him to restart his mind, body and soul. Lee is fortunate that we did the lessons at that time, and he was able to shatter the repetition of being locked down. On lesson five, he was back to normal, and we were able to prepare for the road test by diligently working on parking and other skills. Lesson six, Lee had his best lesson yet. He's back to normal and seems even happier than before the quarantine. On his test day, I pick him up, do a brief warm up and we head to the park to play some catch with my tennis ball. He passes his test with flying colors, and I take him home. He is very appreciative not only for getting his license but, more importantly, that I was able to get him out of the COVID funk! People need to fight the fear of this situation. Yes, many people have suffered and died from COVID but we have to take a stand and fight against the long-term mental damage the lockdowns have caused for this generation. I have seen the severe effects of the lockdown on my students and hope that I have, in a small way, helped them regain their confidence.

50

It's the morning of my 50th birthday, country music was blaring from the speaker of the hotel restaurant. I gingerly walked into the breakfast area looking for food. The waitress sees me struggling, pours me a coffee and asks where I'm from? We had just travelled twenty-four hours straight from Victoria to Poughkeepsie New York to watch Seve play Fall Ball lacrosse.

Love for your son #1

To get to Poughkeepsie, we left our house in Victoria at 7pm and caught the 9pm ferry to Vancouver. The crossing takes 95 minutes, we dock at 10:35pm and drive 30 minutes to my mom's place. Sleep at midnight, get up at 3am. Shower, wake up my bro, Rob, stuff all our bags in his Tesla (low key, if this fucking book blows up, I'm buying this ride!) Arrive YVR at 4:30am, check in for our 730am flight to Seattle. We get into Sea-Tac at 8:15am and head straight to the Delta Lounge. Traveling regularly the last few years following Seve's lacrosse journey, we have been in many airport lounges. The Delta Lounge in Seattle is large and comfortable with amazing staff and has great food and beverage options. The breakfast was simple, scrambled eggs, sausage, rice, and beef carnitas. Average but hits the spot when you're hungry. Though I'm not a big drinker these days, I strolled to the bar to grab a beverage. The host asks me what I would like, and I'm stumped. She sees that I'm confused, takes charge and pours me an IPA. I head back to the table with my beer. Still not satisfied, I order a Shandy. The host looks at me, probably thinking what decade I came from and what cave I crawled out of. I explain that it's ½ beer ½ Ginger ale. The OGs at the Tennis club used to drink this all the time when I was a kid. Maria, also not a drinker, asks wtf this is and takes a sip. She instantly loves it. After an hour, Maria gets restless and walks around to explore the terminal. I was tired and just wanted to sleep so I closed my eyes and charged my fake Air Pods. After 30 minutes, Maria wakes me up. I pack my stuff and look for my ear buds, they're fucking gone! This is the reason I don't buy expensive ones; I lose them all the time. Both a tad pissed but also amused, whoever snatched my buds thought that they were getting $180 air pods instead of $25 knock offs. Still 2 hours from our boarding time, we head back into the lounge. Perfect timing, in a small section of the buffet, there is a featured offering from a local chef. On the menu, they had Vietnamese beef ribs stew, crusty bread and dessert. Having tried this dish growing up in Vancouver, I knew this was going to be delicious! When I took my 1st bite, a nuclear explosion detonated in my mouth (cinnamon, sugary, salty, savory, umami!) It's hard to describe the taste. It's feeling of joy and happiness, like being 16 and making love all night long. I went back 4 times; the chef was so pleased.

Not one to easily give up. As we were leaving the lounge, I asked the counter staff about my ear buds. Luckily, the people in Seattle were honest and they were turned in. I was so upset thinking that I lost my favorite $25 knockoffs! We boarded our 3.5-hour flight to Minneapolis. We land and only have a 15-minute window for our connecting flight to Hartford. Big problem, all the Vietnamese food I ate in Seattle is ready for arrival! I rushed into the bathroom with Maria panicking, she was not impressed with my sudden bowel movement not wanting to miss our connecting flight. Literally, I had one minute to discharge all the stew in my stomach. All you guys know that one minute is not enough time to unload a plane full of cargo! Luckily, the airport had golf carts ferry passengers between gates and Maria managed to commandeer one for us. We make our flight and land in Hartford at midnight. Because I wanted to save some cash, I convinced Maria to just drive straight to Poughkeepsie from the airport without sleeping in a hotel. She was so pissed as we got into the rental. My plan was to stop at a Flying J gas station, take a shower and drive straight to Seve. After 4 hours of driving, we finally reach the Flying J, buy 2 showers for $20 and proceed to get cleaned up from our Odyssey. What a relief to freshen up, use the bathroom and take a hot shower! At that moment, it felt more luxurious than the suite at the Bellagio we stayed at in 2012. Refreshed, we drove two more hours and at last, got to Marist. We travelled more than 24 hours to see Seve!

Love for your son #2

After spending the week with Seve, and watching him play fall ball lacrosse, it was time for us to go home. Because of Canada's strict Covid requirements, Maria and I had to get a PCR COVID test within 72 hours prior to entry to Canada. A big problem, it was hard to find a place in Poughkeepsie to take this test within the 72-hour window. We had to drive three hours to Hartford airport, take the test, then drive another three hours back to

Seve. The trip took 10 hours. We found out later, that the clinic beside Marist offered the same fucking PCR test 😂!

It's time to go home. Three hours to Hartford, sleep in a hotel, fly out at 6:30am the following morning. Hartford to Atlanta to Calgary to Vancouver. Get the car from Rob's house, 2-hour ferry ride and finally back home to Victoria, 24-hour odyssey again!

PSA-it's not only hard to be a parent, but it is also in our DNA to sacrifice everything for our kids.

CHAPTER 9
NAVIGATING ADVERSITY

Becoming a golf professional

I started playing golf in 1990 and I instantly got hooked, the moment I hit my first 300-yard drive. It's that euphoric feeling of hitting the golf ball flush which makes the sport so addictive. In hindsight, if I realized how frustrating this game was, I may have taken up a different sport like pickleball. Nevertheless, three months in, I shot 79. Most golfers will never break 100 let alone shoot 79! I was thinking to myself how fucking hard could this be? I started rapidly improving and began beating players that have golfed for years. In the past, people would always play, with something on the line, from money, food, beers or pride. Some betting games were match play, foursomes, skins, rabbit, birdies, and sandy's. I've even seen golfers play poker and golf at the same time and have witnessed large sums of money change hands on the golf course. Being this ultra-competitive dude, all these games appealed to me. I loved winning but hated losing. When I lost, I was ultra-motivated to get better. It drove me nuts and I would spend the following week practicing all my weaknesses with extra emphasis on chipping and putting to improve my short game. After 3 years, I became a two handicap which is very good as most people's handicap will never fall below twenty. I was considered a good golfer in Vancouver but when I moved back to the Philippines, I was trash. Golf in the Philippines is much different than in Vancouver. Winning was everything and no one wanted to lose. They had very inventive ways to beat you, either through real skill, or fake skill by declaring an inflated handicap which is very immoral. Golfers would even have their caddies or fore caddies place their ball into a perfect spot if they hit their ball into the trees or water. They had no qualms about cheating. There was nothing that people wouldn't do to win and, though I was a top Dog in Vancouver, I became the fish when I first landed in the Philippines. I had two choices at that moment; quit golf and save all my money or learn how to adapt and figure out a way to beat these fucking assholes! First thing I learned was to be HUMBLE. In Vancouver, golfers would generally declare a lower handicap to impress people for their ego. In the Philippines it was the total opposite. Good golfers wanted a higher handicap so that it would give them an unfair advantage when it came to betting. This was such a new and foreign concept to me, but right away I realized that my 2-handicap in Vancouver was more like a 10 in the Philippines. There were a lot of 10-handicaps that I played with, that routinely shot par or under par and they would take my money with a smile on their face! Eventually, I met good golfers who weren't so immoral with their handicaps, but just wanted good competition and tried to play their very best. Guys like Pepot, a flight purser, Commodore an ex-Navy Admiral, Bobby C an educated professional and many others.

We would routinely play and have anywhere between 10 to 15 players for an afternoon golf match. As a 2-handicap, if I didn't shoot somewhere near par, I would probably end up losing a lot of money. And yes! I did lose my fair share of pesos, but I also figured out ways to win some of it back. All the while, we would enjoy each other's company, and I would learn such interesting facts about my playing partners and their lives. It was some of the best competition anyone could ever ask for. We would play for 6 hours as compared to 4.5 hours in Canada. Golf in the Philippines is slower, every three holes, there was a pit stop for drinks. The Philippines is so hot and humid that the snack house was more of a need than a want. They served sandwiches, hot dogs, congee, hard boiled eggs with tabasco(umami), and local Philippine delicacies. For refreshments you had your choice of water, which was always number one, Gatorade, beer, or hard liquor with Red Bull. One of the best drinks I've ever had was water with molasses and lime juice. After our 6-hour round, we would all head into the clubhouse, have 3 beers as we tallied up the winners and losers for the day. Then we would shower, get reenergized, head back into the restaurant and enjoy a feast. Normally the guy or guys that won the most money, would contribute the most into the pot to pay for the bill. By the time we left, everyone was very exhausted but super happy. I did this three times a month.

Back to becoming a golf pro. Because of the harsh competition in the Philippines, I became a really good, seasoned golfer.

When we moved back to Canada, I missed competing with all my buddies. To find that high level of competition, I joined the Canadian Professional Golf Association. This gave me the opportunity to play against the top players in the province. The association represents all the Golf Professionals in Canada who work in the golf industry. Pros would compete against each other in the top local and national professional tournaments. They are also extensively trained to teach golfers of all levels. It is a minimum three-year period before becoming a CPGA Class A golf professional. The first step is to become an apprentice professional. You must work in the pro shop for at least one year and learn from the Head Professional. After a year, you become qualified to take the playability test (PAT.) Every year, would-be apprentices dreaded this day. It was the most pressure packed golf imaginable. If you didn't shoot the required number, you would have to wait one year for the next PAT.

If you are successful, you become an apprentice professional working directly under the head pro. In that time, the head pro will mentor and train the apprentice with all the skills required to become a successful golf professional.

After two years as an apprentice, you become eligible to write the class A exam.

The exam is a grueling 6-hour written marathon and was even more nerve-racking than the playability test. If you fail, you will have to wait one year before the next exam. Today the CPGA has changed this requirement and instituted a college based credit program for Class A accreditation where the written exam is longer a requirement.

My playability test was conducted at Royalwood golf course in Chilliwack BC. It's a links-style track inspired from Scottish golf courses built beside the sea with very little trees, having numerous sand dunes and bunkers. This is challenging because the golfers are very exposed to the elements. If it gets windy, playing gets very difficult. It's much harder to control the golf ball in the air when there are no trees to block the wind. You need to become an expert to play links golf. Strategies would be to hit the ball lower and let the ball run on the ground anticipating where it would stop. In Canada, most courses are tree lined with golfers learning to hit the ball in the air. On the two days of the PAT, the wind was blowing between 20 to 30 km/h. The ground was bone dry after very little summer rain and the conditions were tricky. You could sense the tension and anxiety from my peers trying to achieve the qualifying score. I tee off in the afternoon with two other players. The pace of play is extremely slow. Everybody's grinding and trying not to make a mistake. I've learned through experience that I just have to play one shot at a time and stay in the present. Play each hole, write my score down, and go to the next tee. Though I didn't particularly enjoy playing that day, I shot a really good score of 2 under par, 70. I couldn't believe I shot 70, it felt like an 82, but that's the power of staying in the present. My competitors also played well, shooting somewhere near par. I was optimistic that if I just kept playing the same way, I would qualify and achieve the score needed to pass the playability test. On day two, I remember one particular shot. My ball ended up beside a tree where I couldn't swing right-handed. 140 yards away from the green, my creativity kicked in. I flipped my seven iron upside-down, hit the shot left-handed off the toe of my club, with the golf ball landing softly on the green. This was probably the best shot I've ever hit in my life. I still vividly remember that feeling! Very few golfers would have even dared visualizing that shot, let alone hit it, in that pressure situation. As I said previously, just stay in the present, try your best to make a good swing and not be afraid to fuck up!

When I putted out on the last green, I shot 73, one over. I qualified and had a two-day total of one under, 143 which was safely within the cut margin. I have now achieved the first step to becoming a Class A golf professional.

Now onto the written exam. I hear horror stories from the old pros about this exam. They sweat throughout the 6-hour marathon, with barely enough time to finish. The CPGA conducts extensive seminars for teaching. They also train us how to assess different personality traits, using the Meyers Briggs test, to create lesson plans for our students. Being a golf professional, you meet and are forced to interact with all types of people. While working in the golf shop, I experienced many days where I'd be smiling, but in the back of my mind, I was not pleased with the interaction! Yet I had to stay calm even under the most difficult situations. I try to teach this to my students. Stay in the zone, stay composed and stay calm even under the utmost pressure in any situation, good or bad.

I studied for the class A exam for a week, going over my notes that I learned in my seminars. On test day, thirty of us sit down for the exam. All we have is the test paper, a pencil and an eraser. We're all freaking out. The class A exam consisted of four different scenarios for four different students and creating four different lesson plans. We would be graded on the lesson plans, detailing them from start to finish while using everything we learned in the seminars and in our real-life experiences teaching our students. For my lesson plans, I chose an elderly lady in her 60s, a young 13-year-old girl, who had never golfed before, a top-level amateur in his mid-20s that wanted to turn pro, and a middle-aged golfer with back problems that had limited range of mobility. It took me about four and a half hours to finish. I'm reasonably happy, but not sure how I did.

In the history of the CPGA, they had conducted around 14,000 written exams. The tests were graded with a total score of 132. The passing grade is 75% of 132. On results day, I get a call from the CPGA office. Our rep wanted to talk to me about my test result and for a brief moment, I was worried. To my surprise, he told me that I scored 128 out of 132, 98%! It was one of the highest test scores ever in the history of 14,000 + class A exams. I'm low-key pissed! People would expect me to be happy and I was, but if I knew I was that close to 100%, I would have wanted to be the first one ever to get a perfect score!

That's my story on how I became a CPGA Class A teaching professional. With all the skills and training that I received, I have been able to pivot and help thousands of people become better drivers in Victoria. For anybody wondering, it is so much harder to teach golfers how to hit a stationary golf ball than it is to teach people how to drive defensively!

My student fell from the stands

I got a call from a student and as we were chatting on the phone, I noticed that his speech patterns were quite rigid. Rick was thirty and lived with his sister. A few years back, while watching a hockey game, he fell from the second row of the stands, hit his head on the cement floor and suffered a fractured skull. His neurologist diagnosed that only certain pathways in his brain were working. Right after his surgery, he was unable to speak and formulate words or sentences. Rick underwent a full year of rehab. He had to slowly relearn how to speak, walk, identify patterns and objects.

We start our lesson, and we head outside. They had a basketball hoop in the driveway, and I asked him to shoot some hoops with me. There are times that I chat with a student for 15 to 30 minutes before we start driving. This initial time helps us form a connection and it gives me a chance to lesson plan. As we were shooting, an idea popped into my head. Instead of trying to teach him how he thinks he should learn, I came up with an idea to teach him the opposite. I wanted to stimulate the parts of his brain not working at that moment. I'm not a neurologist, but I've come up with some innovative and unusual techniques that just seem to work. We start driving on this long windy road from his house. Rick drives well but gets anxious as we turn right onto the main road. I tell him not to worry, if we encounter a situation on the road, I'm able to drive us out of danger. His technical skills are good, but our biggest obstacle would be his decision making in busy situations. To loosen up his mind, I have Rick drive while listening to loud music. I choose Allan Holdsworth. His music is a mix of hard rock fused with jazz, his skills are God-like with lightning fast hands. I surprise Rick by cranking up the volume. He thought that he would be driving in silence. I tell him to trust the process. It seems to work. We start driving around and, miraculously, I was able to tap into his subconscious, bypassing his conscious brain. He was able to drive like he did before his fall and was shocked that the driving started to get easier for him. We did four lessons, listening to different types of music. By the end of the lessons his speech patterns and his overall mood was much better. Rick was so appreciative of his newfound driving skills. But, more importantly, he was enjoying life and could look around without feeling trapped by the thoughts he previously had before. I was so happy to help Rick, and it opened my eyes to realize that anything was truly possible. All we need is the will and courage to try things even as unlikely and illogical as they may seem! The following week, I get a text from Rick. He thanked me profusely and said he had no problems with the road test. Rick was very happy with our lessons.

It's important to try the impossible! Don't be afraid to leave your comfort zone and step outside the box!

The Mental Approach

In 2005, I was working as a Golf Pro and was a monthly contributor to The Island Golfer. It's a golf magazine distributed around Vancouver Island. My column was titled "The Mental Approach." I wrote about different mental challenges that golfers faced on and off the golf course. Having played both recreationally and competitively, I was able to offer insights that were original and unique. One of the things I emphasized was the power of visualization. In golf, there is a point where the mental game becomes more important than technique. This happens once you become a low handicap or professional golfer. The importance of visualization cannot be overstated. An example would be hitting a drive with trees on the left side of the fairway and water all along the right-hand side. The fairway, where golfers want to hit their golf ball, does not change in size but the challenge is seeing and being aware of the dangers on the left and right of the fairway. If your mind starts to develop self-talk and fear of hooking your drive into the forest or slicing the tee shot in the water, your body will most likely follow what your mind is seeing (thoughts influence actions!) Therefore, I work extremely hard with my students on the power of visualization and a positive mindset. Even the highest-level athletes will have moments of self-talk and self-doubt, but through all their experiences and highest competition skills, they are able to fight the negative self-talk to get back into the zone. The ultimate goal is for your golf ball to finish on target, not in the hazards lurking left or right. We visualize the flight of the ball takeoff until it safely finishes on the fairway. Sometimes, golfers will want to do this a couple of times to sync what their mind is visualizing with their body. After visualizing the shot, we teach golfers a pre shot routine to set up in a similar way every time to eliminate overthinking. Basically, once you start your routine, all conscious thought should be minimal and all that is left is to swing uninhibited with no fear of fucking up. The ability to free yourself and not worry about the hazards is difference between good golfers to average players. All the effort should be focused on visualization and the pre-shot routine. This is why top golfers will say that golf is 95% mental and 5% physical. For average golfers, that ratio is inverted.

This way of being takes practice and patience. Expect a lot of balls to fly into the woods or into the water but, as we have covered, just keep trying until you make the mental and physical changes needed to eventually hit the fairway and never ever give up!

For dudes, because thoughts influence actions, it is imperative to develop a can-do attitude with no fear of failure. If you fail, just "keep trying until you succeed!" Fight self-talk and self-doubt by trying something over and over again until you breakthrough. You will develop the skill of resiliency and defeat self-talk and self-doubt forever.

Nightlife in Manila

In the 80's and 90's, nightlife in Manila was spectacular. There were endless bars, night clubs, concert venues, and restaurants. I had a blast living in Manila during my late teens and early twenties hanging out with friends and family. Everyone, rich or poor knew how to have a good time. Less well-off people would drink Tanduay Rum and San Miguel Pale Pilsner beer while the more affluent could afford Hennessy, and Johnny Walker Blue. I was friends with both the richest and the poorest people in Manila and was very lucky for the experience! Food was a very big part of Filipino culture, and we ate everything from *balut*, *sisig*, BBQ pork belly (*inihaw na liempo),* sushi, sashimi, BBQ Tuna jaw(*inihaw na panga),* whole roasted pig (*lechon*), live steamed shrimp (*suahe*), and giant prawns (*sugpo*) in a garlic butter sauce. We shared lots of laughs, had lots of fun, and sometimes, one of us, puking our guts out from drinking too much beer!

I think about these experiences now and because of COVID, it seems like we've lost a lot of these opportunities to get together and socialize. Of course, I don't condone breaking lockdown or quarantine, but I am observing the loss of human connections every day and the impact this is having on everyone's mental health. I hope these lockdowns and quarantine measures will slowly be lifted because I'm afraid that the longer we are isolated from one another, serious mental problems will arise, especially with our youth. I can already see troubling signs with my young male students due to this lack of socialization.

Growth Mindset

Throughout my book, I have shared many stories and experiences about myself. Sports have shaped my life profoundly and the most important lessons I have learned from it is the power of a Growth Mindset!

I believe that Growth Mindset is the key to learning. It helps people develop confidence, self-belief, and resiliency in the face of adversity.

Carol Dweck, an American psychologist and researcher, wrote a book called "Mindset". In it, she believes that your mindset can determine the trajectory of your life.

Through her 25+ years of research, Dweck found that most humans will develop into either; a growth or fixed mindset:

Fixed Mindset advocates personal qualities like intelligence, beauty, wealth. And that abilities are innate and hard to change

Growth Mindset believes in the ability to learn and grow without the barriers and pitfalls of failure

These mindsets are shaped from early life by parents, coaches, teachers and environment. How we give feedback and kids receive them are critical to developing a growth mindset. The biggest trap of a fixed mindset is believing that we are special, because of born traits like beauty, intelligence, wealth and privilege. Once a person thinks that these qualities will decide their future, they become brittle in the face of adversity and instead, they rely on them and believe that their future is predetermined due to their fixed traits. People with fixed mindsets are afraid of challenges and will seek out the path of least resistance to achieve a goal. Dweck conducted extensive research on grade school kids about this and found that kids with a fixed mindset would be satisfied with achieving a goal, but they were not as interested to try a harder goal in the next challenge, preferring to do a similar level task. Kids that had a growth mindset not only sought out the harder tests, even if they failed the test, they had no hesitation to try again in the face of failure. They understood that they could learn, adapt, and try again to succeed.

Examples include:

<u>Fixed Mindset Feedback</u>
-You are beautiful
-You are smart
-You're stronger than the rest of the kids
-You're special
-You're talented
-You're rich

<u>Growth Mindset Feedback</u>
-You worked hard
-Great Effort
-Try Again until you get it
-You can't do it, *yet*

-You can try harder next time

-Fail going 100%

In growth mindset, the process is the key to achieving the results. It is essential to not worry about winning or losing but to stay in the present on each shot or skill. You learn from the past to improve future results staying in the present.

Michael Jordan is the ultimate example of a Growth Mindset competitor. He would have a big picture goal, then do everything in practice and games to achieve the said goal. If he lacked a skill, he would tirelessly practice in the gym until he got the skill. Because he practiced harder in the gym, when it came to games, there was no scenario that he hadn't repped out in practice. He knew that he was ready for any situation and did not feel any pressure in the biggest games. And in his mind, the score was always 0-0 meaning that he would play with the same effort whether the score was tied, 0-0, if his team was winning by 30 or losing by 30.

In Mike's most famous commercial for Nike, he proclaimed that:

"I have missed more than 9000 shots in my career, I have lost almost 300 games, I have failed 26 times when trusted to take the game winning shot and missed. I've failed over, and over again in my life. And that is why I succeed!"

His other famous quotes:

"I've always believed that if you put in the work, the results will come."

"I can accept failure; everyone fails at something. But I can't accept not trying."

"If you run into a wall, don't turn around and give up. Figure out how to climb it."

"If you quit once, it becomes a habit. Never quit!"

"Never say never, because limits, like fears, are often just an illusion."

"Some people want it to happen, some wish it to happen, others make it happen."

Not everyone can be like Mike but they "can try" as hard as they can! A good reference is "the Last Dance," a documentary about the 1998 Chicago Bulls Championship season on Netflix

Fixed mindset people will lack the resiliency, and self-belief to keep trying in the face of adversity and failure. The first moment that they lose, fixed-mindset individuals will more easily give up and quit.

It is important to understand your Mindset and how it affects your life!

A lack of babies

The last couple of years I've noticed that a lot of modern people are single, and even the ones in relationships are hesitant to have kids. I saw an article on Global news about fertility rates in Canada. New data showed that the fertility rate plummeted to a record low of 1.26 babies per woman in 2023. A replacement rate of 2.1 babies per woman was the baseline for developed countries for their populations to replace itself from one generation to the next. With that said, 1.26 kids per woman is alarming. There are many scientists who are sounding this population alarm and if it continues, they predict a collapse of the major Western societies around the world. Last week, I was on YouTube watching a channel and they were discussing Japan and its population woes. In the video, it stated that Japan only had 800,000 babies born last year compared to a greater number of aging seniors that were living longer than in previous generations. They theorized that Japan is on the brink of collapse because there are not enough young people to replenish the workforce and to take care of the aging senior population. It further states that this catastrophe may very well happen in a lot of other Western countries, specifically Italy which is also experiencing a lower birth rate. Because Canada has traditionally been an ideal place for immigrants, we have not yet experienced this problem as extensively as in other countries. Canada has made it more accessible for foreigners to get work, student, and business visas to attract younger families and inject younger people into the population. Without this migration, Canada would also be in dire straits.

When Seve started playing lacrosse at 8 years old, there were three house teams and one rep team. Numbers were high, with at least 80+ kids registered in our area. In the rival area, there were 100+ kids. Fast forward 12 years, I ran into his old coach, Rob who was coaching his youngest daughter and son. When I asked how many kids were registering, it was about half of what it was 12 years ago. Maybe it's a combination of a lower interest in lacrosse, but also less kids around to register for the sport. I talked to coaches in other sports, and they are seeing lower registrations across the board for different sports from baseball to basketball, to hockey. Youth participation in sports is at all-time lows. With the current birth rate of 1.26 kids per woman, it's only a matter of time until youth sports will eventually collapse. This is a small but very important example that has much larger implications for Western societies. There will not be enough young people to work, attend schools, replenish the workforce, and in the end, take care of the aging population. People are free to choose to be single and not have kids. I'm not implying that we force people to have kids, but humanity has survived through a number of global catastrophes. The earth has experienced ice ages, sudden warming, the younger dryas cataclysm, disease, famine and devastating wars. Through all these challenges, humans have kept going with their two primary goals, to survive and to reproduce. Now more than ever, it is imperative for people to realize this before it's too late.

When I see a young family, I will always congratulate them and say how lucky they are to have a baby. I give them praise and encouragement because it's not easy raising kids. But the greatest joy I have is seeing my kids do well in life. My oldest son Alex recently started a job as assistant manager for a worldwide clothing retailer. He's two credits shy of getting his sports management degree and will graduate this spring. Yesterday, I picked him up from work and we had a nice chat in the car. I told how proud I was of him. We were discussing his possibilities with that company moving forward and if he was going to do a master's degree. I also spoke with Seve this morning; he's thriving in college and he also wants to do his masters. Knowing that my kids are good, my life is fulfilled. Whatever else that happens to me is irrelevant as long as I know that my sons are going to be fine. I honestly don't need anything else in life! This is the crucial point that modern society is lacking, the importance of family and having kids!

The End of the World

One of my good friends Paul, is a 26-year-old PhD student from San Diego. We met playing tennis, their college team was practicing on the adjacent court. The following week, we played doubles. After the match, he asked what I did for a living? I was in the middle of writing my book. Paul was intrigued but had to go. We exchanged numbers and said that we would do this again. A month later, Paul drops by the hill. I was feeling confident and cocky because my singles game had been steadily improving. I challenged Paul to a set with the loser buying wings and beer. He agreed, not thinking that he would lose but I played really well and I destroyed him 6-2! I was happy to beat Paul! That summer, I started going to clubs and bars to do research for my book. I hadn't been out in 25 years. Paul and I met up at Bard Banker to hang out. Fast forward a few months. Every two or three weeks, we would hang out at Bard, Irish, and Paparazzi. Our friendship grew to the point where I treated him like a little brother. Recently, I've been going out a lot but Paul was missing. I phoned and texted him a few times but I could tell that something was up. He had a virus and was coughing but he also felt depressed about life. In his PhD research and work, he saw many problems plaguing the world which was causing his depression.

He would take data from different sources and create models to predict and forecast the future. He would work with businesses and tech companies in Silicon Valley as well as local, state, provincial and federal governments. They would use his modeling to create policies. What was depressing him was that most of his models showed no hope for humanity. He asked me if I believed in climate change and if I thought a global collapse was imminent. I said there was evidence and he countered by saying if we know that the world is going to shit, how could we possibly think that bringing kids into this world was a good idea? In other words, every model that he created had no positive scenarios. We've been discussing philosophical issues about life for the last year and a half. He sometimes gets frustrated by my viewpoints because I have a more traditional and positive take on things. He asked me what if I had any solutions for all these problems we are facing. I told him that, I firmly believe in humanity and that we should always have hope and faith! And to remember our two primary goals of survival and reproduction. He countered back by saying how could you reproduce when you know that your kids or your grandkids will be going into a hellscape. He kept pushing me until I finally relented and said, "*well maybe there's no antidote or solution.*" We may have to acknowledge that future generations will be fucked. We discussed that about every 20,000 years, a global catastrophe happens, whether it's an ice age, or global warming. With all these catastrophes, even under the most dire climate change events, humans and humanity have still found a way to survive and to reproduce. Paul listened intently. Modern humans think that we can create perfect systems and models to fix everything in the world, but I'll use quantum mechanics as an example. I'm also a science nerd. I love astronomy, biology, and even the study of physics and quantum mechanics. I'm not very advanced in these fields, but while watching a YouTube podcast with Deep Prasad on Jesse Michael's podcast, he was explaining that in quantum mechanics, our current system of physics can only explain about 5% of the known universe and how it works. Why then do we think that humans can create perfect systems? In quantum mechanics, many times, we know things work but can't explain how. Hence the theory of the multiverse. Ok this is too much science, back to the topic at hand: Being content with less than perfect information and not needing to know everything or micromanaging everything. Sometimes we can't fix everything, and accept that things will be less than perfect or may even go to shit. Going back to my chapter about contentment, we may have to lower our expectations. I'm not saying that we shouldn't goal set for a better life, but we should lower our threshold of happiness and contentment. To go back to living a simpler way of life and being. People are going crazy right now thinking about the future, and how their lives won't be the same as their parents. And if we think that the future is going to be fucked, then why not live life to the max, and try to be as happy as possible before shit hits the fan. Because if that's the end result, there's no use worrying about something out of our control!

Baseball in 82

My family moved to Canada in 1979. There were immigrants from all over the world starting to descend into this little slice of paradise. It was an amazing time to grow up, but with all the positives there are also negatives. The local Canadians at that time were predominantly white and indigenous. With so many new faces from different cultures, there were some issues. I don't think it was overt racism but a case of ignorance when encountering people from different parts of the world for the first time. As a 7-year-old Filipino immigrant, I never really thought about this or cared. I know that we had stereotypes about white people too and the feeling was reciprocal. The main difference from the '80s to today is that we were generally okay with this subtle or even overt racism. It wasn't mean spirited but, as I said, I think it was more about ignorance. These days, we've attached so much meaning to the words people use, that racism is stronger in people today.

When I was 11, I joined a baseball team. The sport was popular with most of my teammates being white. There were two minorities and a girl playing on our team, which was rare in 1982. Her name was Mandy, she was stick-thin, small, with short hair and thick glasses. Mandy was very unassuming, but she had one hell of a curveball, and she was a better baseball player than 95% of the guys on the team. She ended up playing for the Canadian Women's National soccer team!

I also had a pretty good curveball, but my go-to pitch was my fastball and I used it to strike-out a lot of batters. Mandy and I would alternate starts on the mound. When I pitched, she caught and when I caught, she pitched. Though I didn't really get to know her personally, we shared similar experiences being outliers on a predominantly white, all-male team. Some of the other kids were not nice to us maybe because we were better players and they were jealous of our skills. These days people would automatically assume that it's racism or sexism, but if I think about it logically, it was probably more based on insecurity from the other boys. I think about that story today because whenever somebody is mistreated, we automatically think of inequality, racism, or sexism. I'm not saying it's not, but it may be more than just that narrow bandwidth of thought. I have extensive experience with diversity, being a visible minority. We think these days that just because we don't say certain words or slurs, that we're not racist or sexist. I'm a firm believer that it's your actions that speak louder than your words or non-words. The true sign that somebody isn't racist, or sexist is when they see everybody the same. If they meet somebody blindfolded, they should be able to treat that person the same once they take the blindfold off.

In the past, we were able to say anything to anybody. I prefer to not say these words out loud now but, 40 years ago, people did so without fearing an instant visceral reaction. People were just not as easily offended back then, and most could take the back-and-forth banter without getting triggered.

These days, everyone in public is walking on eggshells trying not to say anything offensive. People in general seem to act nicer and kinder. But like my chapter about Hong Kong, I miss the days when people were truly transparent and authentic because even if I didn't like what was said, at least I knew where I stood!

Just do it

As I have stated, I'm writing this book for the benefit of young males. Although, I haven't mentioned what the catalyst was to start writing this book.

In February 2021, I was teaching a student, and I shared with her my frustrations about some aspects of modern society. I was noticing less hands-on (kinesthetic) learning going on and expressed my goal of either opening day schools that would teach more traditional hands-on skills or writing a book about my experiences. She said to me, "why talk about it, you should just do it!"

And that is why I'm penning this fucking book! I can't keep giving examples of motivation, will power, goal setting, resiliency and all the other attributes of being a 21st century dude if I'm not going to walk the fucking walk!

If you keep talking about doing something and are fully committed to this action, the hardest thing is taking the first step. It's the leap of faith and belief that you can do it. My earlier examples of exercising, quitting smoking, running the 106th suicide or asking a girl out are possible when you *want* to do it. The most important thing is taking the initiative and having courage to take that first step with the absence of fear.

Patriotism

As a young kid in the Philippines, one of the things I vividly remember taught in schools is our struggle for independence from the Spanish. Our most famous hero was a Filipino named Jose Rizal. There are numerous statues, schools and roads named after him. For his love of country, he paid the ultimate sacrifice, losing his life to the Spanish and becoming the most important martyr in Philippine history. When we moved to Canada, it was the same here. We had so much national pride for our veterans that served in World War I and World War II. In school, we would sing "God Save the Queen" and "O Canada" every morning. Canadian flags were flown everywhere. When Canadians traveled abroad, we would sew a Canadian flag on our backpacks and clothes. People proudly displayed Canadian flag tattoos on their bodies and faces. The Remembrance Day parade was such a big deal. One of the biggest things that I've noticed, especially the last two years, is that the younger people don't seem to be as patriotic. Right now as I'm writing my book and driving around, I hardly see any Canadian flags being flown anywhere. I drove by the Save On Foods Arena which is in downtown Victoria. They had a flag of British Columbia, a flag for the City of Victoria and the flag for the hockey junior team, the only flag they didn't have was the Canadian flag! I couldn't imagine a time in the past where this would have been okay or even being permitted, but here we are. Even 15 years ago, you would drive around and in a lot of shop windows and government or private buildings and you would see the Canadian flag flying proudly everywhere. I'm not really sure how or why it's happened but I feel less patriotism in our society. I often share these ideas with my friends and wonder out loud that if Canada was to be invaded by an outside force, who would protect us? It would probably be people my age that grew up with love for Canada! Is there a correlation between the reduced masculinity and testosterone in young men and them having a lot less of the protector mindset to protect their families, friends, spouses, and ultimately the country? Whatever it is, I hope and pray that there will never be a war on our shores. Because if that ever happens, I'll be fighting tooth and nail and probably die on the front lines! "I would rather die on my sword trying, than give up and be butchered in the slaughterhouse!"

There's a growing number of people today that seem to resent this country. I understand the injustices that have happened in the past, but I want to ask these people that if they hate their country so much, where would they go? Nobody's perfect, and in the past, we've had leaders that did less than perfect things. With that said, if shit hits the fan, where would you go?

Expo '86

In 1986, Vancouver wanted to showcase itself to the world. The city hosted the World Exposition. The 2-week celebration displayed exhibits from different countries which helped attract tourists from around the globe. I was 15, wore pastel pants, spiked my hair with gel, and had zits on my face. I thought that I was so cool in my pastel blue pants (I was delusional!) The Expo was amazing! Each country displayed so much pride in their culture and heritage. It offered them a chance to showcase their heritage to the world. Tourists from all over the world descended into Vancouver. There were food vendors from Ethiopia, Vietnam, Greece, Ukraine, the Soviet Union, and my favorite Big Mac at the gigantic McDonald's kiosk- what an orgasmic sandwich that was! I remember a lot of really good looking girls my age walking around with the nicest summer tans. OMG! OMG! OMG! I was in heaven. My other memory was how united and how hopeful people were at that time. There was less skepticism, drama, and jealousy. The focus of that two-week exhibit was to get the world together in one of the most beautiful places on Earth. You had the embassy staff from each country really make an effort to show how amazing their countries were. This was such a stark contrast to what we see in 2021. Even now, in Vancouver and Victoria, I see unspoken divisions classified by race, ethnicity, gender, religion and money. It's like we can't be genuinely happy for each other and we're always looking at what others have instead of cherishing what we own and who we are. Again, these are just observations, but it just seems like we've lost traits like humility, selflessness, compassion, and unity. They have been replaced with greed, envy, jealousy, and division. With all the progress society espouses, I would 100% live in 1986 instead of 2021.

Going to church

My earliest memory of church was at three years old. I remember my mom sitting near the altar in the front, I was sitting in the back. I got scared and started running towards her crying. In kindergarten, I attended a Catholic school learning to pray, read the bible, and the ten commandments. Our family attended church every Sunday. As a young child, I remember not eating an hour before going to mass. There were a lot of traditions and protocols about going to church and the catholic faith. I wasn't the biggest fan maybe because I found church boring. It was scorchingly hot and humid in the Philippines. Mass on Sundays would take about 1 hour. I would always daydream and couldn't wait until communion which meant that mass was about to finish! After the final blessing from the priest, the parishioners would head outside to check out all the delicious food offered by street vendors outside the gates of the church. They were pastries, cookies and fish balls,and different types of local indigenous delicacies, like tamales, *tapang usa* (Smoked Deer), *quesong puti* (Goat Cheese) and *pan de sal.*

My whole family would head home and enjoy an amazing lunch prepared by my mom earlier that morning. These family gatherings left an indelible memory in my mind. When we moved to Canada, the country was still religious and most people attended church but lacked the same intensity and fervor as we practiced in the Philippines. In Vancouver, we went to a very small and intimate church, St. Peter and Paul. I still hated going and found that mass took way too long. I would incessantly daydream about playing football while the priest was doing his sermon. Usually, Catholics pray every night before going to bed. I didn't do it very often because as I said, I was a fringe Catholic. All the while, not realizing that, I was absorbing all the sermons and the teachings even at a young age. But I still hated going to church. Fast forward to my teen years, when I started driving and had more independence, I would go around twice a month. I would always stand in the back not wanting to sit inside the church. By the time Church ended, I'd be the first one to leave. The other thing I noticed was that there were a lot of very attractive Filipina girls in church. Maybe that was the draw, to check out the girls, but this time I wasn't daydreaming about football but about the pretty ladies sitting on the other side of the pew. In my twenties, I would still follow the same routine, going to church two or three times a month, still not listening to the sermons or the priest. I would still not pray that often, but that changed when I was 21. One night, while I was downstairs in my girlfriend's living room, I started to feel a little bit eerie like there was something I just couldn't explain. The Philippines is a very old country. What I didn't know at the time was that her house was built right on top of an old war site, where close to 50 people died. Around midnight, my girlfriend went upstairs to sleep. Since I lived an hour away, I decided to get some rest before driving home. After ten minutes of sleeping, suddenly my eyes opened but I couldn't move! Remember, I'm this big, strong 21-year-old multi-sport athlete that felt invincible. At that moment though, I was completely helpless! It felt like I was bound, shackled and not able to move, even though my eyes were wide open. I tried to scream as loud as I could, but nothing came out and I started to get really frightened. After about five minutes of struggling, fighting, and trying to get out of this imprisonment, I started praying, "Our Father, who art in Heaven!" Halfway through my prayer, miraculously, I was able to move and get free from whatever was holding me down. I ran outside the door straight into my car and drove an hour with my whole body shaking. When I got home, I called my girlfriend and told her what had happened. There are many unexplained deaths of young and otherwise healthy men and women in the Philippines. Called *bangungot* or *batibat* (in Ilocano dialect), the folklore is of this vengeful demon. It is said to take the form of an ancient, grotesque, obese, tree dwelling female spirit. When a person sleeps near it, the *batibat* attacks the person by sitting on the victim's face or chest, suffocating it, and invading their dream space. The week after, we had a traditional spirit doctor inspect and investigate. He learned that it was an old female spirit that had died 200 years ago in a battle on the property. She had a crush on me and wanted me to die and be with her in the spirit world for eternity. I guess I was pretty hot back in the day, even to dead, female spirits!

When I tell the story here in Canada, most people think that I was just dreaming or having a nightmare. Whether it was a nightmare or an actual supernatural event, it gave me more belief that there is a god and higher power. I am not as religious as other Christians, but I firmly believe in God and have blind faith in him in a life-or-death situation!

This story is just an experience that I had when I was 21. I'm not an evangelist trying to convert people into Christianity. It's just a seminal moment, in my life, that I can't explain. I was able to develop blind faith that when push comes to shove, I have submitted myself to God. It's weird that I am able to help hundreds of people every year not only get their license but also improve their self-confidence, self-worth, and self-belief in themselves. I've helped people that defy explanation, like Rick with the cracked skull, or any number of other students. It just seems like I have this ability to figure out what my students need most, and I'm able to help them with their driving and in their personal lives. It's almost unbelievable the way I can help, it just seems so supernatural. Some of the shit I've been able to accomplish in the last few years has been nothing short of miraculous.

I'm noticing that more and more people these days are having anxious moments, a lack of self-belief, and are unsure about what to believe. It's a very scary proposition, if you become rich and successful, and have 50 million in the bank. These people fear death and are fighting tooth or nail not to die because they don't know where they're going and what will happen to their 50 mil! I won't be worth that much money when I die but because I believe in God, I'm able to live life to the fullest, with no regrets and no fear of death. There are lots of different faiths in the world. It's not about adopting a specific religion but if people can find a higher power that they can truly believe in, I think that it will make a big difference to reduce their anxiety and improve their self-confidence. Most people now think that if you have 50 million dollars in the bank, that you'll be happy. I don't doubt that there's a lot of people with 50 million dollars in the bank that are very happy, but I've seen people with very little or no money that were equally as happy if not more so. They were not as worried about dying and leaving all that money behind!

Having Fun

This is probably the biggest change I have seen in life today. The ability to experience unbridled joy without any limits. In sports development, the most important stage is active start, where athletes start playing sports by just picking up a bat and whacking the ball. It's like the first time a golfer hits a pure shot not knowing how it happened. In this stage, athletes develop a passion for the sport that they are playing. In goal setting, it is so important for people to just have fun and enjoy the sport without worrying too much about technique, rules, competition, and expectations. Their only goal is to hit the ball as hard as possible without worrying about fucking up! Having fun is becoming more difficult today. Modern society is encouraging a more structured way of thinking and being, to not go outside the norm, to be mindful and be kind.

I'm reminded of this when watching the comedians from the past. They weren't as worried about offending the audience, were more creative and most times were super offensive. Comedians like Sammy Davis Jr, Eddie Murphy, Richard Pryor, Don Rickles and Andrew Dice Clay. Late night shows also took more risks and on weekends, people would wait in anticipation to watch the new episode of Saturday Night Live. Everyone could laugh at themselves or others with no reservations. Many times, lines were crossed, and feelings hurt, but it wasn't life or death, and people learned not to be overly sensitive. I am finding the opposite today. My students will generally be quite careful and guarded to be themselves and they default into a vanilla-like personality that resides in a narrower bandwidth. I find it curious that I could have students from foreign countries or different schools, ages, and backgrounds yet, they all communicate in a very similar way. My students are generally nice, polite but afraid to say or act in a way that may be seen as mildly offensive. I only see more substance in their personality once they get more comfortable in the car but still with limits. I will rarely encounter students that have no societal barriers and could take themselves less seriously. In 2019, I had a student travel from Squamish BC, which is a small town north of Vancouver to take her test in Victoria. At the time, road tests were difficult to book, and I had students travel from far away. As we are doing our introduction, I asked where she was from. She says "Squampton", a fun jab at their city. The elites in Vancouver regard the more pedestrian residents of Squamish as lower tier, hence combining Squamish and Compton into Squampton. I started laughing uncontrollably and she reminded me of how carefree and fun people were before. We start driving and her style is aggressive and confident. She is worried about the test as she has failed 3 times. I make recommendations and adjustments to slow her speed down which gives her more time to look around, scan and shoulder check. While doing the lesson, we talk like long lost friends that had not seen each other in years. We laughed, shared stories and were just ourselves with no fear of judgment. The ninety minutes zoomed by like it was fifteen and was the most fun and enjoyable lesson I have had in years. I tell her that she is ready for the test; to be herself and not change the way she drives for the examiner or what she thinks the examiner's expectations are. I loved the way she carried herself, not too seriously, authentic, fun loving. I work with my students to try to develop that same kind of energy. She passes the test with flying colors. We talked on the phone after her test, and I tell her how fucking proud I am of her! Smiling, laughing, and having fun is a mindset that people can achieve. They just have to *choose* to do it and not be *afraid* to do it! With "cancel culture" and an obsession to be non-offensive, this may be difficult to do which I completely understand. But that's why most people today are so fucking miserable!

CHAPTER 10 INSIGHTS FROM DATING, SPORTS, AND SELF-DISCOVERY

Courtship, Dating and Mating Rituals

Dating in 2022 is so much different than in the past. With the combination of technology, social conditioning, time management, and dating apps, these have led to a changes in how people meet and date today. As referenced in the previous chapters, it was so much harder to find a partner or mate in the past. Because it was so much harder, the efforts that men undertook to court and date a woman involved many different dating rituals that have been passed down through millennia. Seeing a woman across the room, making eye contact, a subtle smile, the scent of a woman, an electric feeling in the pit of your stomach, both the anticipation and fear of meeting a complete stranger is present. These actions have been replaced by modern dating apps. The apps are more convenient, have a larger pool of prospective partners and it reduces the time to meet because the bios and pics of the people are readily accessible. In short, it's so much easier to just swipe and bingo, you're all set! Unfortunately, the same rituals that have been tried and tested for over 200k years are disappearing faster than the snow caps on the Kilimanjaro. When talking to my friends and students, they say that hook up culture is now the norm, but most are not satisfied and feel that these are shallow interactions. Even if the hook up goes on to the next steps of dating and partner status, most of these relationships are brittle with less feeling and long-lasting perseverance due to the nature of how the couple initially met. With my chapter about dating in the 80's, guys had to work hard to try to attract a mate and not just write with a killer bio. Believe me, though I have dated various women and have had great success and happiness, this has not come without many failures and rejections. The most important lessons I learned as a kid, is to be authentic and genuinely be yourself. Women appreciate real effort, but the efforts cannot and should not be fake. If it is artificial, makes the guy a simp. Though simping works today, the relationships are often more brittle and superficial than ones that are based on authenticity. It is more ideal to meet a woman organically or be set up by mutual friends than through an app. It is extremely challenging these days to meet organically because modern men are conditioned to not look at or say hi to random women for fear of a me too reaction and to be called a creep. Because of this, men have become extremely fearful to approach, make eye contact or say hello to women they are attracted to. Men therefore become more awkward, clumsy or creepy when they do try to initiate a conversation today because it is not a skill that they have acquired and developed. I often hear my younger female students say that there are no guys in their school. There are still a number of eligible guys, but they act so awkwardly around the girls that the girls get turned off no matter how hot the guy is!

On the flip side, I see a very attractive woman with a guy that is not so good looking but because of his personality, confidence, charm and the mastery of the mating rituals, he is with a woman he has no business being with!

In Victoria, we are on the coast with endless outdoor activities like cycling, walking/hiking trails, skiing, golf, tennis, water sports and gyms! People here are *hella* gorgeous. With that, people still have a hard time meeting partners and keeping them long term. As I write this book and think deeper about this topic, the concepts I keep cycling back to, are appreciation and contentment. Men and women, who I'm around, are always looking for the perfect partner. Maybe due to social media or modern constructs, the invisible bar is so high that any imperfection of a prospective mate is an immediate strike. I was having a beer with Steve. Tall and good looking, he played sports growing up and is now a surfer. My buddy Lee was mentioning my book to him, and we started talking about dating. Steve had a long-term relationship which ended a couple of years ago. Since then, he was saying how hard it was to meet women. Steve tried using dating apps, but he disliked the experience commenting on how shallow the dates were. He asked me what my thoughts were, and I told him that the problem people face is the fear to be or to act in a genuine way. Because everyone feels and senses this very high, invisible bar, people fear that their true authentic selves are not good enough. Therefore, most people in the dating scene try so very hard to show a perfect version of themselves. It causes extreme stress and frustration. Dates therefore become more of a performance rather than a casual, organic way for two people to freely get to know each other. When I run into a couple truly in love, I will stop them in the middle of the street or cafe and let them know how very lucky they are. Couples will always thank me for my honest and heartfelt gesture!

When dating, I always inspire everyone to accept all their human qualities. We all have really good things but also less desirable attributes. We should try to be proud of who we are instead of only presenting the best parts of us. People should instead go back to be more real and authentic. As my Mexican buddy Jorge said *"no somos moneditas de oros*!" If you meet a mate that will love you for you, that's a partner for life!

Foreplay and the act

I'm excited about this chapter, maybe because of my Scorpio tendencies, I don't just view intimacy as sex but it's so much more! Growing up, I've always had an obsession and love for women. I love being around women, talking, smelling their hair, and holding their hand. As our relationships grew stronger, we would be more intimate and start making love. As a Scorpio, I'm very passionate, and I really wanted to please my lover in every way possible; intellectually, emotionally, and sexually. There's a mantra of mind, body and soul, I fully believe this. The act for Scorpios starts even before getting into the bed. As a 20-year-old, I used to date a lot of flight attendants that worked for Cathay Pacific and Philippine Airlines. I remember an ex-girlfriend getting off a flight, all haggard and fatigued from flying for 14 hours. She felt totally gross. I, on the other hand, felt totally turned on seeing her walking, in her flight attendant uniform. I really loved those old uniforms that accentuated their bodies, and especially her black stockings. This was my biggest fantasy, black stockings and taking them off!

I remember the time my girlfriend flew into Vancouver, I was so horny and kissed her from head to toe. It was an act of foreplay. It was instinctual. I did things that felt natural and sensual with no conscious thought. This again goes back to that part about not overthinking and analyzing but just doing it. After a few minutes of cuddling, licking, and nibbling, I slowly took off her uniform starting with her blouse, then I slid off her skirt until she was just in her underwear and stockings. Again, being this very sexual and horny 20-year-old, I loved every aspect of that. I didn't just want to stick my thing in her thing, but those mating rituals and foreplay is an important part of the ultimate act. These days, I hear a lot of people doing casual hookups through tinder, but the hookups seem less genuine and lacking purpose. It's just sticking your thing in her thing and after the act is finished swiping to the next picture. Because of the lack of emotion in these hookups, the act itself becomes very meaningless and in the end, both parties leave feeling unsatisfied from the experience. This is why traditional mating rituals are extremely important! These include foreplay, kissing, nibbling, holding and caressing, smelling, touching and feeling, emotion, biting and all the other things that people freely do when in love. These are my own experiences about intimacy. We have a lot of ancient books and texts that talk about this very same thing. The problem today is that most people use porn as the guide to intimacy. I suggest that people go back to basics, learn how to reignite their instinctual behavior and if things are consensual, enjoy the beauty of intimacy and not just to stick your thing in her thing!

Making Love

Many people think that having sex is making love. Though you can make love by having sex, they are not one and the same. Having sex is primarily the physical act of oral and sexual intercourse. It is a very important facet of humanity, the act to procreate and reproduce. The physical attraction between a man and a woman is sparked by many factors which leads us to a more primal and carnal state. Like dogs in heat, humans traditionally have also felt this sensation with the ultimate end goal for a man's sperm to fertilize a woman's egg. This doesn't sound very romantic but frankly, is needed for humanity's ultimate survival. Having sex has fueled reproduction for humanity since the dawn of our existence! With that said, as a Scorpio, having physical sex isn't fulfilling for me without also establishing an emotional, mental and spiritual connection. It just feels hollow and empty. Though I have had lots of sex, being an extremely passionate dude, I love making love! Finding the right soul mate is very rare but if you are lucky enough to do so, the sex becomes magnified by an infinite factor. Through personal experience, by having true connection, the act of making love is ethereal. Our subconscious surrenders our own needs for that of our partners which leads to this very special moment of bliss. Because I love my partner, I become fully selfless, and my only goal is to give her maximum pleasure. It stimulates my body when I see her experience the most magical and intense orgasms. This act of selflessness is often reciprocated by my lover and all the emotions heighten the primal and carnal act of sex which leads both of us to Nirvana. A magical realm that many couples desire but few ever achieve. Again, let me reiterate that there is nothing wrong with fucking. But if you are fortunate enough to experience true love and how that strongest human emotion affects lovemaking to the highest degree, casual sex will never ever be good enough. In modern times, with the continued degradation of humanity and our emotional connections with one another, reaching Nirvana and experiencing total bliss is becoming almost impossible. Yes, people have orgasms and enjoy the sex but because I have experienced the difference between having sex and making love, I will always treasure the moments when I experience this eternal bliss.

What is love

Marie and I came back from Victoria last night and we had a great time. It was her first time there, so I wanted to show her the day in the life of Alex Cordero! We had happy hour at Ferris seafood restaurant. Marie is obsessed with fresh oysters, so we inhaled 30 of them plus fish and chips and 4 mojitos. Afterwards, we went dancing and she met my musician buddies; Brett, Louis, Sascha, and Steven. The next day, we grabbed coffee at Parsonage cafe in the morning and Calamari for lunch at Fig Mediterranean deli. After lunch, she watched me play tennis at Beacon Hill and met a bunch of my buddies. Finally, we spent a couple of hours laying on a rock in front of the water, facing the Pacific Ocean! It was such an amazing experience, especially embracing your true love while watching the waves crash into the rocks on the beach! We took the ferry back to Vancouver and enjoyed a late dinner with her mom and daughter. Marie ordered sushi. The four of us had an amazing family dinner with her daughter constantly roasting me at the dinner table. But she also gave me the biggest compliment when she said that her mom and lala had *old energy* while I had *young energy*. Marie was not impressed! That night, we had the most explosive love making session. When we make love, I feel true love. It feels so natural because nothing is ever forced! I feel my whole emotion and always wanting to be beside Marie! It's so hard to quantify. What love feels like, you'll just know. The following morning, after another amazing love making session, I asked Marie how she knew she loved me? She pondered the question and started saying that she loved me because she was more caring with me, more loving with me, more patient with me and more understanding with me. Basically, she gave me the best versions of herself at the peak of what she could give! These were all amazing thoughts and emotions, but then she started thinking a little bit more and she said to me, that for the first time ever, she felt selfless. Where she would willingly give herself for the love of me where herself was not more important than me. That floored me because in the past few weeks, we would sometimes have disagreements. I would say to her that I didn't keep a ledger or a tally in our relationship. I know that in modern times, we are taught to expect something from our partners when we do something nice for them. It's like a back-and-forth score and more often, you'll need a chartered accountant to keep track of the supposed love that couples have for each other! So, when Marie shared her take about love, it started giving me thoughts about where love came from in the past. And because of our Catholic roots in the Philippines, Jesus Christ was always present in our lives. We are taught from an early age about Christ's love for man. In fact, it is written in the Bible that Christ endured excruciating pain, humiliation and suffering because he wanted to absolve all of man's sins. After 3 days of torture and humiliation, he sacrificed his life to absolve all our sins for his love of man. It was the ultimate act of selflessness, and that is what's missing in the world today! Instead, we live in a me society where it's my pleasure, my time, my body, my Instagram page, my ego. If people today want to experience true love, they will probably have to do self-reflection and go back to a more basic time when they were more selfless and gave all of themselves to their partners. After a few weeks of courting, Marie and I finally reconnected in an intimate way for the first time after 36 years. On that special night, my only purpose was to pleasure her as much as possible without any thought or desire for me. It was my purest expression of my love for her!

Banfield Park

When I got back into tennis in March 2021, the first person I called was Abner, my Filipino tennis buddy. We started playing regularly at Banfield Park which is in Vic West, an older part of town. The courts are not the best. The surface is bumpy, with ant hills and weeds growing on the cracks. Beside the court is a trail where mothers would regularly walk their kids going to the playground. Joggers and families use it as a thoroughfare to get to the waterfront. Across the street is Fry's, an authentic French bakery, Spiral Cafe, an eclectic coffee shop, a barber shop and a used clothing store. It was a great place to start playing tennis again. People would sometimes stop to watch us while on their walks. It was nice to play in front of a crowd. Most of the players at Banfield were of Filipino, and I knew some of them through basketball. One of Abner's good friends is Gary. We played each other in the Filipino basketball league a decade ago. He is as tenacious and tough as they come. When we were playing, his only job was to shut me down and try to deny me the ball. Gary would follow me from one end of the court to the other. I was the point guard and main facilitator for my team. Gary would use all the tricks in the book whether they were legal or illegal. I remember games where he would hold me, elbow me, grab my shorts or shirt, and when the ref wasn't looking, tackle me like we were playing football! So, it was great to play tennis with him because he couldn't do that shit like in basketball, but we could still be ultra-competitive on the tennis court. This helped my game rapidly improve because as I've said in the past, people

30 years ago hated losing! I think the reason people would stop and watch us play is how competitive we were against each other. They found it enthralling to see us cuss, swear, moan and groan and exhibit raw emotions that are not normally seen today. Tennis is a very confrontational sport. On every point, there's a winner and loser, mano e mano. It can get heated, but it's also a great sport to develop grit, determination, passion, intensity and sportsmanship. Sportsmanship is key because eventually if you exhibit all the other traits but do not play with sportsmanship and honor, you're going to run out of tennis buddies that will want to play with you.

We play to win, but do it with honor, discipline and sportsmanship. In dating, this is chivalry and acting like a gentleman. There are no line judges or umpires when we play. When balls are close to the line and the battle is heated, one's true character shows on how you make these line calls. We experience so much emotion in wanting to win, that all your deepest traits, flaws and attributes will show while playing tennis. There's no time to think. Everything's instinctual and subconscious. I have a read on everybody when I play, and I get to know them down to their last cell. I've had lots of great matches not remembering if I won or lost, but what I remember fondly is the blood, sweat, tears and camaraderie I've shared with all my boys at Banfield Park.

Beacon Hill

After playing for a few months, my tennis game started taking off. Though I was still rusty, and my backhand not 100%, but with my ultra-competitive streak, I wanted to challenge myself against the best. Beacon Hill Park has three tennis courts that have been around for over a century. Most of the top players in Victoria have played there. "The Hill", as it is fondly called, is the place to play for locals or tourists visiting Victoria. It's a special venue where anyone could drop in and find a game. This is unique because normally, it would be difficult to find good caliber players to play with without scheduling a match ahead of time. This is the charm at the hill, show up and most likely, you'll find a good game.

I played junior tennis but for various reasons, I stopped at fourteen. Fast forward twenty-five years, one of my friends, Ed, invited me to play at the Hill. He was a local legend and had played there for over forty years. Everyone knew Ed and was he so nice to invite me to play. At that time, I was really rusty after my long hiatus from the sport, but Ed said no worries Al, just try your best! So that summer, I started playing at the Hill with him and his friends. I was average and nowhere near as good as I was as a junior. Because I was busy with life, a wife and 2 young kids, I couldn't play too much but, with my limited time playing, I was able to get my level up to about a 4.0 which is decent. For the next few years, I would play for a few months and take a couple years off, play for another few months and take another few years off. Last year was the first time that I really committed to playing tennis again but this time because I didn't want to feel old and out of shape, I stuck with it for longer than a few months. Wanting to test myself against the best, I found myself back at the Hill. There were a lot of new faces, and I didn't recognize any of them. When I get there, I see a regular standing beside the fence. He suggests that I hit with this younger guy sitting in the bleachers. I introduced myself and asked if he wanted to hit. His name was Matt. Little did I know that *Pizza Matt* was one of the top players at the hill and a regular. Normally, good players hesitate to hit with a random stranger, but Matt didn't think twice, and we rallied for about 15 to 20 minutes. More people show up, and he asks me to play doubles with them. The courts at the hill are a lot faster than Banfield so it took me time to adjust, but luckily Matt was such a good player that we won with ease. After that match, my competitive juices started flowing and I wanted to go back and play more of the regulars there. Because we were still in COVID lockdown, more people than usual were playing tennis. It was one of the few places that you didn't need a vaccine passport. The courts were busy in the afternoons, and it was so easy to find a good game. But in this competitive environment, there is a hidden hierarchy especially when the place is packed. I learned this harsh reality. If the top players needed a player, I was welcomed to play but I would be bumped down in busier times. This pissed me off but motivated me to get even better! Like my example of Captain's picking teams on the playground, you had two choices; to quit, or to keep your mouth shut and work your ass off to get better. I chose the latter and I really poured myself into trying to be the best tennis player I could be. These guys were a level better than the players at Banfield which was saying something because the Filipino crew were solid players! Slowly but surely, my level got better, and I started to win sets against some of the stronger players. And through meritocracy, they started inviting me into the top games. By the end of the summer, my game was almost back except for my backhand which was still suspect. I would hit some sublime backhands but hit some really shitty ones too and it really drove me crazy. That's a good learning moment for everybody. Even though I had weaknesses in my game, I wasn't afraid to play the best. I was able to overcome my faults through determination, belief in myself and the ability to adapt. I was quick enough that if people tried to get to my backhand, I could run around and hit my forehead. That took a lot of effort, but then I was able to adapt and find a way to still be competitive.

I have regular buddies I play with; Geoff, Pizza Matt, John, Han, Nick, Nathan, Tyler, Vegas Dean, Garrett, Patrick, Jonas, Josh, James, Selkie, and my biggest fan, Stanley. They come from diverse social, economic and educational backgrounds, as well as from different places in Canada and the world. It is a great place to play. My only regret is that I couldn't split my body into two. Since I started playing more at Hill, I have played less at Banfield, which is unfortunate because I love my Filipino buddies. But being this ultra-competitive alpha, I had to play the very best and that's at the Hill!

The Beagle

After another writer's block moment, it took me a whole year to start writing again. Earlier this spring, I started going to the Beagle with Mark, and my other tennis buddies for Tuesday wing nights. Their wings and beer were to die for! It's a great neighborhood pub with an amazing vibe and awesome staff. Because it's so close to the Hill and the surrounding neighborhood, lots of regulars would go there after playing cricket, softball, and tennis. The place was always packed.

One day after tennis, I was sitting by myself, drinking beer on the patio. I was in the middle of writing a chapter when two guys asked me to join them. Lee and his brother-in law were there hanging out. He asked me what I was up to, and I mentioned my book. He was curious and asked for more details. Lee was very intrigued and said that he really liked the premise. A week later, my buddy Mark and I ran into Lee again. He then asks us if we wanted to join their group for their Wednesday volleyball. They set up nets on the grass beside the cricket pitch at the hill. We initially hesitated to join them because we play tennis on Wednesday evenings. A few weeks have gone by, and he invites us again. I tell Mark that it might be a great place for him to meet a partner organically. I arrive around 6:00p.m. While waiting for Mark to arrive, I went around and say hello to everyone. I get into the next game. Most people were playing in bare feet, so I took off my shoes and sprang into action. As in all other sports, I only have one gear which is 1,000%. Our team gets into the groove. We win the set, high fiving and fist bumping each other. I started diving for balls and for a brief moment, felt 18 again. People were stunned that I'm playing with such passion and tenacity, constantly, on the ground digging balls and blocking the opponents up at the net. After volleyball, we head to the Beagle for some beers. I get props from everyone. The following day, my back seizes up cuz I am 50! Everyone says that age is just a number except the day after volleyball.

This group seemed like any other friend group from 30 years ago. Music blasted loudly from the speakers. Guys were brash and talked a lot of trash. The ladies hung out with each other, sitting on the grass, watching the action. Most of the people were buzzed by the beers and ciders and generally, everyone was able to be themselves. There were still some barriers but not on the same level as I normally see everywhere else. It was great to be in a place where guys were free to be guys and girls to be girls. I was happy for Mark to experience this organic group of disparate friends. Though he was not the best in volleyball, he really appreciated this opportunity to slowly come out of his shell. It's a shame that I don't see this type of openness more often these days.

I was walking at a local beach last summer and though people were having fun, I noticed how reserved and quiet the people were in their small groups, cognizant not to be loud and intrusive to the groups beside them. In the past, the beach behavior was like spring break in Tampa. Though it can be annoying with the loud and brash behavior, modern people are at times too moderate and measured. A balance between both extremes would be ideal and could foster an environment where people could be themselves and meet others organically instead of relying on dating apps.

The Beagle is a special place where people could be themselves. Unfortunately, when I am around town, most places are the exact opposite.

Falling Down

One of the biggest differences that I have noticed over the generations is the ability to fall down and get back up. As a 4-year-old kid in Manila, we would often be left alone to play in the backyard by ourselves with minimal supervision. One morning, I was doing tricks on my skateboard. I fell down hard and hit my chin on the cement driveway. With no one around and my chin bleeding profusely. I slowly got up, dazed and walked into the house. My mom was cooking and as I stumbled inside, she asked what had happened and if I was, okay? She quickly patched me up as she was scolding me for being an idiot. And said, "next time, be more careful!" as I went back outside to do more board tricks. It's the same when I'm playing sports. In tennis, there are plenty of times that I will make an error and lose a point. What separates really good players is the ability to overcome the mistake instantly. In other words, when you fall down, just get the fuck back up! This seems simple enough, but modern high-performance coaches have a different take on this. I was having a beer with a tennis buddy who holds a master's degree in high performance. He was taught that if his athletes fall down, there are several steps to take for self-reflection: how and why we fell down, what we were feeling while we were down, processing the emotion of falling down and, after doing all this self-reflection, this would be the right time to get back up. He said that if we fell down, and just got back up, that we would miss the opportunity to self-reflect. We discussed back and forth for a few minutes; he asked if I had sufficient self-reflection time by getting up so quickly. I told him that since athletes in the past had experienced more failure and learned how to process them, that the self-reflection was already happening as we were falling down. We were allowed the freedom to explore and try to do a skill and, if we failed, we just tried again. Today, if an athlete fails, there are so many coaches and parents hovering around the kids that they are not able to instantly try again if they fuck up. There is too much emphasis placed with the failure and the factors that led to falling down that the athlete will start to overthink and second guess themselves before getting up. They will retain the negative feeling longer than they would have, if they just got the fuck back up.

Golf

I started playing golf in 1990, when I moved back home to Vancouver. Instantly, I fell in love with the sport, and was hooked, after hitting my first 300-yard drive over the fence in the driving range. It is the ultimate sport that combines technique, mental strength, patience, and determination. Golf is a sport that very few have conquered and when you start thinking that you are good, it has a karmic way of humbling and humiliating you!

Being a pretty good athlete, I was able to develop quickly and after 3 months shot 79. Most golfers will never break 90 or 100. The common theme was my desire to be the best. I could never just play golf for fun. I loved competition, and I had to always find someone to beat. Whether it was family, friends or strangers, the thrill was always to come out on top. I would go crazy trying to improve to the point of obsession. Looking back, the sport has taught me so many lessons in life. A typical 18-hole game takes between 4-5 hours. A golf shot will take about 15-30 seconds to execute from approaching the ball, visualizing a shot, picking a club to hit then hitting the ball. The actual swing happens in less than half a second, then you wait between 5-10 minutes before your next shot. Everyone in your group does the same process of hitting and walking to their next shot. Golfers learn patience, and courtesy as they wait for everyone in their group to play. Players are also given the space to talk and communicate. This develops interpersonal skills sorely lacking today in modern people. Golfers communicate face to face instead of using their devices to snap or DM. Another benefit is the self-reflection time you have when you walk to your ball. Our lives are so chaotic with societal pressures, always being connected by technology. Golf gives people a chance to breathe and exhale! I would definitely recommend golf to all young people as it is an amazing way to become a more mature, well-rounded person. By the way, I forgot to mention how many clubs I broke when I started playing this fucking game at 18.

Playing Catch

When my students take their road tests, most are very nervous. I try to calm them down by playing good music, speaking more calmly and going to a park. At the park, I will have my students sprint or jog to get their heart rate up, then take a number of deep breaths to relax. My goal is to release their restless energy. Another thing we do is throw a tennis ball for a couple of minutes. For a lot of my students, throwing the ball invokes memories of their youth playing catch with their parents, siblings or friends. My goal is to help them touch and feel the ball in their hands. The throwing action helps them not overthink and to become more instinctual for their test. In the last couple of years, I have noticed that my younger female students are more coordinated and more skilled in passing and catching the tennis ball than the dudes. I always remark and share with them my joy in how athletic they are. Conversely, a growing number of my male students are less coordinated and really don't enjoy or have the skill to pass and catch with me. Don't get me wrong, there are still athletic young men, but that percentage is so low that it's actually shocking! I often joke to my students that in my generation, we would give guys a hard time by saying, *"you throw like a girl!"* But now, the joke is *"you throw like a boy!"*

It is imperative that parents and their sons start playing catch with balls when they are young. This will give them the foundation and coordination to be decent at any sport that they may want to play in the future. As they get older, they will feel less awkward when playing sports. This is the reason many young boys are not interested in playing sports - they become super conscious about their lack of skills. Even if they decide to play, eventually they just give up.

ITF Masters 100 tennis

It's late October 2023. This year, we had some of the nicest weather that I can remember in Victoria! I played 6 times a week. The only negative was my body being a little bit sore from all the wear and tear. Tennis is a very physically demanding sport.

I was playing with my buddy Jason last week and he told me about the ITF Masters 100 tournament being played in Victoria in November. The International Tennis Federation (ITF) hosts tournaments all over the world! Tournament players will travel nationally and internationally to play in these events. With my health scare back in August, and change in diet, I became much fitter and lighter. This helped me move faster around the court and gain increased stamina. I don't get tired as easily and I'm much quicker covering more of the court. I played a singles tournament back in September and had a good win, beating the number two seed at the Victoria open. But I wasn't planning on playing the ITF because, I wanted to give my body a break. Two days before the deadline to register, Jason gives me a call. He's an ex-high level baseball player and has recently turned fifty. Jason a bit shorter than me, standing 5'8 with a stocky build. His game is tenacious, gritty, with lots of fight. He's got that dawg in him! He asked me to play doubles with him, I didn't think twice and said yes. Jason is a very solid player and is tough as nails. He's very consistent with very good ground strokes. His only weakness is up at net. But I didn't think twice to partner up because I knew even with that slight weakness, I would want a partner like Jason beside me in the heat of battle! He would never fold or collapse like Sam did in the Victoria Open back in September. I signed up for both singles and doubles and was excited to play the tournament because I felt really good about my game. The week before the tournament, Jason and I set up a practice match against Carlos and John. They were playing in the over 30's division, while Jason and I were in the over 50's. These guys were younger, stronger and fitter, but it was a great way to practice and prepare for the tournament. We got destroyed, 6-1, 6-4, 6-2. But it was okay, because it gave Jason and I the chance to play with each other and create chemistry on the court. I was excited for our team's chances to win!

Because my body was sore leading up to the tournament, I didn't touch a racket for 3 days. It gave me a chance to rest and heal. My first singles match was Thursday afternoon vs Dan, a local player that I had played once before. He was a good player that I couldn't take lightly. I went down to the courts an hour early to warm up for my match. Surprisingly, I felt no pain and started hitting the ball clean. I played well and won 6-1 6-1! I was happy with that win, but I had very little time to celebrate because my next opponent was my dubs partner Jason! The next day, I was lucky that my body was pain-free because Jason and I had the most grueling match! In the first set, he was playing very well hitting powerful shots from the baseline. I was committing some errors because of the pressure he was applying on me. This played right into his hands! He won the first set 6-3. I was concerned because he had all the momentum. I had to regroup and adjust my strategy for the second set. If I kept playing the same way, he would have steamrolled me but instead, I tried to think of a way to disrupt his momentum and flow. I decided to switch tactics to a more conservative and non-traditional way of playing which is to get the ball back with more slices, chips and lobs. In other words, I became a pusher which is not the prettiest way of playing but can be very effective to counteract players that are more used to hitting topspin shots. I would chip the ball and wait until I got a short ball, then attack and finish the point up at the net! It's not the easiest way to play tennis because I would have to cover the whole court and run down balls but it's what I needed to do to try to give myself a chance to win! We had some very long rallies but it slowly started working. I was able to break Jason on one of his service games to take the lead in the 2nd set, eventually winning it 6-3. After the set, both Jason and I took a water break but in reality, we needed a timeout! We were both struggling physically with my right calf cramping and his right ankle sore from all the running. This is what happens when you get older gladiators battling it out on court with the no quit, never say die attitude! We both took our time stretching and hydrating before the start of the third set. But deep down inside, I knew I had the advantage with my newfound fitness! I kept the same strategy and eventually wore Jason down winning the match 3-6 6-3 6-3. He fought and battled till the end! We shared a very warm and respectful embrace at the end of the match! It's how it should be, leave everything on the court and win or lose, show grace and the utmost respect for your opponent. He wished me luck moving forward, reminding me to rest up for our doubles match the next day. The respect I had for Jason grew immensely not only by the way he battled but also how he reacted immediately after such a tough loss! This is something I wish more young people could see and learn from. I'm sure deep down inside, Jason was extremely disappointed losing such a close match, but he competed and carried himself in a way that I would want my readers to do too! To play as hard as you can, give it all on court but after a loss, be able to accept that loss without being salty, angry, dejected or depressed.

My opponent for the semifinals was Greg, originally from Vancouver, he has played a lot of tournament tennis. He has a much more serious demeanor than most of the guys I know with tennis being his life and identity. We played a lot of doubles at the hill this past summer and as partners, we often struggled due to a lack of chemistry. As with Jason, if I played Greg straight up giving him normal topspin balls, he would have an advantage over me. He's 6'2, possessing a long wingspan. He had solid ground strokes and a big serve. He had lots of game, and his only real weakness was that he could get frustrated and lose his composure. My plan was to exploit this! Tennis, specifically singles, is such a mano e mano sport! It's only you and your opponent, there's no outside coaching allowed and once your match starts, it becomes much more of a mental than physical battle! I didn't know exactly what would set Greg off, I would just play the match and make adjustments real time. Sometimes, people will game plan tirelessly before a match and will stick to this game plan even if it's not working. The most seasoned competitors have a basic idea of what they want to do but will be malleable and adapt on the fly if they're original plan isn't working! This skill and ability to switch gears and strategies real time is something I'm seeing less and less of with young people today. And the problem is that schools, coaches, and society are not encouraging this dynamic way of thinking and competing. Instead, they only focus on – *Technique! Technique! Technique!*

Our match begins and as I predicted, we have some good points. Greg is hitting well with lots of big forehands and serves. The first set was close, and I was up 6-5 with Greg serving. I was also playing well and sticking to my strategy which was to hit big forehands and hit soft slice back hands to Greg's backhand. Though this shot isn't very powerful, it can be very annoying for opponents because they're not getting the usual pace that most people will hit with. So, with that change in pace from heavy forehands to a soft slice backhand, Greg wasn't able to get into a nice rhythm and groove for his shots. All I needed was to break Greg's serve once and I would win the set. Greg was getting frustrated and tight. On the 1st point, he double faulted, I'm now up 0-15. 2nd point, we have a long rally which ends with him hitting a ball into the net, 0-30. Now clearly imploding, I had Greg right where I wanted him! I closed out the 1st set and won 7-5. He's pissed and frustrated, I knew if I could just keep my foot on his neck, that I would be able to win the match. Unlike my match with Jason where I needed to adjust my strategy. When you find something that's working, you just need to keep doing the same thing over and over again!! As harsh as it sounds, frustrating Greg was the key to winning for me. It wasn't personal, but strictly game theory! He still hit a lot of great shots but with his frustration level at almost 100%, I was able to win the second set 6-4 to close out the match, 7-5 6-4! I couldn't believe that I was in the finals of an ITF Masters singles tournament! It was a big accomplishment but my reward in the finals was internationally ranked Hannes Blum! He is a member of team Canada and plays all over the world in high level tournaments. I realistically gave myself a 3% chance of winning and the only way I could was with him sustaining some sort of injury or physical ailment! If I rated myself as a tennis player, I would be a 4.5 in singles and probably a 5.0 in doubles which is a very high level! Hannes is a solid 5.5-6 international level player. I have rarely played against this caliber of player. The only time I have was last year in Provincials, Hannes killed me 6-2 6-0. But in my mind, I still had a shot even if it was only 3%. Leading up to the finals, my friends asked me what my strategy was. I said that I would try my best and play each point as well as I could. Maybe try and frustrate Hannes, but I was at a major disadvantage. Though my game is good, he's just a much better player. I was hitting, moving and playing extremely well! I would play points that I would normally win but every time I had Hannes on the run, he hit counter shots that would win him the point! I tried switching strategies and tactics, I ran around, scrambled and gave it my all! In the end, nothing worked because he was just too damn good! I never gave up and fought till the very end but with me playing well, he killed me 6-0 6-0. The points and match were closer than the double bagel score would suggest. After the match, my buddy Shaun asked me if I was disappointed or embarrassed. He was shocked that I was okay! I would have been pissed off if I didn't try, and just gave up. But because I truly gave it my all and played as well as I could, I am able to accept losing 6-0 6-0 with my head held high! I wasn't embarrassed, I was very happy and proud of how I played. Hannes was just a better tennis player than me and I could accept it. The loss motivated me to work on the finer details, to improve my technique and to get the reps I needed to move up to national and international level! These are very important learning moments I want my readers to see and learn from! That the effort is so much more important than the results! I was an ITF Masters singles finalist with a trophy in hand because of the effort and attitude I had. And if someone is better than you, understand what things you need to improve and let the loss motivate you to improve for the next match!

The thing about competition is that you don't have time to feel sorry for yourself after a crushing defeat. Our doubles finals were up next with me only having 15 minutes in between matches to prepare! Jason and I were taking on Glen, our head coach for the vets and Steve. Both these guys are seasoned veterans winning multiple tournaments nationally! Glen is a current member of Team Canada and just came back from the World's in Portugal last month! They would be extremely tough to beat. Even though I just got destroyed by Hannes, I was playing really well, and I knew that if I played the same, it would give us a 50/50 chance to win. My game is more suited for doubles, and I'm known in Victoria as a doubles specialist. I'm serving to start the final and immediately get broken. After Glen holds serve, they are out to a 2-0 lead. I wasn't worried and knew that doubles is a game of runs and momentum. The other thing I realized was that I needed to attack the net and get closer to finish points off quicker. The closer I could get to the net, the easier it would be for me to kill my volleys. In the very next game, we had some amazing net exchanges but with me closing the net, I was able to win a bunch of points for us.

Jason was playing very well, hitting hard forehands and running down balls! We had great chemistry and came back to win the next 6 games winning the 1st set 6-2. As the saying goes, "if it ain't broke, don't fix it!" We played the exact same way on the second set. In the end, we wore down Glen and Steve winning the match 6-2 6-4. On match point, as Glen's ball sailed out, I yelled, yesssssss!!!!!!! It was a huge accomplishment for Jason and me! This was an ITF Masters 100 doubles title, and we are now ITF doubles champions! We beat two extremely tough, battle tested team Canada players. Jason only started playing tennis several years ago and I had been out of the game for years, so this was a very big deal! There are lots of things to take from this tournament, the biggest takeaway is the old school competition skills that Jason and I showed in winning and in losing, and the importance in sharing these with young dudes today!

CHAPTER 11
MASTERING CONFIDENCE AND COMPETITION: THE ART OF WINNING

Self-talk and Self doubt

Everyday, I notice people with a lack of confidence and belief. At the golf course, coffee shop, dentist's office, in the grocery store, schools or when teaching my students. I look at body language, speech patterns, people making eye contact, or lack thereof, and overall communication skills. Though at first glance, people seem aloof and unbothered, the reality may be deeper and more complex. Modern societal expectations and constructs shape behavior in people. Many people I know today go to therapy, meditate, do yoga, all in an attempt to center their lives. There is a growing trend for people to use cannabis, edibles, psychedelics and other products to help them feel better daily and temporarily improve their self-worth. In the past, people were told and expected to suck it up and move on. Today, society deals with this issue with a softer, gentler approach. If our expectations of ourselves and others around us were not so high, it may lessen the pressure and anxiety that lead to all these problems in the first place. Imperfections are what makes us perfect and the ability to accept these faults could help people improve their overall confidence by not being imprisoned by the ridiculously high bar set for us and others by modern society.

Live life to the fullest

Because I sit a lot in the car when teaching, I have not been exercising much. After feeling sluggish and weak in the winter, a blizzard hit Victoria dumping 8 inches of snow. The following morning, I had to shovel our driveway to be able to get the car out of the house. After five minutes of clearing and shoveling the snow, my whole body seized up and I could hardly breathe due to extreme exhaustion. All my life, I have felt strong, playing multiple sports. If five minutes of shoveling wrecked me like this, I knew that I had a problem so I decided to start slowly getting active again, by walking. The first day was the toughest, I woke up at 5:30am and forced myself to go for a walk. It lasted 45 minutes and I was dead tired. This is the same fucking guy that felt like super human at one time on his life! Day 2, I walked for 45 minutes again, this time just fatigued. Day 5, I walked for 1 hour and 25 minutes, with my stamina getting better. Three weeks in, I call my tennis buddy Abner and ask him to play. It's my 1st set in years, and he destroys me! Being this competitive dude, I'm motivated to get better because I hate getting my ass kicked. I am now religiously waking up at 4:30am before work with the goal of 20,000 steps a day. Abner and I start playing more. The following week, I met his buddy, Mike. He was in his late 60's and was pretty fit for his age. We warm up and I'm really impressed with his skills. Abner and I play a set and, again, I get killed. Mike was sitting on his blue lawn chair, watching our match. I drop by the next few weeks, Mike always sitting in his blue chair or playing tennis with the boys. Then, one Saturday, I found out that he suffered a massive stroke during an afternoon match. The next day, his wife Joy comes to the court and gives us an update for Mike. He passed away and was only briefly able to open his eyes. She gathered us around for 15 minutes sharing both her sadness on how to proceed with her life but also thanking all the boys that Mike had gotten to know at the park. It was such a powerful moment that left an impression on me. She went on to say how special Mike felt about his tennis friends and that he was happy and ready to go to heaven when the time came. Though I was not particularly close to Mike, I wanted to share this story to everyone. A lot of my students have self-talk and self-doubt. They get imprisoned by fear, but they should realize that life can be taken away at any time. We should live life to the max with no fear or anxiety. I learned from Dr. Sean Richardson in his Ted Talk on YouTube, "fail going 100%!" We don't know when our time will come, so make sure you do everything in your power to achieve your goals. Finally having finished writing this fucking book after numerous writer's block moments, it proves that anything is truly possible! Carpe Diem.

The Inner Child

As a tennis player and all-around athlete, I have always enjoyed everything about competition from winning, playing, persevering, trash talking, and all the other things associated with sport! My enjoyment fully manifests as the stakes increase. But all these emotions come from memories as a child playing pickup sports in the playground. Some coaches call this the sandlot playing. Lacrosse coach Jamie Munro will often reference the importance of sandlot development. Initially playing a sport with less structure. The rules are made up by the kids on the playground instead of parents or coaches. This type of environment encourages a freer, more creative way to play that helps kids learn a sport or activity with less boundaries and it helps develop the freedom and love for the sport which is essential in later development stages to become an elite athlete. I describe this as the inner child, the time when kids could just be kids. Being able to play without the confines or barriers that are present in a more structured environment. Too often today, youth athletes are taught good technique and rules, but they are not given the space to try, fail, and try again. It is important to play many different shots without any thought of technique or rules and be able to display raw emotion. Instead, kids are expected to work on proper technique and abide by a more uniformed code of conduct or decorum. While this may aid in refining and achieving an elite level at an earlier age, it may sacrifice true enjoyment and happiness for the sport and may lead to burnout in the future. I see this a lot in many different sports and activities. Sometimes, while taking our dogs to the park, I would see young kids using the slides or swings. Parents would be close to their kids supervising and making sure that their kids are behaving and sharing. Though these traits are good, what's being lost is their child being able to freely explore and communicate with other kids. Instead, they are learning to behave and share but with so much rigidity that they are fearful to explore the different social boundaries of the playground. Not all parents will agree with this and may even be proud to be raising upstanding, rule-abiding children, but what's lost is the ability to conceptualize and think outside the box in a fluid, organic way. This may seem insignificant, but this behavior plants the seeds to a fixed mindset. To promote equality and fairness, game play is closely monitored by the supervisors/coaches/teachers and if 1 or 2 players are always succeeding, they will pause or stop the game and start over. And they will enforce strict rules for kids to play fairly and act properly. Again, I need to stress that these are good things and excellent traits to promote, but what is being lost is the opportunity to be more creative and learn these traits organically instead of being forced upon these kids all the time. As parents, coaches, teachers, we should mentor and teach these core values, but also give equal time for sandlot development.

An example is when Seve was starting out in lacrosse. In youth box lacrosse, the nets are tiny. It's hard to score goals because of the small nets and goalies with jumbo padding. Therefore, coaches would religiously teach and encourage young players to shoot the ball with an overhand release. This was the safest and most accurate way to hit the net. Other forms of shooting are side arm or subshot with the release being from different angles instead of an up or down angle of the overhand shot. From ages 5-12, most coaches would drill into the players, "overhand, overhand, overhand!" If a side arm shot was taken, coaches would start yelling immediately "overhand!" If it happened again, the player would most likely be benched for the period or the rest of the game. Too much importance was placed on trying to score and win. Though it is important to score and win, long term skill development of the young player would most likely be stunted if they were not able to or allowed to explore different ways to shoot and score. An accurate overhand release is imperative for any lacrosse player, especially the best and highest-level players in college and professional leagues, but equally as important or even more so, is the ability to shoot sidearm, subshot, backhand, tommy twister or any other ways to shoot. In the highest levels, the defenders and goalies are so good that it becomes too predictable to only have an overhand shot. Having variety in your arsenal will separate the good from the great and the average from the good.

Back to my playing style. Having played multiple sports with pure joy and love, I will go 100% all the time! Not only do I go hard, but I will sometimes take riskier shots and make moves that deviate against standard game theory. It's because of the lack of fear in making a mistake and instead owning a more carefree, creative way of playing. In tennis, I might try hitting a drop shot from the back of the baseline or hit a forehand through an opponent when safer options exists.

In golf, I am able to visualize and see multiple approach shots into the green. Whether hitting a high shot that lands softly and stops quickly near the hole, a mid-flight shot, that lands further away from the pin and rolls to the hole or even running a shot on the ground and trundling the ball on the fairway until it rolls onto the green. In extreme cases, I have even flipped my seven iron upside down and hit the ball left handed with the toe of the club when I was stymied by a tree. Each decision comes with its own risks. The shot I choose is based on how I am feeling and performing on that day. Golfers that are more rigid will not be able to conceptualize the different shots and will play with a more predetermined strategy. If they are able to visualize a different shot, they may not try it for fear of failure. With that said, I am not always successful and will also fuck up from time to time. If this happens, I can brush off the bad shot immediately, learn from it and not have any residual frustration for the next shot. The key to being creative is to have a short-term memory of the failure but be able to analyze the error and make the necessary adjustments when a similar situation arises in the future. Try the shot again! Fail going 100%!

Curriculum

The last three or four years, especially after COVID, I've noticed a really big shift in both mindset and masculinity with my young male students. When I first started teaching driving 9 and 1/2 years ago, most of what I taught were hard skills such as turns, shoulder checks, parallel parking, and all the other maneuvers that were required on the road test. It was simple enough and most of my students were very receptive and could easily learn the material. Though recently, as much as 80% of what I teach are soft skills like observation, face to face communication, being comfortable in a random setting, and taking up space on the road. Most of my students today are uncomfortable in big crowds and need to focus on looking not just at turn signals and traffic lights, but actually observing facial expressions of pedestrians, body language of cyclists, and looking inside the car to understand what the other motorists are potentially thinking. I'm sure that the lockdowns contributed to the general population being less comfortable with face-to-face communication, but there must be more to this. It's almost like my students have invisible walls that inhibit them from even turning their head or if they do look in a certain direction, they're only registering about 20% of the information that they see. An exercise that I do with them is to get out of the car and go to a very busy intersection. We just hang around and observe the cars, the people walking on the sidewalk, and all the other cyclists and road users. I inspire my students to not only focus on the hard skills but to really judge and profile every road user and pedestrian on the sidewalks and on the road.

We try to assess and interpret their intentions through their body language, their eyes, using our natural intuition and not always relying on conscious thought. I've noticed especially the last two years, that the majority of my students are relying on a very defined yes or no answer, right or wrong, left or right, but many of my students are not comfortable with the premise of "maybe". I call this the maybes of driving, or the maybes of life in general. My theory is that the school system and curriculum today is so focused on rigid, politically correct learning objectives, that any sort of ambiguity or unknowns are not tolerated. Therefore, most people today only seek the hard facts and want me to teach them what's right or wrong. As an example, a question I get asked all the time is "when do I shoulder check?", or "how many times should I use my mirrors?" Instead of answering them with a fact, I instead ask them why we shoulder check or use our mirrors. This way, they're not just waiting for me to tell them what to do, I'm able to encourage them to think more freely. I often quote Thomas Sowell, a modern philosopher. He states that he's not trying to teach people what to think but the ability to be able to think. Modern society and school systems seem like they are teaching people what to think and not how to think. Though this has had an impact on everyone, it has had the biggest impact on my young male students. Many of them seem frozen and unable to make the simplest decisions on the road. They often ask me what to do without any initiative to try and figure out how to do something. They're always asking for permission. It's good in society to have rules and regulations, but what's being lost is that human spirit to try. I fear that we will have a generation of males that, without guidance or a different perspective, will lag behind females in terms of motivation, self-belief and confidence. As I stated in my introduction, it's good to empower females in modern society, but it doesn't mean that males have to be emasculated and become weak and fearful. There are some prominent social media personalities that are trying to inspire young men. Some of what they say seem beneficial, but the problem is that to attract more likes and clicks, their message becomes more polarized and maybe influencing young males to have a jaded and toxic outlook. We have lost most of the traits and traditional values of what it is to be a gentleman. Hopefully, this book inspires young males to learn to be masculine and confident to become the very best man he can be.

Building Character through sports

After 10 months of no showing in the Tuesday-Thursday vets training group, I decided to go this morning to get exercise, to see all the boys and most importantly, to chirp our head coach Glen a bit for beating him in the ITF doubles final! I should really try to show up more because my strokes felt amazing right after the training! Glen congratulated me for playing well and having an awesome tournament. We went over my matches and he gave me his assessment of my performance. All my matches were tough! I enjoy it when something is on the line. It's what sports is all about, the challenge, fight, perseverance! I cherish and live for these moments! The players I beat were all disappointed, but they were also gracious in defeat! Then, I shared something that happened in one of my matches. An opponent called one of my balls out that was actually in! Glen wasn't surprised when I told him who it was, and he shared something very interesting with me. Before retiring in Calgary, Glen worked as a financial advisor, and he had a team of advisors working under him in his office. When he had a prospective new hire, he would invite the hire to play pickup basketball. He did this because he could learn a lot from a person by the way they played sports. During the game, he could assess if someone was an individual or team player. If they were selfish or would make good decisions and pass the ball. During a game, Glen would observe their mannerisms and how they reacted under pressure. In sports, as the competition and pressure ramp up, people will default into their subconscious core traits. It's hard to mask, fake and hide who you are. Your true character comes out when facing pressure in the heat of battle. After playing basketball, Glen gained the insight he needed about these guys, and it played a major role in his hiring decisions as well as future opportunities for promotion in the company! It's also why I'm able to judge someone's personality while they're driving because in a chaotic situation, their true selves naturally show. Playing golf is also a great barometer to see someone's character. This is why it's imperative for young people, especially young guys to play sports! It will teach them the true meaning of sportsmanship, hard work, grit, resiliency, teamwork and all that comes with winning and losing! I've played multiple sports at a high level, I'm ultra-competitive but also very enjoyable to play with and against. I rarely have problems finding people to play with whether in individual sports like tennis or golf or team sports like basketball, volleyball. I'm able to play pickup at Crystal pool or Beacon Hill and I'm always welcome to join! The main reason is because people enjoy competing with me and being around me. I play hard but also exhibit great sportsmanship. From time to time, I make bad line calls. It's not on purpose to cheat my opponents but due my 52 year old eyes! If my opponents make a bad call, I'll look at them, but I rarely complain and instead try to beat them even if they're cheating me. This gives me the ultimate edge in competing because even if my opponents will try to cheat, they know that they can never gain the advantage psychologically and in the end the people who have less morals and values will crumble under pressure. I will keep playing hard no matter what the circumstances are and the adversities that I face. In my other chapters, I talk a lot about always giving it 100%

and to never expect fairness and equality. The biggest thing you win playing sports is the character it builds in you! In the end, it's not the trophies and medals that are important but the person you become from playing sports!

Women's responsibility in a good man

Everything that I've written so far is guy-centric and the onus is on guys to better themselves, but women also have a role in this. Actually, they have a massive role how men develop which is precisely one of the reasons why we're in this situation today. Growing up in the '70s and '80s, one of the core movements was feminism and female empowerment. I fully support and embrace empowered women. My mom was a very strong woman, and in all areas, led our household.

But feminism has in many ways, weakened men. The movement has disrupted and almost destroyed the traditional nuclear family and patriarchy. Our societies for 200,000 years have always had roles for men and women, fathers and mothers, brothers, and sisters. Yes, we would like to strive for equality and a level playing field. With that said, humans are inherently different through their physical, emotional, psychological, and biological traits. We were not meant to be fully equal, and these differences are what make us special. Without these differences and unique traits, society would have collapsed a long time ago because we would not be able to procreate and have babies, if everyone was the exact same. With all the progress of feminism, women will have to make a choice right now. I guess when I say women, I mean society. The choice that women will have to make is to 1. Understand and be okay with the patriarchy and importance of roles in a nuclear family 2. Be okay and accept that men are not perfect and to lower the exceedingly high bar that modern society has created for men.

Of course! We want men to be the best men that they can be, but in the end, the expectations are so high that a lot of men have just given up! Women ask me and wonder why there are no more men. It's hard for me to explain to them how much they have had a hand in the eradication of men.

Mansplaining and fractured masculinity

Over the past few years, especially post COVID, I have both heard and observed many instances of mansplaining and fractured masculinity. Truly immersing myself in different social settings, it has become clear that modern dudes lack real confidence to take a loss and admit that they don't know everything and generally don't know that much at all.

Guys have been so beaten down that any sort of affront to their ego becomes magnified to an almost nuclear level. I have experienced many examples of this recently. A couple of weeks ago, I was at Darcy's dancing in front of the stage with a buddy. To my left were four young ladies having a good time. The Prowl, a local band, was killing it playing cover songs. The dance floor was packed with mostly, young, and vibrant people pulsating with Doug and Avian masterfully shredding their guitars, Ces cooly slapping the bass, Amber doing her thing on the drums and Gill, the lead singer, serenading us with her angelic voice. Halfway through the set, a guy, in his mid-twenties, aggressively bumps me to get to the ladies to my left. He starts to grind and dance like a total fucking loser. The ladies were ignoring him because he was so crass with his gross attempt to pick them up. As he is doing his spastic moves, he repeatedly hits me without any apology or acknowledgement. I pushed him back with a stiff forearm shiver. He was surprised that I stood my ground, he instantly got into my face, toe to toe and said to me "you don't want any of this bro, not tonight bro!" I looked him straight in the eye without flinching. He kept talking then tried to push me back but even at 51, I'm really strong and he couldn't really do much. Next, he tried to piss me off by touching my hand. I just ignored him and after a few more seconds, he backed off and left the dancefloor. It was great for the guy to shoot his shot and try to dance with the girls, but unfortunately, most guys I have observed recently try way too hard to show their masculinity that they end up looking weak or just creepy. When confronted, these guys want to act tough but most of the time, it's all talk.

Another time while in line to get a beer at Bard & Banker, a similar thing happened. After waiting for a minute, I was next to order when four young guys tried to sneak in front of me. With my left arm, I shivered the guy, and I pointed my left forefinger up to signal for him to wait. The guy was shocked and pissed off. The bartender understood what was going down and took my order first. After ordering, the guy got into my face arguing with me. He was clearly wrong but, again, his ego could not let him take an L! He thought that I would back down, but I stared him down eye to eye and calmly said to him that "he was being a little bitch!" I was expecting him to throw his fists, but he kept whining until, finally, his three other buddies deescalated their friend. I later found out that these guys were ex junior A hockey players.

These examples could have played out much differently if the guys had more confidence and just acknowledged that they were wrong in that situation. A simple, my bad, sorry, fist bump or even a nod of the head would go a long way for these guys. Instead, their fractured ego can't handle the perceived sleight and often they lash out and compound their error, double down and start "mansplaining".

In the modern school curriculums, I hear students are taught to debate and keep defending their point even if they know that their position is clearly wrong. Though it is important to stand up for yourself, it is equally, if not more, crucial to be self-aware and back down when your position is clearly wrong! Learn to take a loss, take ownership and improve yourself instead of acting like a little bitch!

Respect

The Philippines is an old country with a lot of tradition stemming from the original Malay culture to the 400+ years of Spanish and American colonization sprinkled with Chinese and Japanese influences. Growing up, we had a deep respect for our family, including elders, teachers, priests, police, and politicians. People were very community based with lots of activities centered around church life, schools, and basketball. To show respect to elders when speaking, everyone would use a prefix, either ho or po. So, if we spoke with an uncle or parent, an example would be: "good morning uncle Roger, *ho*" or good morning uncle Roger, *po*." The *ho* & *po* are almost the same and it was added in the end of a sentence as a sign of respect to the person you were speaking to. Very similar to when I was growing up in Vancouver in the late '70s and '80s, our teachers in school would teach us to be polite especially to older folks and when speaking, we would always say "Good morning, sir or Good morning Ma'am". These traditions and values have been ingrained in me that even now at 51, if I am speaking to someone older than myself, I will automatically call them sir/ma'am or in Tagalog use *ho/po*. Those times in the past seemed to have more order and structure. People in positions of authority generally felt a responsibility to try to be better and to lead by example to the younger generation that looked up to them. Equally, the younger generation tried so hard to be better to impress and make the older generation proud of them. This symbiotic relationship wasn't perfect but worked very well and there were generally less problems with more connection and understanding between generations. These days, it seems like the inverse has happened where there is little connection and interaction between different generations and the mutual respect is almost nil. I am fortunate that I can connect with most people but that is so uncommon these days. Parents have very little understanding of what their kids are doing in school. Kids have little or no interest in what their parents are also doing. It's the same in school, work, sports, and overall society. We are so fractured that we hardly know anyone around us. People will greet each other with the customary, "hello, how are you doing?" "I'm doing good, how about you?" "I'm doing great!" "Have a good day, you as well!" And then, the interaction is over. Just like our human connections, it's almost OVER!

Body count

I was doing a lesson with my 18-year-old student, Elle. On our way back to her house, saw one of her friend's ex-boyfriends. He was on her kill list because he was a total douche when they were going out. He also tried to hook up with her other friends and asked them for nude pictures. Guys would typically say, "do you send?" or "you send?" to ask for naked photos. As an older dude, I had no fucking clue what the obsession is with nudes. Apparently in this generation, a vast majority of guys will ask girls through Instagram, Snapchat, or text. They will show the nudes to their friends to brag about their supposed sexual exploits and body count. Because of the insecurity of a lot of younger males today, one thing that is important for their ego is body count, the number of sexual partners that they've had. They associate their body count with their worth as a man and will brag and compare with friends about their sexual conquests. There would seem to be an invisible hierarchy in which guys compare themselves with their friends or classmates in school. These guys are known as "fuck boys". It's not enough to attract and date the prettiest, most desirable girls, a growing number of modern males feel a need to show off and therefore exhibit more toxic tendencies that probably would not have existed or be an anomaly in previous generations. Many students have told me stories about fuck boys destroying friend groups by hooking up with multiple girls in the same friend group creating drama and infighting. This book is written to inspire confidence for young guys to become gentleman and good boyfriend material, not to be fuck boys.

A couple of months ago, one of the servers I know started dating a fuck boy. Both were in their late 20's, and she seemed really happy. After a couple of months, the dude couldn't stop flirting with other girls at parties or at work. My friend was so hurt and couldn't handle her boyfriend still being a fuckboy. She thought he was "the one". After the breakup, my friend was devastated. She dropped out of school, started to drink heavily, and do coke again. She had been sober - for years. Luckily, her friends and family were able to support her through this difficult time. Without this, she probably would have self-destructed and gone into a very dark place. For all you fuck boys in your mid to late 20's or older, please be aware of the pain and damage that you may cause to women and understand what these women are in this for. If it's casual, that's fine, but if it's serious, stop being a fuckboy!

As I have written in the earlier chapter about overconfidence, there is a very fine line between confidence and arrogance, be disciplined and be a good guy.

Hockey Culture

Hockey is the fabric that bonds our country. From St. John's Newfoundland, Saginaw Quebec, Thunder Bay Ontario, Flin Flon Manitoba, Saskatoon Saskatchewan, Red Deer Alberta, to Victoria BC Canadians, from every corner of the country, love hockey. For generations, going to the rink at 6 a.m., with a double double from Timmies and a dozen doughnuts was the morning ritual for many families around the country. Hockey night in Canada was a Saturday night ritual most people planned around. Games from coast to coast were televised and families would gather around to turn on the TV at 5 p.m. I hated the Habs or Oilers. In the '80s, they would always destroy my beloved Canucks! Watching Wayne Gretzky score a gazillion points from behind the net and Guy Lafleur skate through our whole defense, those memories were painful but memorable. I vividly recall where I was during each one of the Canucks Stanley cup runs in: 1981, 1994, and 2012. The "miracle on ice" in the '80 Olympics, Canada cup in '87, Olympic Gold in 2002 & Sidney Crosby's golden goal in 2012 in Vancouver. Don Cherry held court over the nation on coaches' corner, every Saturday night, talking about hockey and preaching about his love of veterans and Canadian patriotism.

Hockey is the lifeblood of many small communities in our country. Families centered their lives around the rink. Games and activities were the focal point in their respective communities.

Hockey is also a very violent and brutal sport! Though these days, we emphasize skill and scoring goals, in the past the physicality and toughness of players were equal if not more valued. And the team aspect and camaraderie were second to none. Teammates were most times brothers for life, bonded together by seasons of playing, sweating, and persevering together to achieve a common goal. This may have been the reason that the Canadian forces were the most feared in WW1. For their toughness, and willingness to fight for not only their country but for others.

But as hockey in this country became a business, changes began to chip away at the purity of the sport and the innocence of a nation. With the expansion of the NHL in the 70's to the present, there was a push to integrate and change those smalltown values into a more commercially viable product for the US market. When Wayne Gretzky, the GOAT, who had won 4 Stanley cups in the '80s, was traded to the Kings in 1990, it was probably the defining moment that hockey in Canada had changed forever. Gone was the naive belief that it was *our* smalltown game. It was replaced by the glitz and glamour of Hollywood. The NHL headquarters soon followed and moved from Canada to NYC. The brutality and violence that had been ingrained in the NHL were now primed to be reduced and lessened to a more palatable level. "Slapshot", starring Paul Newman, is a movie that encapsulates everything about this change. A cult classic with hockey players, it is both extremely funny but also, eerily accurate in depicting the transformation from a smalltown game, along with the traditional values, to a big city business.

The crass, low brow nature of players are now being replaced by more hockey academy robots. The smalltown values and "the player's code" in hockey are now policed by league rules instead of the players on the ice.

With a combination of society's push to eliminate toxic masculinity and to encourage guys to embrace their feminine side, an interesting trend has occurred recently.

A couple of years ago, I was teaching a grade 12 girl going out with a hockey player in her school. She did several lessons and during our drives, she would talk about her boyfriend. She said that he was really kind and nice and not really like the traditional "hockey bro". At the same time, I was chatting with my tennis buddy's daughter who was going out with a guy on the same team. Both girls shared with me stories of the hockey dudes.

I was surprised to hear from both girls that at a party last weekend, the guys got drunk and started to fool around. It's standard for teammates to get wasted after a long road trip. What was different was that as a joke, the teammates started kissing and making out with each other. And they also joked around by sticking their fingers in their teammate's butts! She shared another story during math class where two teammates randomly started making out. These things may have happened in the past too, but I think the meaning and reason may be different these days.

I have also seen this firsthand. Back in February, I was at Irish times on the dancefloor. A group of guys and girls joined me and started dancing. They looked like 19 and 20-year-old hockey guys.

The girls were very attractive, and the group was having a great time. After a couple more songs, two dudes that were completely hammered, jokingly started to kiss right in the middle of the dancefloor. At that moment, all I could think about was "why the fuck were they kissing each other when there were the lovely ladies right beside them?" The girls were looking at each other and seemed to be thinking the exact same thing!

How to win

It's now been exactly two years since I started playing tennis again. In that time, I played lots, had ups and downs, and competed in a few tournaments with varying degrees of success. I have gotten to know most of the tennis community here in Victoria. My level is pretty high and though I've primarily been playing doubles, this past year I played a lot more singles. I prefer playing doubles because, frankly, I don't have to run as much to cover the whole court. With that said, I used to be an exclusive singles player as a junior and I even won a few tournaments. With tenacity, grit, effort and hard work, I was able to find ways to grind and beat my opponents. As I've written in the previous chapters, I love to compete regardless of whether I win or lose.

My chapter today talks about how to win and how to conduct yourself when you're winning. With the social media generation, we are always trying to find that perfect moment and show people the best sides of ourselves. This unfortunately has seeped into how people compete and show their need for validation. When I first started playing singles last year, I would go up against one of our training partners, Mike. He's about the same age as me but has been playing consistently for the last 30 years. A big strong guy, he looked like a very athletic linebacker. Mike played tennis with the same aggressiveness and athleticism. I could never beat him whether it was just a tiebreak or a full set. He was just too damn good, and my singles game was really rusty. But as everyone knows by now, I hate losing. I didn't take those losses in a negative way, I just knew that if I stayed with the process and kept improving, eventually I would get my singles game back. Saturday morning, I strolled down to the Hill around 11:00 a.m. This is quite early in February for the regulars to be playing so I didn't expect anyone there. As I drove into the parking lot, I saw Mike rallying with two young ladies. He was coaching his tenants that lived in his basement. I got out of my car and said hello. I had no intention of playing but he insisted that I help him coach the two ladies. We hit for about half an hour and played a few games. The ladies had to go but Mike and I both agreed to play a set. Mike hadn't played as much this past winter, but I had been playing and my game was good. After I won the first four games, Mike didn't know what had hit him. He tried to adapt and adjust his game, but I was just playing too damn good and I steamrolled him in the first set 6-3. Mike, the competitor that he is, asks for a rematch and we play a second set. Again, in that set, I was playing well but the score was much closer. In the end I prevailed 7-5. I have never beaten Mike in a set before and as we're playing, we joke around but we are also 100% competitive. In the end, he said "good job buddy I'm going to try again!" I said to him "good set," not wanting to show him how excited I was inside and happy about winning. I tried to be more low key in our handshake. That's a pretty big difference to today. With the internet age and social media, you see outlandish celebrations when people win. Not saying we can't celebrate or shouldn't celebrate, but as I said to Seve in lacrosse, act like you'd been there before. A couple weeks go by, I see Mike at the hill again. Time for a rematch! I got up to a four-nothing lead. He stormed back but I won 6-4. In the second set, Mike level ups his game and he beats me 7-6. We play a rubber set for a beer at the Beagle. We played some amazing points, and in a see-saw last set, I won 7-5. As with all matches, we shook hands. I'm very respectful with my head down and not wanting to seem overly jubilant. I joked around with him, but I wanted to show him the utmost respect by playing as hard as I could while, at the same time, not acting a fool during or after the match. After the hard fought 3 sets, we headed to the Beagle. Mike bought me a beer and we had many laughs. And we talked about my book and the state of modern guys. He was shocked by some of the things I shared with him, but he also agreed with most of it. In the end, this is how competing and winning should be, respectful, tenacious, and graceful, with a couple of beers in hand at the pub.

Last night, I'm with another one of my buddies, Ray, who I'm doing a project with. Ray and I have had some competitive games, but we've never played a set. We'd always play games to five or to 11 and the results have been pretty even so far. Ray took up tennis just a few years ago but his level is high for the short time he's been playing. I have everything going. I was in the ultimate zone, and I couldn't miss a shot. It felt like I could do anything which is pretty rare because there's so many different shots and strategies in tennis. Being able to do everything that you want is something that happens maybe once in 10 years. I go up to a 5-0 lead and Ray can't do anything. He's playing well but my level was just too high. I literally could do anything just like Neo in the matrix. Because of his pride, he plays a good game and wins one before I close out the set 6-1. In modern times, we are taught to have mercy when we are blowing out the opponent.

I've also felt this at times in my competitive career and have lost a match or two because of it. I have realized that letting up and showing mercy could give your opponent a chance to come back. It would also be very disrespectful to Ray, like throwing him shade. As Michael Jordan said, the score is always zero-zero. I'm a super nice guy and very giving and helpful. With that said, we've overcompensated for that hypercompetitive nature to one that is more participatory in nature. This is why we have mercy rules in a bunch of different sports. They say that a three-goal lead in hockey is the most dangerous because the team leading, if they let up, will stop playing hard, giving their opponents a chance to come back and win the game. While I'm thoroughly demolishing Ray, I show no emotion. I hit a lot of good shots that were college level and literally played the best that I could possibly play. But with each passing shot and winner, I just played on like the score was 0-0 and was emotionless even though I hit the most tremendous shots possible. We play a second set, nothing really changes and again I win 6-1. In my mind, this game was good for me but equally good for Ray. The reason is that with me playing that well and Ray being helpless, it gives him a lot of things that he could work on and build and improve on his game. This is one of the reasons why we have such mediocrity in modern society. We are not pushing people to their limits but instead taking it easy on them and when we do push people to the limits, it is done in a disrespectful and unsportsmanlike way. We have forgotten the true meaning of competition, society has demonized it and viewed anything mildly competitive as bad. Throughout history, steel hardened steel, the training would sometimes be more ferocious than the real war while simulating and preparing their troops for battle. It's important to be able to succeed without seeking fame or the adulation that comes with winning. Ray and I talk a lot about ego and how it leads to the destruction and downfall of people. This was an example of me absolutely dominating both Mike and Ray but without the need to brag or share my wins with anybody. I don't need to stroke my ego. What I enjoyed the most was battling with my good friends and even if I had lost, just being able to share the battlefield with them. Playing with honor is much more important for me than just winning!

How to lose

After a busy week of work, I finally took a day off and dropped by the hill to play some doubles. I was teamed up with Greg and we took on the Korean duo of Nick and Han. All of us play at a really good level and on any given day can compete and win against anybody at the hill. On this day, Greg and I were playing well but for whatever reason, we lost the first set 6-3 after leading 3-1. Always the competitors, we try again. The second set was equally intense as the first with lots of amazing points. Again, we lost the set 6-4, and I'm not amused! But with the Michael Jordan mindset, the score is 0-0, we try again and play a 3rd set. Unfortunately, we get killed 6-2. This rarely happens to me and understandably, I'm pissed off at myself. I try to see what I could have done better and say sorry to Greg for not playing up to my usual level. I shake everyone's hand and sincerely congratulate them for kicking our ass with no anger, frustration or animosity.

It's late in September, and usually, the weather starts to get wet and cold this time of year in Victoria. Luckily, we had a mega bonus warm sunny Sunday. Everyone was out to soak up the last remaining days of sun this year! The big hitters were all there, Geoff, John, pizza Matt, Han, the UVic team, and my doubles partner Sam. He had recently made their school team, and this gave him a massive ego boost. I was happy for him but also saw some of the negative changes in his mindset.

We played our 1st set on court one. Me and Andriy, a recent Ukrainian immigrant, took on Sam and Miguel, a young tennis coach. Andriy had been coming to the hill recently but only wanted to rally and hit lots of balls. He found doubles boring and thought that his game wasn't match ready. Miguel had good skills passed on through his dad, an ex-national player in Europe. Basically, Sam and Miguel had a slight edge in our matchup. It was a seesaw battle with Sam and Miguel coming out on top 7-6 (9-7) in a close tiebreaker. I had set point on my racket but missed a standard volley. We all shook hands and waited for the next court. It took a while but after an hour, we had our chance to play again. This time, I was partnered up with my buddy Corey. The match up was an even tossup. While we were waiting to play, Sam asked me for some Advil as his back was a little sore.

We started our set strong and won the first 2 games easily. With every error that Sam made, he threw in an excuse about his back, the shadows on the court, or some other reason for missing his shots. He also starts to labor with his movement and stretches his legs a bit. Remember, he said that it was his back that was in pain. We play the next two games hard and have some long rallies and excellent back and forth exchanges. We won both games and went up 4-0. This is where Sam again stretches his legs and back. But this time he says, I need a "sub" because my back is too painful to continue playing. Well, what the fuck? When we lost 7-6, he was fine, flying around on the court but 0-4 down, suddenly, his 20+ year old body starts fucking breaking down? It was such a bitch move but becoming the norm with younger competitors now. When they're winning, it's all smiles and high fives, but when they're losing, it's every fucking excuse in the book. Now, he could very well have a sore back but if his back is good enough to win, it's good enough to lose! This is not how you lose. You lose on the battlefield fighting all the way.

I understand that in competition, you will sometimes lose. How you lose, what you learn from the loss and the motivation that it gives you for the next match are all extremely important. Again, I hate losing but I'm able to accept it, with my head up and can give props to the victors like a man. These days, guys are afraid of losing because in their minds, it's an assault on their egos. I think the key to being a solid competitor is to take ego out of the equation whether you win or lose. Without ego, you just play the game as hard as possible without the extra baggage that comes with playing the game for your ego.

"I would rather die on my sword fighting than be butchered in the slaughterhouse!"

CHAPTER 12
BECOMING A TRUE DUDE: EMBRACING IMPERFECTION, STRENGTH, AND PURPOSE

I almost killed a cyclist

I was on my way to one of my local coffee hangouts, Parsonage Cafe. I'm in the final stages of finishing my book, it's a long weekend holiday Monday in February 2024. I parked my car on the street and without thinking, started to open my door. Either through luck or through intuition, I stopped opening it just in time for a cyclist to pass by. He gave me a dirty look. One of the ten commandments of my driving lessons is to check your mirror and shoulder check before opening a door to make sure to see what's behind you, especially a cyclist passing by. There have been many instances of cyclists getting doored by an open car door and that's a $368 fine. For the cyclist, it's dangerous because if they crash into an open door, they can fly off and severely injure themselves or even be killed. Once I got out of the car, I rushed to try to speak to the cyclist. He parked his bike in front of the coffee shop, I approached him and said sorry bro my bad! You could tell he was a little bit upset but he also said that I was one of the good ones for acknowledging my mistake. I went on and told him that I taught people how to drive and one of our core teachings is to shoulder check before opening the door. Additionally, I really felt bad because I drill this into my students every time but as I mentioned to the cyclists, I'm not perfect and I'm only human. Even people that have been training every day to do something that's right, will sometimes have a moment of weakness and do something that's not right. This leads into my chapter about nobody's perfect. We can try our best to do all the right things and train ourselves to do the right things. But because we are imperfect, sometimes we will accidentally slip up, not on purpose, but just because we are human.

My night at the Roxy

It's July 2024 and I finished my book! I'm doing my final edits before submitting my draft to my publisher. After 3 years, many struggles and bouts with writer's block, I feel so blessed to be finished. I recently reconnected with my first love Marie. It was 1988 all over again just like the first time I met her at Duffin's Donuts. We randomly bumped into each other at JJ Bean, which is a local cafe chain in Vancouver. Serendipitously, it's only 15 blocks away from Duffins! Our love has not only continued but blossomed into a Romeo and Juliet like love story and saga. We've been on numerous dates. Last night, she wanted to go dancing and looked for places to go. She chose the Roxy. It has a long-standing reputation in Vancouver for the place to be when you're single and you want to meet somebody. I was excited as I've been hearing about the Roxy for decades but had never been there before. It's famously known for the Roxy Flu. NHL teams would arrive in Vancouver the night before, party it up at the Roxy and have an awful game the day after. So, in my mind, the place would be filled with the hottest girls and the best looking alpha guys. We set out and took an Uber from Marie's and got to the Roxy around 8:15 p.m. We went there early because she didn't want to line up, Marie hates lining up! We got to the front door; they asked for our IDs and we found a booth in the back beside the bar. It was a great place because we had a little bit more privacy to make out just like it was 1988. I ordered a pair of vodka cranberry drinks, and we sat down in the booth. There were a couple of people inside, but it was still pretty empty, so Marie and I had time to kiss and make out. She was having a great time reminiscing about the past and telling me stories from when she was in her twenties working as a teacher right across the street. A few more people arrive, and we both start noticing something pretty interesting. A group of girls sat beside us on the next table but what we really noticed was when the guys started arriving. Remember, the Roxy had a reputation for being the IT club where you could meet beautiful people. It was scary that everything I had written in this book was on full display at the Roxy. The guys did not look like guys! Marie was commenting on how scrawny and weak they looked and how they seemed to smell bad displaying poor hygiene and wardrobe selections. In other words, the guys did not look like guys and instead look like what I've written in the book, weak, emasculated, insecure, facsimiles of men! It was so disappointing for me to see because I was also expecting to see a bunch of strong alpha dudes. It was so bad, that as Marie and I were dancing, girls were checking me out and even trying to get my attention. This is not good because it shows the sad state the guys are in in 2024. I was both disappointed, upset and angry that this is the case. Marie shared our experience with her friends, and they were equally shocked to hear the sad reality of men in the 21st century. We had a fabulous time, but I can't imagine what these vibrant women there were thinking. Trying to meet a guy and being left to choose from a pile of broken, unattractive, weak men. I sincerely hope that my book can in small part revive masculinity, chivalry and how to be a gentleman. Because if not, I really fear for the state of the next generation. We may actually not have a next generation because there won't be any men left to procreate with all the strong women wanting to get pregnant.

Guilt and Company

It's 10 p.m. on Friday, Marie and I were looking for places to go. We decided to go to Guilt and Company. It is in the heart of the Gastown district in Vancouver. The area is a popular hangout for locals with Guilt and Co being my favorite place to go. It's an intimate jazz bar situated in the basement of a historic 100-year-old building. The ambience is second to none, dark and rustic, it feels like a man cave on steroids. I've watched numerous shows and have always been blown away with the musical talent we have on display in Vancouver! We arrive at 10:30 p.m., the place is packed and standing room only. We head straight for the dance floor; Marie loves to dance and so do I! The band for the night is called *The Matinee*, they mostly play original songs but also belt out a couple of covers. We were packed like sardines on the tiny dance floor in front of the stage. It was such an awesome vibe! As we were dancing, I noticed a couple of things:

1. a couple of guys were trying their best to attract and meet the pretty ladies beside us
2. They were having a heck of a time keeping the women's attention!

It was weird because it seemed like most of the people were single but for whatever reason, I would see them meet and dance for half a song, then, game over for the dude. He was doing all the right things, looked good, respectful, masculine but the opportunity for couples to organically meet is dying a slow death. I dunno, maybe I'm just being too judgy about modern dating! I hope that

I'm wrong because if I'm right, we are facing a dating apocalypse that will wipe out most of the ways to meet partners in person and we'll be stuck exclusively using these less human dating apps instead!

LTAD To Be a Dude

Throughout the book, I have shared my life stories from the time I was born in Manila all the way to 2021 in Victoria. In my introduction, I professed that I did not know everything, and I am the first to admit when I'm wrong. This last section of the book is my own thoughts on how to become a dude in the 21st century. This LTAD is not rigid and can be fluid to suit the wants and needs of the readers. As we have gone over on numerous occasions, the most important thing is for the dude to *want* to develop the traits and characteristics described in the book and take a level of ownership. Don't trust this blindly. Scrutinize the material and come out with your own conclusions.

"I'm not trying to teach you what to think, I'm trying to teach the ability to be able to think!"

Long Term Athlete Development and the Long-Term Development (LTD) framework was created as a way to develop athletes from the initial stages until the active for life stage in order to reach the greatest heights of sport achievement as outlined by Canada Sport 4 Life.

I will outline LTD to be a dude in the 21st century:

There are 7 stages for LTD

1. Active Start
2. Fundamentals

3. Learn to Train
4. Train to Train
5. Train to Compete
6. Train To Win
7. Active for Life

1. Active Start

As we have discussed throughout the book, this is the most important stage. I call it buy-in. Are you interested in the premise of being a modern, masculine dude? You should _want_ to do this and be willing to make every effort no matter how difficult it is to make the changes necessary to be a dude in the 21st century.

2. Fundamentals

Learning chivalry and how to be a gentleman

Examples would be:
- Being attracted to a woman
- Opening a door for a stranger at the coffee shop, school or restaurant.
- Opening the car door for your mate
- Looking people in the eyes when talking to them
- Good Athletic Body Posture
- Looking up
- Be Willing to Communicate
- Be an active listener
- Waiting for your girlfriend to sit down at a restaurant first
- Being respectful to your mate's family

- Playing a sport
- Group activities; band, dance class, gym, yoga
- Volunteer
- Don't expect or demand equity or equality
- Stop gaming or reduce substantially
- Get a haircut, shave and start to show your face and yourself to the world
- Start shaking hands with your parents/siblings to practice a firm handshake

3. Learn to Train

Of course, change is not easy, and you want to slowly adopt some or most of the fundamentals. In the beginning, it will be difficult because your mindset is hardwired with procedural and emotional patterns that you have learned over the years. When I teach students, we must be patient in breaking habits. I call it exponential growth. Take baby steps and, eventually, we will hit an explosion of learning in the later stages. Setbacks in the Learn to Train stage are normal so don't bail out at the first sign of adversity.

- First, start with improving your posture while standing, have your feet shoulder width apart, leaning back with your head up, shoulders back and chest out. This will promote an athletic stance which I teach in all sports that I coach.
- Start making eye contact with your parents, siblings and teachers when you talk to them. This may take some time

to get used to and you'll probably feel awkward in the beginning.

- Join and take up a sport of activity. Try to immerse yourself in a team sport. No matter what your skill level is in that sport. Participation is the key at this stage, not the skill level.
- Leave your house for an extended period of time, whether going to study in a cafe, watching a basketball, football or lacrosse game. Watch live music at a festival or club
- Never complain about a bad call or unfair treatment or conditions
- Start looking up and around when walking on the street or in the school hallways
- Start to open doors for people at school or at the mall
- Play board games at home with family or friends
- Start talking more to your mate's family/younger siblings
- Start to notice girls that you are attracted to and casually flirt with them by making eye contact, smiling. Read books and online articles about flirting.
- Start to call and talk on your phone, many modern people lack the skills to effectively call or answer their phone
- Shake hands or fist bump with teammates after practice and with teachers (firm)
- Never complain about a bad call or unfair officiating. Don't expect or look for equality.

4. Train to Train

At this stage, we start to increase repetition and add competition to learn to train skills. It is essential in this stage to embrace trial and error (kinesthetic) learning without being disappointed about the results. Risks will be introduced slowly. Winning and losing will take on a larger role in this stage.

- Start to make eye contact and smile to strangers on the sidewalk, bus or in the hallways at school
- Make sure to always maintain good posture when outside
- Start making eye contact and talking to acquaintances in school, work and teams you are in.
- Start talking to girls casually at work or school. Ask how their day is going and learn how to listen to them making sure to make eye contact and maintain eye contact.
- In class, raise your hand to answer a question from your teacher, sit in the front of the class and be seen in class, not in the back, chat with coworkers during breaks, ask what kind of music they like, what they're doing on the weekend.
- Make eye contact and talk to your coaches and teammates, get on the same page, shake hands after practice with coaches and teammates (hard handshake, no limp wrist)
- When at a live music venue, try to meet and say hi to people. Without being over the top, say hello to a woman and ask her to dance or buy her a drink without being overly pushy or aggressive. Be more low-key.
- If an opponent makes an incredible shot to beat you, shake their hand with no frustration. Learn to accept greatness from your opponent with sportsmanship. You may not like

losing but give 100% effort. Shake their hands after the game (firm and with respect!)

- Never blame officiating or outside conditions for losing
- In bed, try to engage in more foreplay and teasing. Don't just go to the point. Read books like Kama Sutra and others about the art of lovemaking.
- Start competing more in sports. Try harder to win. If you lose, start to feel it and not like that feeling. Watch *The Last Dance Documentary* about Michael Jordan to see and learn what it's like to be an Alpha Competitor.

5. Train to Compete

In this stage, we intensify all the aspects in the Train-to-Train Stage by introducing winning and losing in every activity. I encourage you to try new things that will make you uncomfortable, adapt, learn and refine. Risks of failure must be embraced in this stage. There will be successes, but the growth will come from how you deal with and adapt to failure.

- Start walking around everywhere with your head up, good posture, engaging strangers and saying hello. You will find that most people you encounter on the street or school hallway will look away, try to make eye contact until they look back at you, then give a friendly smile. At stores, briefly ask the cashier or host how their day is going. It may even feel like you are flirting which it probably is. Don't be discouraged if you do not get a response, for every failed attempt, you will learn to refine your approach for next time. Don't harass them if you don't get a response. Back off and reassess in private what you did and what things you can improve with your flirting.

- At school, be fearless and start talking to everyone, especially girls. If you like a girl at school or work, go up to them and casually ask if they would like to hang out. Girls will be more receptive today as less guys are willing to step up to the plate and she may say yes. If they say no firmly, move on, reassess what happened and try again with another girl. Try to not be upset because you were turned down, she may be already taken or is not interested in you.
- Less thought (conscious thought) and more action (instinct)
- On your sports team or activity group, try to be more vocal and non-vocal in your communication with your teammates or group mates. It is imperative that you improve your communication and interpersonal skills. If you are an introvert, you may need to just dive in headfirst and just do it. In a game or practice, be vocal and communicate where you are, ask for a pass or call out for help. Non-verbal communication can be high fives, fist bumps, eye contact, nods of approval, nods of disapproval, elbowing your opponents, facing and not backing down from opponents.
- In tough losses, have your head up. Shake hands with your opponent (hard). Show the utmost respect to them. Improving your skills that were lacking for the next game to get revenge. Never complain about officiating or other outside things. Take the loss and try again!

- At work, volunteer your time, always look your coworkers in the eyes while talking to them, be comfortable talking and answering your phone and from time to time, phoning in an order instead of ordering food online, phone your parents and talk to them longer than usual.

- When making love, really make love with all your emotions. Be unselfish and try to give as much pleasure to your mate as you can before for yourself. Use all the foreplay and flirting techniques learned to add variety to your sexual arsenal and to keep things fresh and exciting. Be adventurous.

- Relish the chance to compete against the best. If faced with a monumental task with little chance of success, try your best and see what happens. Even in no win situations, compete as hard as you can without giving up. "Die on your sword not in the Slaughterhouse!"

- Try to compete in all sports or any activity with a winning and losing outcome. Enjoy the competition and always try to win and come out on top. If you lose, contemplate and reassess instead of just being ok with losing. You should start to dislike and hate losing, this will motivate you to make changes in your strategy and try again. Have no residual emotion after a loss, learn that losing is part of winning. Once you can embrace that losing is a possibility, you will not be afraid if you lose. This will free yourself from the fear of losing and you will be much more instinctual in your behavior. This is called "the zone" in sports - the absence of fear of fucking up and just playing.

*It's crucial to learn how to lose so that if a girl says no, you will have the processes and capacity to deal with the rejection!

6. Train to Win

In sports, this stage has world class competitors who compete in the highest levels of competition i.e., Olympics, World Championships, Or top pro leagues. By the time you reach this stage, you will have all the characteristics to be a dude in the 21st century. This stage is where you are liberated and free from all the fear and anxiety that most modern males are feeling today. At this stage, you will be supremely confident in yourself, be assertive in all aspects of life, not be easily offended and will take everything in stride, have initiative in life, have amazing decision-making skills, be disciplined and in control, probably be in a relationship with a girlfriend having amazing sex. You will be at an automatic stage in your interpersonal communication skills and will be at ease in any situation anywhere in the world. You will challenge yourself and seek out uncomfortable goals to conquer. You will be a high achiever and goal set to the moon. You operate mostly with your instincts with less conscious thought required. Your foundation is rock-solid, few people will ever reach these heights of being a dude.

7. Active for Life

This is the end of LTD. At this stage, you have accomplished everything that you set out to be. You can mentor and help younger dudes, be a counselor, teacher, or even a "driving instructor". At this stage, you can seamlessly communicate and enjoy everyone's company, make people at ease with your presence, be instinctual and comfortable. Lastly, the dude of the 21st century is confident and in control, a guy other men admire, and ladies want to be with. He is 100% genuine and authentic with no fear of living life.

Carpe Diem!

Nobody's perfect

I thought that I would finish the book with the LTAD chapter and steps on how to be a dude in the 21st century. After much contemplation, self-reflection and frustration in writing this book, I have come up with more.

After 3.5 years of me going out, experiencing modern life, playing multiple sports, listening to my friends & students, talking to everybody, and watching talks about men on YouTube, Twitter, Instagram that I possibly could. I've come to realize what the problem is and offer some solutions. The expectation for men is exceedingly high! With the push to eradicate toxic masculinity and to eliminate any sort of inequality and power imbalance with men against women, we have in society set out and defined an expectation that is both exceedingly harsh but also unattainable for men. We've asked men to change, to become more vulnerable and emotional, to become weaker, to not be so strong or aggressive or competitive, to become less sexual and more thoughtful, to ditch their instinctual behavior that has been hardwired in them for over 200,000 years. The modern expectation of men is to never ever make a mistake. To not display behavior remotely toxic, never ever act in a way that's deemed toxic or never even feel in a way that's toxic. It is the same expectation we have of our leaders in society like priests, politicians, leaders of industry, celebrities and sports stars. The problem with these expectations is that it is impossible to achieve. We are all human, and humans are imperfect. We can try our very best to be good people but unless there is a second coming of Jesus, that perfect human may never ever exist.

In the goal to eliminate toxic masculinity, we are eradicating all masculinity in the vast majority of men, not just in Victoria but around the world. It is not too late to reclaim some of the traditional traits and values of males, but if we keep insisting on eradicating toxic masculinity, we might inadvertently destroy ourselves in the process due to a lack of men. There won't be any men to fight for their country, protect their family, community or clan, men to be interested in a woman, start a family and have kids. All these things will lead to a catastrophic societal collapse.

I just finished writing this fucking book

It's 6:30am on September 20ᵗʰ, 2023, I am sitting in Starbucks finishing my last five chapters. For my very last chapter about Jordan Wallace, I wanted to finish it at Parsonage Cafe, in front of the Ukrainian Church.

So, on my drive to the cafe, I feel a complete sense of euphoria and accomplishment which is indescribable. After two and a half years of frustration, several bouts of writer's blocks, 80,000 words and the multiple fights with Maria to the breaking point of our marriage, it's very surreal to know that I am almost finished writing this fucking book!

The feeling is just like winning a big tennis tournament, a major poker tournament, passing the playability test, or meeting and getting the phone number of your first love at 16. Of course, getting married to Maria and having Alex and Seve are the pinnacles of my life but finishing this book is damn close. When I first started writing it back in March 2021, I thought that it would take me 3 weeks. Little did I know that it would take two and a half years of my life and almost end my marriage!

I want dudes to know that if you put your mind to something, feel passionate about something, be motivated to make a change in yourself or the world and really put in max effort, great things can be accomplished. What's needed is the ultimate belief in yourself, to take that first step, that leap of faith, that things will work out. I'm not a writer or an author but I just have the utmost belief in myself that I can make this happen. In accomplishing this monumental and herculean task of writing this book, I hope I can help dudes in the 21st century become dudes. Even when I go to Darcy's or Irish Times or play volleyball with my buddies, I don't really know how it's happening. I'm an average middle-aged Filipino dude that has just made things happen. So, for all you there thinking that you can't do it, let this book and my journey be an example that anything is truly possible.

In memory of Jordan Wallace

I've been writing this book now for about two and a half years and felt like I was finished but, every time, it seemed somehow incomplete. I felt this after three months, six months, a year and two years of writing.

I felt like I had written everything I needed to, but the book was missing something. Little did I know that the reason why I couldn't finish this book is because even though I had noticed and observed changes in young men and the effects it was having on them, all these signs that I was seeing weren't nearly as important as what my friends and I had experienced three months ago - the loss of a friend, comrade and brother. If the stakes weren't so high and the decrease in confidence and masculine men was just that, then it wouldn't be as important as what's happening in the world today. The problem with the attack on men is that it's having the greatest impact on the mental health of young men today. There is an assumption that men will always be strong and that they can handle anything thrust upon them. Throughout time immemorial, through 200,000 years plus of human evolution, men have always fought, protected and been the backbone of the patriarchal family. It was perceived that there could be nothing done to men whether physically or psychologically to dull or weaken them. Therefore, with the rise of feminism and equality, there was a push to empower women to be equal if not greater to men. As I have stated in my previous chapters, not only is this understandable but it should be celebrated to empower women.

The problem is that in the movement's attempt to empower women to find equal footing, it also sought out to weaken and emasculate young men with the thought that these men can take and will be able to handle the attack on them because they're strong. The early signs of what I was seeing a few years ago is now mushrooming into an avalanche of frail, weak, scared and more suicidal young men. It is affecting society in every way from relationships, workplace dynamics, reproduction, post-secondary enrollment, the ratio of female to male doctors and therapists, and the overall lack of direction for these young men. The movement and push for equality had very few, if any, checks and balances. Society may not have foreseen the signs that it had gone way too far. There are certain advocates today like Jordan Peterson and Andrew Tate. Their original messages were pure and were able to help men. But coming from a dude, it seems like they have succumbed to the pressure of the hype by changing their original message. It has been hijacked to get more clicks, likes and more attention. If their message was left pure and they didn't try to seek more attention but just focused on the message, I think that they wouldn't be attacked as much by the feminist movement or the equality movement and now the LGTBQ. An honest and non-emotional conversation or dialogue is needed to stem the tide of this growing suicide and mental health epidemic. We first need to acknowledge what is happening, why it's happening and what factors have led to it happening. Admitting culpability on all sides and finding a way for some to acknowledge their direct hand in this, may slow the attack on men.

As I have written in this book and on my Instagram @alexlovesjazz, I have been out and about town and have gotten to know a lot of people through sports, music, and everyday life. Last summer, I started playing volleyball with the Beagle crew: Lee, Donnie, Jordan, Eli, Jurrell, Guy, Falco, and the rest of the gang. Being a complete outsider, they were so welcoming and pretty soon, I was one of the gang! The games were reasonably competitive because most of the group had played high level sports like lacrosse, golf, hockey, soccer, basketball, and volleyball. These guys were mostly in construction and still fit in their twenties and thirties. There were also a bunch of girls that played, and the atmosphere was amazing. It was one of the last places in Victoria where people could still reasonably be themselves and not be so worried or be politically correct. Not saying that some weren't but it had a much more down-to-earth, organic vibe than most places in town. Wednesday volleyball was a very special place, a very welcoming and unpretentious atmosphere. It was BYOB, so guys would always bring coolers full of beer. We would have music being played by Charlito, @fundipz on IG, who is a local DJ in town. If he wasn't around, there would be an Iphone plugged into a speaker blasting tunes the whole time we played. For whatever reason, at 51, I was still one of the better players at volleyball. I don't know why since the last time I played was on the grade 7 team. Because of my competitive drive and passion for sports, I can play at a pretty high level. Therefore, in these spirited games, I would develop friendly rivalries with the other dudes like Eli who played in school, and Jordan who was an all-around fucking stud athlete. Jordan was a guy's guy and a ladies' man. Charismatic, good looking and very popular. Jordan had it all plus he was probably the best athlete at volleyball having played high level lacrosse with Donnie. In volleyball, he could get up super high, and spike the ball or jump up and block one of my hits. And every once in a while, when he would do something phenomenal, he would do a backflip on the grass from a standing position which was crazy because if I'd had tried to do this same backflip, I probably would have broken my back and been in the hospital for a year! Jordan was always the center of attention with his larger-than-life personality, infectious laugh and smile. When I first started playing volleyball, I would see a bunch of different girls by his side, embracing him, flirting with him, playing with his very manly beard, and just trying to get his attention. As I've mentioned, Jordan is one good looking dude. When volleyball season wound down last year, I saw less of the guy but from time to time, I would run into him at the Beagle. I would see Jordan with Donnie, Quinn, Eli, and Lee having beers, flanked with women, always by their side. The one thing I did notice when I would see Jordan was that, depending on his mood, he would always seem like the same guy. But every once in a while, I would notice him saying a backward remark to me. It kind of surprised me but it also gave me pause to think of what he was really feeling inside, not the optics he was showing the world. I went back to the Beagle in the spring, I ran into Donnie, Jordan and his new girlfriend, Jen.

Donnie's New Year's resolution was to be booze free. Three weeks in, we message each other, and he asks me to meet him for coffee at Moka House, a local cafe close to the Beagle and the hill. We sit down and catch up on how things are going. Donnie's feeling great and has clarity from being sober and taking dips in the frigid water at Oak Bay in the mornings.

We call this the polar bear dip, submerging in freezing water for a few minutes, then immediately sitting in a hot sauna for 15-30 minutes. Russian doctors that I have talked to swear by this and how therapeutic and healthy it is for men. This swim is meant to increase their testosterone production.

He asked me how my winter went, and I told him about the progress of my book, my tennis and life in general. He then shared with me an idea he had for a business- a gym in Cook Street Village, the area that surrounds the Beagle, Moka and Beacon Hill Park. I was thrilled and excited for him and told him that it was a great idea. Donnie is such a great guy and a solid friend with amazing energy. He had been in a serious car crash a few years back which has defined and affected his life the past few years. So, for him to start conceptualizing and dreaming of owning a gym was dope. He also wanted to have a place for younger dudes to go and be themselves. Though he didn't say it, I sensed that he wanted to mentor and be a big brother to these guys. I was pumped for Donnie and would check up on him by dm or dropping by the Beagle every few days. I felt like his guardian angel, like I was sent by God to watch over him. I couldn't understand why or the significance that would play out later in the summer. As I would pass by and see the boys at the Beagle, Donnie would be ecstatic having me there. More subtly, I could tell that Jordan was good with me, but I had a feeling that he was a tad jealous of my attention to Donnie. I was also at fault because I thought Donnie needed more of my help and mentorship, blindly ignoring Jordan. I assumed that he was a happy, strong dude that didn't need my guidance. We had the nicest spring and summer weather in Victoria in a very long time. The weather gets really nice earlier than normal, and I start playing tennis at the Hill in February. Wednesday volleyball resumes in April. I was thrilled to see the gang again. We hit the ground running with a lot of highly spirited, competitive games. Everyone is stoked to play with and see friends, get some much-needed vitamin D from the sun after a long, cold, dark snowy winter and to share some beers and laughs. At the same time, I was going heavy at bars and clubs and from time to time, I saw the gang at Irish, Bard or Darcy's. I fondly remember dancing with Josh and Donnie at Darcy's with my shirt being absolutely soaked from the sweat going full tilt, 100%. I thought I was going to collapse from exhaustion. Remember I'm 51!

Victoria is having one hell of a summer, beautiful weather, outdoor concerts, festivals, and numerous events. Tennis and volleyball were top notch. The bars, musicians and bands were going crazy busy with tourists and locals. The economy was humming, and the mood and vibe was electric. There was an outdoor block party in Cook St. Village. They closed off several blocks with street vendors, food trucks, a beer garden, and an outdoor stage for bands to perform and energize the crowd with the most amazing live music! I played tennis in the morning and right after, I asked Seve if he wanted to come down, grab a beer and meet Lee. He was sponsoring Seve for the season and Lee's company name and logo was sewn on the back of Seve's lacrosse jersey. We got to the party around 3pm and headed straight to the Beagle seeing Donnie and Jordan. Seve, Donnie, and Jurell had played lacrosse the week prior with Seve scoring 4 goals as a call-up. Donnie liked Seve a lot and would always rave about him. He bought us drink tickets for the beer garden, we grabbed some ciders and started walking around. We then bump into Jordan; I introduce Seve and they chat for a bit. Finally, we see Lee. He and Seve talk for a few minutes. It's the first time that they meet, and Seve is very thankful for Lee's generosity and season-long jersey sponsorship. It's not really Seve's scene so after a few more minutes, we head home. Little did I know that it would be the last time that I would see Jordan.

I had a very busy week and missed volleyball. The following Wednesday, I showed up but when I arrived, I noticed something was off. People were more muted than normal; the music wasn't as loud and the game hadn't started yet. Everyone was in small groups. Finally, we start the game. Halfway through the first set, I yelled at Donnie asking where the fuck he was last week. Seve played for Donnie's team again scoring 4 goals, but he was a no show. I was giving him a hard time about it and wanted to flex about Seve's goals. He approaches me during a break in the game and whispers to me, "you don't know what happened to Jord?" I said "no!" stunned in complete silence. I gave Donnie the warmest hug and we continued playing. The game had a very solemn and sad vibe. The gang was grieving and the volleyball area felt like a morgue. As always, spiritual things happen and in the next game, we are in a long rally with Donnie and I facing each other up at the net. After a furious rally with multiple digs and spikes, the ball flew up right between Donnie and me. With me thinking that Donnie would jump to block my spike, I soared up as high as I could, and unleashed the hardest, most thunderous spike I have ever hit! Unfortunately for Donnie, he didn't jump and instead waited on the ground. The ball exploded from my hands and hit Donnie right on his head knocking his Ray Ban's ten feet in the air. That spike was vicious, ferocious and much needed as it shattered the morgue-like vibe that was being felt that afternoon. With Donnie laying on the ground, I ran to him both sheepishly but also losing it because it was an epic play. He wasn't mad at all and said, "that was awesome!" He really saw the humor in that spike and I think it was Jordan sending a message from up above for the gang to stop being sad and instead to just play and enjoy the volleyball.

Jordan took his life on Monday, the day after the block party. It's a very sad and unfortunate ending to a most beautiful life! He seemingly had it all, good looks, great friends, solid job and great girlfriend. Jordan was a natural in sports and in life. 99% of the dudes would think that he led the perfect life. And with all that he had going for him, it wasn't enough. Why the fuck wasn't it enough? Who said it wasn't enough? What pressures are being placed on dudes that are saying "it's not enough"? I knew Jordan reasonably well, not as well as Donnie, who had been his very best friend since they were kids, but well enough to say stop. Stop with this attack on men! Stop with the weakening of men! Stop with the vilification of men and of their masculinity! If society doesn't stop with this unrealistic and unattainable expectation of men, we will see many more tragic deaths in the world, just like our dear brother Jordan Quinn Wallace! RIP bro!!

PiNK DAY
When? APRIL 15 2010

PiNK DAY
SUNSHINE
WOODS GOLF
SOUTH
18
SOUTH

Garden Group
oil, Mulch.
nd & Gravel
778-TOP   IL
SOIL - MULCH - SA
NURSERY ST
ALLY OWNED & OPERATED BY NEW
ASK US ABOUT TEAM FUNDRAISIN
CORDERO
8
FRENETTE
EXTERIORS

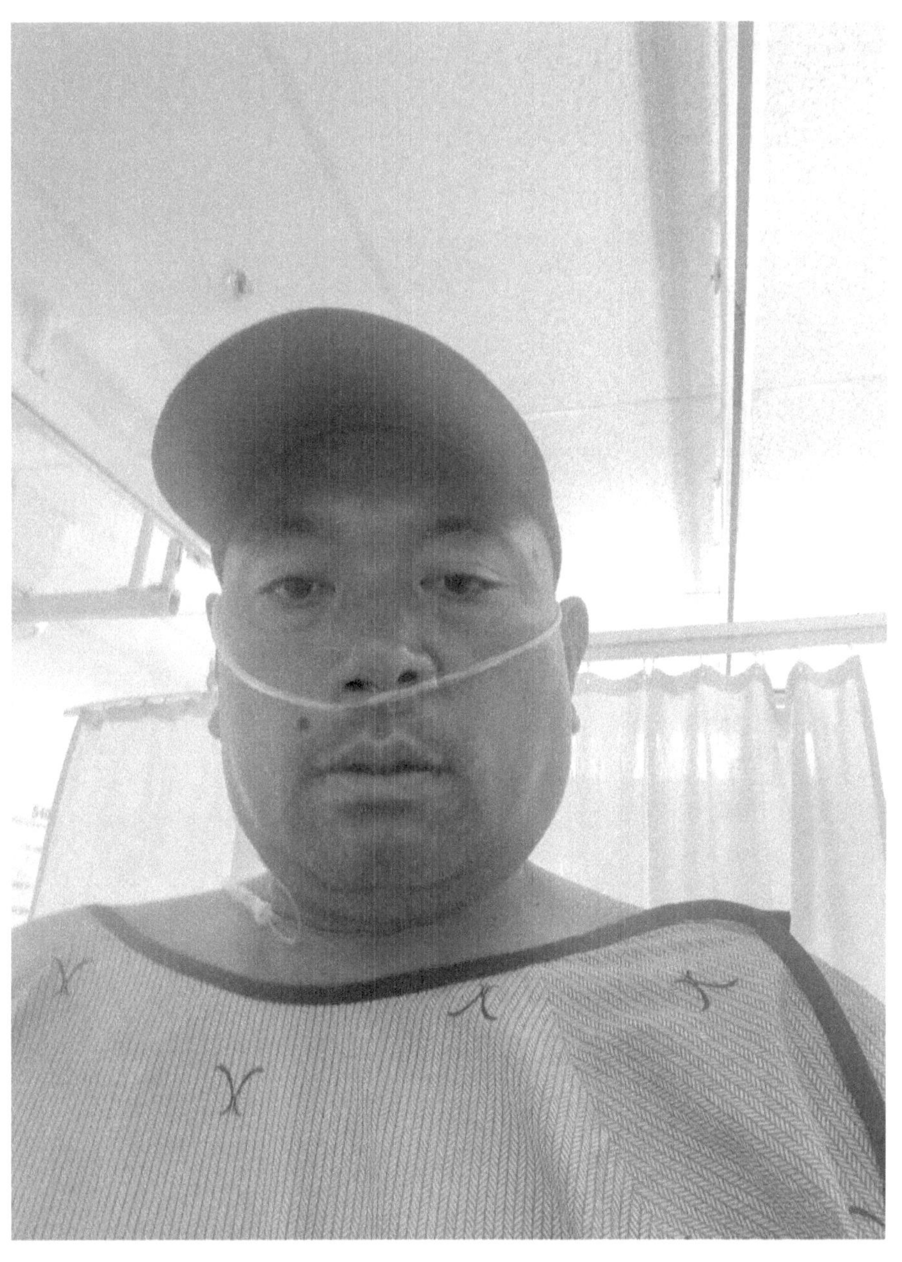

STUDENT
DRIVER
COROLLA
JIM PATTISON
Beautiful British Columbia
CV6 39F
JUN 2019
TRPG SCHOOL.ca
GP

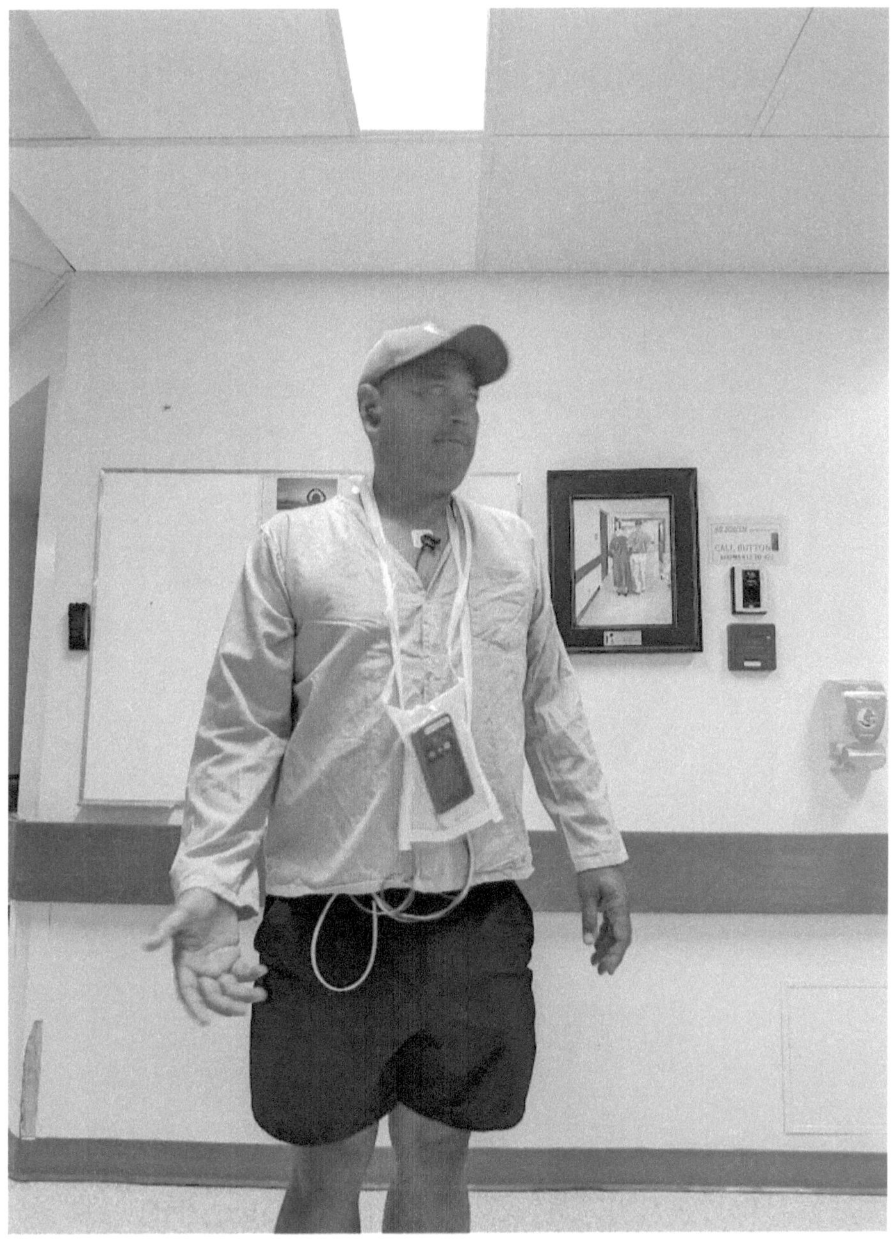

Duffin's donuts
SUB ▪ NOODLE SOUP ▪ CHINESE FOOD

KETBALL

♥ my Boo

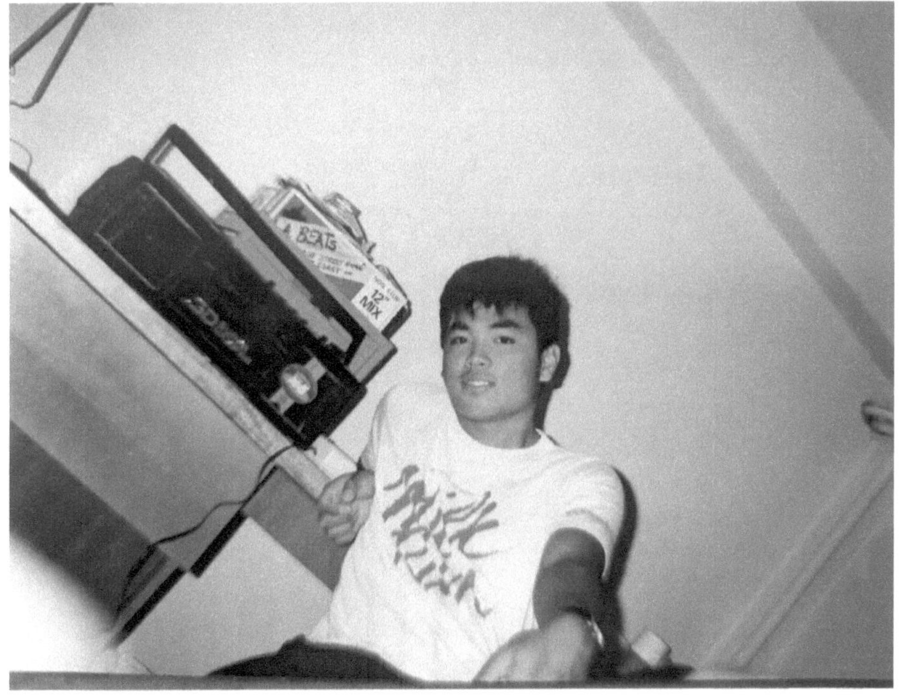